BRITISH LITERATURE UNLOCKED
Vol IV: Transition to The Romantics

A Complete Guide for UGC NET

ANKIT SHARMA

TO THE POINT NOTES BASED ON PREVIOUS
YEARS QUESTION PAPERS

Table of Contents

<u>Foreword</u>

The journey through British Literature is one marked by profound ideas, artistic transformations, and socio-political upheavals, all of which have shaped the literary canon as we know it. In "British Literature Unlocked: A Complete Guide for UGC NET," this literary heritage is meticulously unpacked, volume by volume, to serve as an essential resource for UGC NET English aspirants. Spanning six volumes, this series guides readers from the ancient foundations of the Greco-Roman period all the way to the nuanced expressions of the Modern and Postmodern ages. With each era, readers will find to-the-point notes, questions from the last decade of UGC NET exams, mnemonic codes, and strategic insights designed to simplify and streamline the study process, making preparation not only thorough but also deeply engaging.

Volume by Volume Breakdown

Volume I: Greco-Roman to Chaucer

Dive into the roots of Western literary thought, tracing the influences of classical antiquity up through the Middle Ages and Chaucer's groundbreaking contributions. This volume introduces foundational concepts and sets the stage for the evolution of British literature.

Volume II: Elizabethan to Jacobean

Enter the vibrant Renaissance period, where the works of Shakespeare, Marlowe, and their contemporaries reflect the artistic flourishing and complex socio-political shifts of the time. Each page delves into the drama, poetry, and prose that defined these eras.

Volume III: The Age of Milton, Restoration, and The Augustan Age.

Explore an age marked by poetic grandeur, the restoration of the monarchy, and the Augustan pursuit of clarity and wit. This volume captures the transformations in language, form, and ideology as literature moved into a reflective phase of transition.

Volume IV: The Age of Transition and The Age of Romanticism

Witness the emotional and imaginative power of the Romantic movement, a response to the rigid rationality of the previous era. This volume celebrates the Romantic poets and novelists who embraced nature, individualism, and emotion in revolutionary ways.

Volume V: The Victorian Age

This volume covers the prolific Victorian era, an age of dramatic change and conflict that grappled with industrialization, social reform, and expanding empire. Here, readers can explore the complex morality, realism, and unique characters of Victorian prose and poetry.

Volume VI: Modern and Postmodern Literature

The journey concludes with an in-depth look at Modern and Postmodern literature, where literary form, narrative structure, and thematic depth are pushed to their limits. From the experimental techniques of Modernism to the playful and questioning nature of Postmodernism, this volume brings British literature into the contemporary era.

Why This Book is Essential?

Designed for aspiring NET scholars, "British Literature Unlocked" offers a unique blend of academic precision and strategic insight. With mnemonics that transform complex historical timelines and literary movements into memorable codes, this guide ensures that vital information is readily accessible. Each volume is filled with analysed questions from the last ten years of UGC NET exams, helping you understand not only what to study but also how to approach the exam strategically. This guide offers a structured pathway through the vast landscape of British literature, reducing overwhelm and empowering students to confidently tackle their preparation.

An effective study companion, "British Literature Unlocked" is the result of years of dedicated analysis, scholarly research, and an in-depth understanding of the UGC NET requirements. The goal is to provide readers with more than just a study guide—it is to offer them a roadmap that navigates through the richness of British literary history with ease and engagement. As you turn these pages, may you not only prepare but also find joy in the timeless world of British literature, its stories, and its legacy.

This series invites you on an enlightening journey, guiding you through the ages and unlocking the potential for both academic success and a deeper appreciation of the literary arts. Welcome to "British Literature Unlocked: A Complete Guide for UGC NET."

CHAPTER 1

THE AGE OF TRANSITION (1740-1800)

THE HISTORICAL BACKGROUND (1740–1800)

- **Decline of Party Feud**
  Tory weakness; Whigs dominate mid-century; Tories regain power under George III.
- **Commercial and Imperial Expansion**
  Empire grows under Whig ministers; Burke's work reflects imperial challenges.
- **The French Revolution**
  Revolutionary ideas influenced English literature significantly.

THE AGE OF TRANSITION

- **The Double Tendency**
  - **Classicism**: **Samuel Johnson** as its main figure.
  - **Romanticism**: Began with **Thomson's Seasons**.
- **The New Romanticism**
  - **Return to nature** over artificial pastoral.
  - Focus on **man's position** in nature.
  - **Sympathy for the poor** (Cowper, Burns).
  - **Revolt against conventional** techniques (heroic couplet).
  - Romantic themes: **The Ancient Mariner, La Belle Dame.**
- **The New Learning**
  - **Revival of Romanticism**: Ballad research, **Percy's Reliques.**
  - **Shakespeare and Chaucer** editions reflect **archaic interests.**
- **The New Philosophy**
  - **Skepticism and inquiry** shaped Romanticism by clearing old beliefs.
- **Growth of Historical Research**
  - Led by **Gibbon**, history gained importance in literature.
- **The New Realism**

- o **Rise of the novel**: Domestic life explored with **Romantic freshness**.
- ➤ **Decline of Political Writing**
  - o **Pamphlets lost influence**; rise of **independent writers** like Johnson.

SAMUEL JOHNSON (1709–84)

His Life:

- ➤ **Born in Lichfield**, son of a Tory bookseller.
- ➤ Inherited **strong Tory views** from his father.
- ➤ **Suffered from a skin disease** throughout life.
- ➤ Disease affected **his sight and hearing** severely.
- ➤ Privately educated; attended **Oxford University**.
- ➤ Endured **poverty and indignities** as a student.
- ➤ **Failed at school-teaching** after leaving Oxford.
- ➤ Married a **woman twenty years older**.
- ➤ Moved to **London in 1737** to Grub Street.
- ➤ Experienced **miseries of Grub Street life** deeply.
- ➤ **Macaulay described Johnson's hardships** vividly.
- ➤ Johnson **hated recalling** his early life struggles.
- ➤ Slowly **rose from poverty** through hard work.
- ➤ Became **noted poet with "London"** in 1738.
- ➤ His **Dictionary (1747–55)** boosted his fame.
- ➤ Emerged as **literary leader in London**.
- ➤ Gained a **State pension in 1762**.
- ➤ Spent final years **socializing and conversing**.
- ➤ Boswell captured **Johnson's quirks in biography**.
- ➤ Notable for **humor, bearishness, and goodwill**.
- ➤ Known for **physical oddities and superstitions**.
- ➤ Displayed **piety, vocal Tory prejudices** often.
- ➤ Renowned for **immense conversational abilities**.
- ➤ **The Club or Literary Club:**
- ➤ **A London dining club founded in February 1764.**
- ➤ **Founded by the artist Joshua Reynolds and essayist Samuel Johnson.**
- ➤ The nine original members were:

- o Joshua Reynolds: artist
- o Samuel Johnson: essayist, lexicographer
- o Edmund Burke: writer, later M.P.
- o Christopher Nugent
- o Topham Beauclerk
- o Bennet Langton
- o Oliver Goldsmith: author, playwright, poet
- o Anthony Chamier
- o John Hawkins: author

Notable Works:

> **Code:**
> **First Work:** *Messiah* (1728) and *London* (1738)
> **Second Work:** *Life of Mr Richard Savage* (1744)
> **Savage Wishes Irene**
> *The Rambler* (1750–52) and *The Idler* (1758–60)
> *A Dictionary of the English Language* (1755)
> *The History of Rasselas, Prince of Abissinia* (1759)
> **Second Last:** *The Plays of William Shakespeare* (1765) and *A Dictionary of the English Language* (1755)
> **Last Work:** *Lives of the Poets* (1779–81)

Essays

- ➢ *Birmingham Journal (1732–33)*
- ➢ *Plan for a Dictionary of the English Language (1747)*
- ➢ ***The Rambler (1750–52)***
- ➢ *The Adventurer (1753–54)*
- ➢ *Universal Visiter (1756)*
- ➢ *The Literary Magazine, or Universal Review (1756)*
- ➢ ***The Idler (1758–60)***
- ➢ ***The work titled "The Pernicious Effects of Revery" by Samuel Johnson***
- ➢ *The False Alarm (1770)*
- ➢ *Thoughts on the Late Transactions Respecting Falkland's Islands (1771)*
- ➢ *The Patriot (1774)*
- ➢ *A Journey to the Western Islands of Scotland (1775)*
- ➢ *Taxation no Tyranny (1775)*
- ➢ *The Beauties of Johnson (1781)*

Poetry and Drama
- ***Messiah (1728),*** *a translation into Latin of Alexander Pope's Messiah*
- ***London (1738)***
- ***Prologue at the Opening of the Theatre in Drury Lane (1747)***
- ***The Vanity of Human Wishes (1749)***
- ***Irene, a Tragedy (1749)***

Biographies
- *A Voyage to Abyssinia (1735), by Jerome Lobo, translated from the French*
- ***Life of Mr Richard Savage (1744)***
- *Miscellaneous Observations on the Tragedy of Macbeth (1745)*
- ***"Life of Browne" (1756) in Thomas Browne's Christian Morals***
- *Proposals for Printing, by Subscription, the Dramatick Works of William Shakespeare (1756)*
- ***Preface to the Plays of William Shakespeare (1765)***
- ***The Plays of William Shakespeare (1765)***
- ***Lives of the Poets (1779–81)***

Dictionaries
- ***Preface to a Dictionary of the English Language (1755)***
- ***A Dictionary of the English Language (1755)***

Novella
- ***The History of Rasselas, Prince of Abissinia (1759)***

Poetry:
- Johnson wrote **little poetry**, none of it first-class.
- **"London" (1738)** is a powerful, somber poem.
- Depicts **city life's vanities** through a bitter poet's view.
- **"The Vanity of Human Wishes"** (1749) is his second notable poem.
- **Inspired by Juvenal's Tenth Satire**, gloomy outlook.
- Examines **human endeavors** with bleak pessimism.
- Written in **heroic couplet**, like "London."
- **Emotion and conviction** add weight to the work.
- Shows **stern immobility** in pessimistic outlook.
- Contains **lines of solemn grandeur** and power.
- Both poems reflect **Johnson's pessimistic worldview.**

London (1738)

- ➤ **"London" by Samuel Johnson** was written shortly after moving to London in 1738.
- ➤ Johnson's **first major work**, a 263-line poem, imitates Juvenal's Third Satire.
- ➤ **Thales**, the poem's character, leaves London for Wales.
- ➤ Johnson followed the **Augustan trend** of imitating classical poets like **Pope**.
- ➤ **Published anonymously** in 1738, it received praise, notably from **Pope**.
- ➤ **Johnson and Garrick** lived in London with Richard Norris in 1737.

Do You Know?

"London" by Samuel Johnson (1738)

A **satirical imitation** of Juvenal's Third Satire in heroic couplets.

"London" by William Blake (1794)

Critiques **oppression and industrialization** in society.

"London, 1802" by William Wordsworth

Opens with: **"MILTON! thou shouldst be living at this hour."** Wordsworth **laments England's decline** and praises Milton.

"London" (novel) by Edward Rutherfurd

Spans **2,000 years** of London's history, following multiple families.

The Vanity of Human Wishes (1748)

- ➤ **Full**: *The Vanity of Human Wishes: **The Tenth Satire of Juvenal Imitated.***
- ➤ **"The Vanity of Human Wishes"** imitates **Juvenal's Satire X.**
- ➤ Johnson sympathizes with subjects, unlike Juvenal.
- ➤ Focuses on **human futility and greatness**, emphasizing **Christian values**.
- ➤ Johnson's **second Juvenal imitation**, after *London.*

- Emphasizes **philosophy over politics**, unlike *London*.
- **Not financially successful**, but highly praised by critics.
- **Walter Scott** and **T.S. Eliot** called it Johnson's **greatest poem**.
- Howard D. Weinbrot labeled it a **great English poem**.
- *London* focused on politics; **Vanity** on philosophical ideas.
- Changed publisher from **Edward Cave** to **Robert Dodsley**.

Life of Mr. Richard Savage (1744)

- **Full Title:** An Account of the Life of Mr. Richard Savage, Son of the Earl Rivers.
- The first significant biography published by Johnson.
- **Johnson's biography of Richard Savage** was anonymously published in **1744**.
- It details Savage's **controversial life**,
- Claims of **illegitimacy** from a noble family.
- Johnson used the biography to explore **ethical questions**.
- Later included in **The Lives of the Poets** (1779)
- It marked Johnson's rise as a biographer.

Drama:

Irene (1726 and 1749)

- Johnson brought the manuscript of "Irene" to London in 1737.
- **David Garrick** staged the play in **1749** at Drury Lane Theatre.
- "Irene" ran for nine nights but was unsuccessful.
- The play **marked Johnson's only attempt** at drama, and it soon disappeared.

Prose:

- **Johnson's prose** is considered his best writing.
- Early work involved Parliamentary reporting for Cave.
- Johnson **fabricated speeches** for legislators' benefit.
- Produced various **hack-work** before major projects.
- **Johnson's Dictionary** was completed over eight years.
- Wrote **The Rambler** (1750–52) and **The Idler** (1758–60).
- Both periodicals followed **The Spectator** in style.
- Essays in these periodicals are **dense and abstract**.
- **Johnsonese** style features long, Latinized sentences.

- ➤ **Rasselas** (1759) was written to fund his mother's funeral.
- ➤ **Rasselas** is a philosophical novel with **little plot**.
- ➤ Characters in Rasselas are basic and underdeveloped.
- ➤ The book contains shrewd observations and somber clarity.
- ➤ Johnson's later years produced little literary work.
- ➤ Engaged in a **quarrel with Macpherson** over Ossian.
- ➤ Journey to the Western Islands shows narrative skill.
- ➤ His last major work was **Lives of the Poets** (1779-81).
- ➤ Lives of the Poets contains strong, insightful criticism.
- ➤ His criticism is influenced by classical school ideals.
- ➤ **Johnson's prose** remains influential for its **virile style**.

Johnson's Dictionary (1755)

- ➤ Published on 15 April 1755 and written by Samuel Johnson.
- ➤ The most influential dictionaries in the history of the English language.
- ➤ Dissatisfaction with existing dictionaries led to Johnson's commission.
- ➤ Johnson was paid **1,500 guineas (£1,575)** for the dictionary.
- ➤ He took **seven years** to complete the work, not three.
- ➤ Worked **single-handedly**, with only clerical assistance.
- ➤ Produced **several revised editions** during his lifetime.
- ➤ **Johnson's Dictionary** was the leading dictionary for 173 years.
- ➤ Walter Jackson Bate called it a monumental scholarly achievement.
- ➤ The Dictionary included language history and grammar.
- ➤ Contained words based on **London conversation** and respected writers.
- ➤ A **one-volume version (1756)** was popular into the 20th century.
- ➤ Johnson used European lexicographical techniques with skill.
- ➤ It remained the standard dictionary until Noah Webster's (1828).
- ➤ Johnson's Dictionary was highly influential and enduring.

The Rambler (1750-1752)

- ➤ The Rambler was a periodical by Samuel Johnson.
- ➤ Targeted the **rising middle class** of the 18th century.
- ➤ Aimed to help integrate middle-class into aristocratic circles.
- ➤ Published **Tuesdays and Saturdays** from 1750 to 1752.
- ➤ Johnson's most consistent and sustained work in English.
- ➤ The Rambler totaled 208 articles.

> ➢ Differed in **style of prose** from other periodicals.

The Idler (1758–1760)

> ➢ **The Idler** (1758–1760) was a series of **103 essays**.
> ➢ Mostly written by **Samuel Johnson**, with some contributors.
> ➢ Published in the **Universal Chronicle** weekly.
> ➢ **Johnson wrote some essays** quickly, like casual letters.
> ➢ Popular essays were reprinted without permission.
> ➢ Johnson threatened to **reprint competitors' work** for charity.
> ➢ **The Vulture** essay was omitted due to **anti-war satire**.
> ➢ Replaced by an essay on **imprisonment of debtors**.

The History of Rasselas, Prince of Abissinia (1759)

> ➢ Full: The Prince of Abissinia: A Tale, though often abbreviated to Rasselas,
> ➢ **Rasselas** is a philosophical novel with **little plot**.
> ➢ The book's original working title was "*The Choice of Life.*"
> ➢ The book was first published in **April 1759 in England**.

Preface to Shakespeare (1765)

> ➢ The following are the four components of Johnson's *Preface to Shakespeare*:
> ➢ Describe Shakespeare's "greatness,",
> > ➢ Particularly his **"portrayal of human nature"**;
> ➢ The "faults or weakness" of Shakespeare;
> ➢ The relationship between Shakespeare's plays and contemporary poetry and drama;
> ➢ A history of "Shakespearean criticism and editing down to the mid-1700s" and what his work intends to do.
> ➢ It has **72** Pages.
> ➢ "*Antiquity, like every other quality that attracts the notice of mankind, has undoubtedly votaries that reverence it, not from reason, but from prejudice.*"
> ➢ "*What mankind have long possessed they have often examined and compared, and if they persist to value the possession, it is because frequent comparisons have confirmed opinion in its favour.*"
> ➢ **Shakespeare was a poet of nature.**
> ➢ **His plays are neither tragedies nor Comedies.**

> ➢ **Poetry should instruct and delight.**
> ➢ **Shakespeare's genius in Comedy.**
> ➢ **People naturally like justice.**
> ➢ **Johnson was critical of Shakespeare's poetic justice.**
> ➢ **Shakespeare's drama plots are loosely formed.**
> ➢ **Shakespeare is guilty of violating the chronology of time and place. Example: Hector in Troilus and Cressida.**
> ➢ **Unnecessary repetition of language.**
> ➢ **Language.**
> ➢ **Violation of all unity.**
> ➢ **Shakespeare as Homer.**
> ➢ **Harmony of Blankverse.**

Important Paragraphs:

Johnson begins:

"That praises are without reason lavished on the dead, and that the honours due only to excellence are paid to antiquity, *is a complaint likely to be always continued by those, who, being able to add nothing to truth, hope for eminence from the heresies of paradox; or those, who, being forced by disappointment upon consolatory expedients, are willing to hope from posterity what the present age refuses, and flatter themselves that the regard which is yet denied by envy, will be at last bestowed by time. Antiquity, like every other quality that attracts the notice of mankind, has undoubtedly votaries that reverence it, not from reason, but from prejudice.."*

"To works, however, of which the excellence is not absolute and definite, but gradual and comparative; to works not raised upon principles demonstrative and scientifick, but appealing wholly to observation and experience, no other test can be applied than length of duration and continuance of esteem. ***What mankind have long possessed they have often examined and compared, and if they persist to value the possession, it is because frequent comparisons have confirmed opinion in its favour.***

"Of the first building that was raised, it might be with certainty determined that it was round or square, but whether it was spacious or lofty must have been referred to time. ***The Pythagorean scale of numbers was at once discovered to be perfect;*** *but the poems of Homer we yet know not to transcend the common limits of human intelligence, but by remarking, that nation after*

nation, and century after century, has been able to do little more than transpose his incidents, new name his characters, and paraphrase his sentiments."

*"The reverence due to writings that have long subsisted arises therefore not from any credulous confidence in the superior wisdom of past ages, or gloomy persuasion of the degeneracy of mankind, but is the consequence of acknowledged and indubitable positions, that what **has been longest known has been most considered, and what is most considered is best understood**."*

Johnson then introduces Shakespeare:
NOTHING can please many, and please long, but just representations of general nature. Particular manners can be known to few, and therefore few only can judge how nearly they are copied. *The irregular combinations of fanciful invention may delight awhile, by that novelty of which the common satiety of life sends us all in quest: but the pleasures of sudden wonder are soon exhausted, and the mind can only repose on the stability of truth.*

Shakespeare is above all writers, at least above all modem writers, the poet of nature; the poet that holds up to his readers a faithful mirror of manners and of life. *His characters are not modified by the customs of particular places, unpractised by the rest of the world: by the peculiarities of studies or professions, which can operate but upon small numbers; or by the accidents of transient fashions or temporary opinions: they are the genuine progeny of common humanity, such as the world will always supply, and observation will always find. His persons act and speak by the influence of those general passions and principles by which all minds are agitated, and the whole system of life is continued in motion. In the writings of other poets a character is too often an individual; in those of Shakespeare it is commonly a species.*

*It will not easily be imagined how much Shakespeare excels in accommodating his sentiments to real life, but by comparing him with other authors. **It was observed of the ancient schools of declamation, that the more diligently they were frequented, the more was the student disqualified for the world, because he found nothing there which he should ever meet in any other place.*** The same remark may be applied to every stage but that of Shakespeare. The theatre, when it is under any other direction, is peopled by such characters as were never seen, conversing in a language which was never heard upon topics which will never arise in the commerce of mankind. But the dialogue of this* *author is often so evidently determined by the incident which produces it, and is pursued with so much ease and simplicity, that it seems scarcely to claim the merit of fiction, but to have been gleaned by diligent selection out of common conversation and common occurrences.*

*Characters thus ample and general were not easily discriminated and preserved, yet perhaps no poet ever kept his personages more distinct from each other. **I will not say with Pope, that every speech may be assigned to the proper speaker, because many speeches there are which have nothing characteristical; but, perhaps, though some may be equally adapted to every person, it will be difficult to find, any that can be properly transferred from the present possessor to another claimant.** The choice is right, when there is reason for choice.*

*Other dramatists can only gain attention by hyperbolical or aggravated characters, by fabulous and unexampled excellence or depravity, as the writers of barbarous romances invigorated the reader by a giant and a dwarf; and he that should form his expectations of human affairs from the play, or from the tale, would be equally deceived. **Shakespeare has no heroes; his scenes are occupied only by men, who act and speak as the reader thinks that he should himself have spoken or acted on the same occasion: Even where the agency is supernatural the dialogue is level with life.** Other writers disguise the most natural passions and most frequent incidents: so that he who contemplates them in the book will not know them in the world: Shakespeare approximates the remote, and familiarizes the wonderful; the event which he represents will not happen, but if it were possible, its effects would be probably such as he has assigned; and it may be said, that he has not only shewn human nature as it acts in real exigencies, but as it would be found in trials, to which it cannot be exposed.*

***This therefore is the praise of Shakespeare, that his drama is the mirror of life; that he who has mazed his imagination, in following the phantoms which other writers raise up before him, may here be cured of his delirious ecstasies, by reading human sentiments in human language;** by scenes from which a hermit may estimate the transactions of the world, and a confessor predict the progress of the passions.*

"The poet, of whose works I have undertaken the revision, may now begin to assume the dignity of an ancient, and claim the privilege of established

fame and prescriptive veneration. He has long outlived his century, the term commonly fixed as the test of literature merit. *Whatever advantages he might once derive from personal allusions, local customs, or temporary opinions, have for many years been lost; and every topic of merriment, or motive of sorrow, which the modes of artificial life afforded him, now only obscure the scenes which they once illuminated. The effects of favour and competition are at an end; the tradition of his friendships and his enmities has perished; his works support no opinion with arguments, nor supply any faction with invectives; they can neither indulge vanity nor gratify malignity; but are read without any other reason than the desire of pleasure, and are therefore praised only as pleasure is obtained; yet, thus unassisted by interest or passion, they have past through variation of taste and changes of manners, and, as they devolved from one generation to another, have received new honours at every transmission."*

Lives of the English Poets (1781)

- ➢ This volume contains short biographies
- ➢ Critical assessments **of 52 poets** who lived during the 18th century.
- ➢ Johnson divided his biographies into **three** distinct parts:
  - ➢ **A narrative of the poet's life**
  - ➢ **A presentation of his character (summarized traits)**
  - ➢ **A critical assessment of his main poems**
- ➢ The names were arranged roughly according to the **date of death**.
- ➢ It is not arranged by the date of birth.
- ➢ They range in length from a few pages to an entire book.
- ➢ There are many notable lives among them:
  - ➢ Abraham Cowley,
  - ➢ John Milton,
  - ➢ John Dryden,
  - ➢ Joseph Addison,
  - ➢ Alexander Pope
  - ➢ William Collins
  - ➢ William Shenstone.
- ➢ Johnson's dislike of John Milton and Thomas Gray.
- ➢ The blank verse makes some approach to that which is called the "lapidary style"; has neither the easiness of prose nor the melody of numbers, and therefore tires by long
- ➢ These have been cited as evidence that he was prejudiced against their poetry.
- ➢ However, this argument has been overstated.

- ➤ His opinions about a poet and his work differ from time to time, as in the case of Collins.
- ➤ Johnson disagreed with the poet's poetic manner:
- ➤ "he puts his words out of the common order, seeming to think, with some later candidates for fame, that not to write prose is certainly to write poetry."
- ➤ He was particularly proud of the *Life of Cowley:*
  - ➤ Included a comprehensive discussion of the 17th-century Metaphysical poets.
  - ➤ According to Johnson, Cowley may have been the last representative.
  - ➤ *"But wit, abstracted from its effects upon the hearer, may be more rigorously and philosophically considered as a kind of* **_"discordia concors;" a combination of dissimilar images,_** *or discovery of occult resemblances in things apparently unlike. Of wit, thus defined, they have more than enough. The most heterogeneous ideas are yoked by violence together; nature and art are ransacked for illustrations, comparisons, and allusions; their learning instructs, and their subtilty surprises; but the reader commonly thinks his improvement dearly bought, and, though he sometimes admires, is seldom pleased."*
- ➤ *The Life of Pope* is the longest and best.
  - ➤ Pope's life and career were fresh.
  - ➤ It was public enough to provide ample biographical material.
  - ➤ Johnson found Pope's poetry highly congenial.
- ➤ Johnson agreed to write **"little Lives and Prefaces"** for English Poets in 1777.
- ➤ He defended **Pope as a poet**, despite common criticism.
- ➤ "It is surely superfluous to answer the question that has once been asked, whether Pope was a poet? otherwise than by asking, in return, if Pope be not a poet, where is poetry to be found?"
- ➤ Johnson considered **Dryden greater than Pope** in poetry.
- ➤ He separated a poet's **life from their work.**
- ➤ Believed a **good poet** wasn't necessarily a **good man**.
- ➤ Acknowledged contradictions between life and writing.
- ➤ Sought to promote Piety through biographical parts.
- ➤ Johnson was ready to chastise failings, commend virtue.
- ➤ He favored poets from **Dryden to Pope** the most.
- ➤ Skeptical of contemporary poets like Gray and Collins.

> ➢ Admired Gray's "An Elegy Written in a Country Church Yard".
> ➢ Used his method to assign **different purposes** to life and poetry analysis.

Quoted Phrases:

1. **"little Lives, and little Prefaces, to a little edition of the English Poets"**
   (Johnson's initial thoughts on the project)

> ➢ **"he puts his words out of the common order, seeming to think, with some later candidates for fame, that not to write prose is certainly to write poetry"**
> (Johnson's critique of William Collins' poetic style)
> ➢ **"It is surely superfluous to answer the question that has once been asked, whether Pope was a poet? otherwise than by asking, in return, if Pope be not a poet, where is poetry to be found?"**
> (Johnson's defense of Pope's status as a poet)
> ➢ **"a manifest and striking contrariety between the life of an author and his writings"**
> (Johnson's belief about the divergence between a poet's life and work)
> ➢ **"in such a manner, as may tend to the promotion of Piety"**
> (Johnson's intent in writing the biographical parts of his work)

Questions:

Question 1

Who among the following observed that "Nothing can please many, and please long, but just representations of general nature"?

(1) Philip Sidney
(2) Samuel Johnson
(3) S.T. Coleridge
(4) William Wordsworth

Explanations:
Answer: Samuel Johnson

*"**NOTHING can please many, and please long, but just representations of general nature. Particular manners can be known to few, and therefore few only can judge how nearly they are copied.** The irregular combinations of fanciful invention may delight awhile, by that novelty of which the common satiety of life sends us all in quest: but the pleasures of sudden wonder are soon exhausted, and the mind can only repose on the stability of truth."*

Question 2

Choose the correct chronological sequence in which the following works were published:

> A. Vicar of Wakefield
> B. Life of Johnson
> C. Johnson's Dictionary
> D. Lives of the Poets
> E. The Life of Nelson

Choose the correct answer from the options given below :

> (1) A, E,B, C, D
> (2) C, A, D, B, E
> (3) B, A, E, C, D
> (4) C, B, A, E, D

Explanations:
Answer: (2) C, A, D, B, E

Here are the publications listed in chronological order:

> **C. Johnson's Dictionary – 1755**
> **A. Vicar of Wakefield – 1766**
> **D. Lives of the Poets - 1779-1781**
> **B. Life of Johnson – 1791**
> **E. The Life of Nelson - 1813**

Question 3

Which among the following is not a work of Samuel Johnson?

> (1) The Rambler

(2) The Idler
(3) The Journal of Stella
(4) The Pernicious Effects of Revery

Explanations:
Answer:
The Rambler: A series of essays by Samuel Johnson, published between 1750 and 1752.

The Idler: Another collection of essays by Samuel Johnson, released from 1758 to 1760.

__The Journal of Stella:__ A series of letters by Jonathan Swift to Esther Johnson, nicknamed "Stella." This work is not by Samuel Johnson.

The Pernicious Effects of Revery: A lesser-known work attributed to Samuel Johnson, discussing the negative effects of idle fantasy and daydreaming, reflecting his moralistic and didactic style.

Question 4

Who said of the blank verse, quoting an unnamed critic, that it is -... verse only to the eye", adding further that it "has neither the easiness of prose nor the melody of numbers"?

1. Samuel Taylor Coleridge
2. Alexander Pope
3. Samuel Johnson
4. John Dryden

Explanations:
Ans: Samuel Johnson

ESSAY ON POETIC THEORY from Lives of the Poets BY SAMUEL JOHNSON

"LIFE OF MILTON"

Poetry may subsist without rhyme, but English poetry will not often please, nor can rhyme ever be safely spared but where the subject is able to support itself. **The blank verse makes some approach to that which is called the "lapidary**

style"; has neither the easiness of prose nor the melody of numbers, and therefore tires by long continuance. Of the Italian writers without rhyme, whom Milton alleges as precedents, not one is popular; what reason could urge in its defense has been confuted by the ear.

But of all the borrowers from Homer, Milton is perhaps the least indebted. **He was naturally a thinker for himself, confident of his own abilities and disdainful of help or hindrance;** he did not refuse admission to the thoughts or images of his predecessors, but he did not seek them.

Question 5

Arrange the following in the chronological order of publication:

    A. Advancement of Learning
    B. The Origin of Species
    C. On Heroes and Hero Worship
    D. The Lives of the Poets

Choose the correct answer from the options given below:

    1. D, A, C, B
    2. D, A, B, C
    3. A D, C, B
    4. A D, B, C

Explanations:
Answer: 3. A D, C, B

"Advancement of Learning" is a work by Francis Bacon, published in 1605. It is considered to be one of Bacon's most important works, and it outlines his ideas about the nature of knowledge and how it should be acquired.

"The Lives of the Poets" is a collection of biographical essays by Samuel Johnson, published in 1779. The essays provide detailed accounts of the lives and works of several important English poets, including John Milton, Alexander Pope, and John Dryden.

"On Heroes and Hero Worship" is a series of lectures by Thomas Carlyle, published in 1841. In the lectures, Carlyle discusses the concept of heroism and examines the lives of several notable figures from history, including Muhammad, Shakespeare, and Napoleon.

"The Origin of Species" is a book by Charles Darwin, published in 1859. It is considered to be one of the most important scientific works ever written, and it outlines Darwin's theory of evolution by natural selection.

Question 6

Arrange the following 18th-century magazines in the chronological order of publication:

> A. The Critical Review
> B. The Monthly Review
> C. The Gentleman's Magazine
> D. The Rambler

Choose the correct answer from the options given below

> 1. A, D, B, C
> 2. D, A, B, C
> 3. B, A, C, D
> 4. C, B, D, A

Explanations:
Answer: 4. C, B, D, A

The Critical Review, The Monthly Review, The Gentleman's Magazine, and The Rambler are all significant periodicals in the history of English literature.

> ➢ **The Gentleman's Magazine, founded in 1731.**
> ➢ **The Monthly Review, founded in 1749.**
> ➢ **The Rambler, a series of 208 essays written by Samuel Johnson between 1750 and 1752.**
> ➢ **The Critical Review, established in 1756.**

Question 7

Arrange the following critical works in their chronological order of publication:

> A. "Preface to Lyrical Ballads"
> B. "A Defence of Rhyme"
> C. "Life of Cowley"
> D. "The Frontiers of Criticism"

Choose the correct answer from the options given below:

> 1. A, C, B and D

2. B, A, C and D
3. B, C, A and D
4. C, A, D and B

Explanations:
Answer: 3. B, C, A and D

- ➢ **Samuel Daniel (1562–1619)** wrote the essay *A Defence of Rhyme (1603).*
- ➢ **"Life of Cowley" by Samuel Johnson and first published in 1779..**
- ➢ **"Preface to Lyrical Ballads by William Wordsworth and originally published in 1800"**
- ➢ **"The Frontiers of Criticism" essays by Matthew Arnold, published in 1961.**

Arrange the following in the chronological order of their publication:

A. Past and Present
B. Leviathan
C. Unto This Last
D. The Life of Samuel Johnson

Choose the correct answer from the options given below:

1. (B) (D) (A) (C)
2. (B) (A) (D) (C)
3. (C) (D) (A) (B)
4. (C) (A) (D) (B)

Explanations:
Answer: 1. (B) (D) (A) (C)

- ● Leviathan
- ● The Life of Samuel Johnson
- ● Past and Present
- ● Unto This Last

- ➢ *Leviathan* **by Thomas Hobbes was published in 1651.**
- ➢ *The Life of Samuel Johnson* **by James Boswell was published in 1791.**
- ➢ *Past and Present* **by Thomas Carlyle was published in 1843.**
- ➢ *Unto This Last* **by John Ruskin was published in 1860.**

Which two of the following are Samuel Johnson's statements about metaphysical poets?

(A) they were singular in their thoughts
(B) they were careful in their diction
(C) they affected combination of dissimilar images
(D) they avoided occult resemblances

Choose the most appropriate answer from the options given below:

1. (B) and (C) Only
2. (C) and (D) Only
3. (B) and (A) Only
4. (A) and (C) Only

Explanations:
Answer: 4. (A) and (C) Only

Samuel Johnson made two statements about metaphysical poets:

(A) they were singular in their thoughts: Johnson praised the metaphysical poets for their unique and original thinking. He admired their ability to explore unconventional ideas and delve into complex intellectual realms.

(C) they effected a combination of dissimilar images: Johnson recognized the metaphysical poets' skill in creating surprising and imaginative connections between seemingly unrelated images or concepts. He appreciated their ability to merge disparate elements in their poetry, resulting in striking and thought-provoking metaphors.

Johnson's statements highlight the distinctiveness and innovative nature of metaphysical poetry, emphasizing its intellectual depth and unconventional style.

Arrange the following periodicals in the chronological order in which they started publication:

A. The Spectator
B. The Tatler
C. The Rambler
D. The Critical Review

Choose the correct answer from the options given below:

1. A, B, C, D
2. B, A, C, D
3. B, C, D, A
4. A, D, B, C

Correct Explanations:

B. The Tatler was a British literary and society journal published between **1709 and 1711.**
A. The Spectator was a British daily publication that ran from **1711 to 1712.**
C. The Rambler was a British literary magazine that was published between **1750 and 1752.**
D. The Critical Review was a British literary magazine that was published between **1756 and 1817**.

In "The Life of Cowley", which two of the following criticisms were made by Samuel Johnson against a group of writers he termed the 'metaphysical poets'?

A.   They made an inappropriate combination of wit and imagination.
B.   Instead of writing poetry, they only wrote verses.
C.   They neither copied nature nor life.
D.   They never tried to be singular in their thoughts.

Choose the correct answer from the options given below:

1. **A and B only**
2. B and C only
3. B and D only
4. C and D only

Correct Explanations:
Samuel Johnson in his essay "The Life of Cowley" was critical of the group of poets known as the metaphysical poets, whom he accused of being too focused on using wit and elaborate language at the expense of genuine emotion and meaningful content. Johnson felt that they were more interested

in creating clever verses than in writing real poetry and that their work lacked the beauty and grace that characterized the great poets of earlier eras.

"The metaphysical poets were men of learning, and, to show their learning was their whole endeavour; but, unluckily resolving to show it in rhyme, instead of writing poetry, they only wrote verses, and, very often, such verses as stood the trial of the finger better than of the ear; for the modulation was so imperfect, that they were only found to be verses by counting the syllables."

Question 11

Which two among the following condemned transporting 50000 slaves into England in 1771?

    A.   Samuel Johnson
    B.   Alexander Pope
    C.   Horace Walpole
    D.   Thomas Gray

Choose the correct answer from the options given below:

1. **A and B only**
2. B and D only
3. B and C only
4. A and C only

Correct Explanations:
It is true that both Samuel Johnson and Alexander Pope were outspoken critics of the slave trade, and condemned the transportation of slaves to England.

Johnson, in particular, was a well-known abolitionist who wrote a number of essays and pamphlets condemning the slave trade. He was also a member of the Literary Club, a group of writers and intellectuals who were active in promoting social and political reform. Pope, too, was critical of the slave trade, and used his poetry to raise awareness of the issue.

Question 12

"It ought to be the first endeavour of a writer to distinguish nature from custom or that which is established because it is right from that which is right only

because it is established; that he may neither violate essential principles by a desire of novelty, nor debar himself from the attainment of beauties within his view by a needless fear of breaking rules which no literary dictator had the authority to enact",

The above passage considered to be the death- knzll of the neo-classical criticism is attributed to

1. John Dryden
2. Alexander Pope
3. **Samuel Johnson**
4. Joseph Addison

Correct Explanations:
This quote is from Samuel Johnson's "The Rambler," a series of essays published in the mid-18th century. In this particular passage, Johnson is arguing that writers should strive to distinguish between what is natural and what is merely a product of custom or tradition. He believes that writers should not be afraid to break from established rules or conventions if doing so will allow them to more fully capture the beauty and truth of the world around them. At the same time, Johnson cautions against novelty for its own sake, and suggests that writers must be guided by essential principles that are grounded in the nature of things, rather than blindly following the dictates of literary fashion or convention.

Question 13

Given below are two statements:

Statement I: Dr. Johnson had an inclination toward the Tory political ideology,
Statement II: Dr. Johnson strongly believed in transcendental scepticism.

In light of the above statements, choose the correct answer from the options given below:

1. **Both Statement I and Statement II are true**
2. Both Statement I and Statement II are false
3. Statement I is true, but Statement II is-false
4. Statement I is false, but Statement II is true.

Correct Explanations:
Statement I suggests that Dr. Johnson had a political inclination toward the Tory party, which was a conservative political party in England. This statement is related to his political beliefs and affiliations.

Statement II suggests that Dr. Johnson had a philosophical belief in transcendental scepticism, which is a philosophical position that emphasizes the limitations of human knowledge and the difficulty of knowing things with certainty. This statement is related to his philosophical beliefs.

While it is possible for an individual to hold both political and philosophical beliefs, there is no necessary connection between the two. Therefore, the truth of one statement does not necessarily imply the truth of the other statement.

Question 14

Dr Johnson's Dictionary of the English Language was published in

1. 1751
2. 1753
3. **1755**
4. 1757

Explanations:

Dr Johnson's Dictionary of the English Language is a landmark in the history of English lexicography. **It was first published in 1755** and was the most comprehensive dictionary of its time, **containing more than 42,000 words and their definitions..**

Question 15

Find the chronological order of publication of the given works:

A. Boswell's Life Of Johnson
B. Hobbes's Leviathan
C. Pepys's Diary
D. Bunyan's Pilgrim's Progress
E. Locke's Human Understanding

Choose the correct answer from the options given below:

1. **BCDEA**
2. ACDEB
3. CDABE
4. DEACB

Explanations:
1. Bunyan's Pilgrim's Progress, published in 1678
2. Hobbes's Leviathan, published in 1651
3. Locke's Human Understanding, published in 1689
4. Pepys's Diary, published in 1825 (though written in the 1660s and 1670s)
5. Boswell's Life of Johnson, published in 1791.

Question 16

An Account of the Life of Mr Richard Savage, Son of Earl Rivers (1744) was the first major biography published by

1. Alexander Pope
2. Joseph Addison
3. Samuel Johnson
4. James Boswell

Explanations
Answer: 3. Samuel Johnson

Samuel Johnson's Life of Mr Richard Savage, also known as Life of Savage, is a **significant biography that marked Johnson's debut in the genre.** Published anonymously in 1744, it portrays the life of Richard Savage, a London poet and close acquaintance of Johnson, who passed away in 1743. The biography delves into Savage's own account of his life, including his assertion of being the illegitimate child of a noble family who disowned and abandoned him shortly after his birth.

Question 17

Arrange the correct chronological sequence of the publication of the following texts:

A. Essay of Dramatic Poesy
B. A Room of One's Own
C. Culture and Anarchy
D. The Lives of the Poets
E. "Preface to the Lyrical Ballads"

Choose the correct answer from the options given below:

1. A, D, E, C, B
2. D, A, E, B, C
3. A, C, D, E, B
4. E, D, C, A, B

Explanations:
Answer: 1. A, D, E, C, B

A. John Dryden's *Essay of Dramatick Poesy* was likely written in 1666 during the Great Plague of London and published in 1668.

D. *Lives of the Most Eminent English Poets* (1779–81), alternatively known as Lives of the Poets, is a work by Samuel Johnson that includes short biographies and critical appraisals of 52 poets who lived during the eighteenth century. The poets are arranged roughly by the date of death.

E. *The Preface to Lyrical Ballads* is an essay by William Wordsworth, first published in the second edition of the poetry collection Lyrical Ballads in 1800 and later expanded in the third edition of 1802.

C. *Culture and Anarchy: An Essay in Political and Social Criticism* is a series of periodical essays by Matthew Arnold, first published in Cornhill Magazine from 1867 to 1868 and later collected as a book in 1869. The preface was added in 1869.

B. *A Room of One's Own* is an essay by Virginia Woolf, published in 1929, based on two lectures she gave in 1928 at Newnham College and Girton College, the first two colleges for women at Cambridge. In the essay, Woolf discusses the status of women, particularly women artists, and argues that financial independence and a dedicated space are essential for women to pursue their creative endeavours.

Question 18

Who among the following was NOT one of the original members of Johnson's Literary Club?

1. Oliver Goldsmith
2. John Dryden
3. Edmund Burke
4. John Hawkins

Explanations:
Answer: 2. John Dryden

The Club, also known as the Literary Club, is a renowned dining club in London that was established in February 1764. Its founders were artist Joshua Reynolds, essayist **Samuel Johnson, and philosopher-politician Edmund Burke.** The original nine members included prominent figures such as Reynolds, Johnson, Burke, Christopher Nugent, Topham Beauclerk, Bennet Langton, **Oliver Goldsmith,** Anthony Chamier, and **John Hawkins.** The Club served as a gathering place for intellectuals, writers, and artists, fostering lively discussions and camaraderie among its esteemed members.

Question 19

Arrange the following writers chronologically in accordance with their years of birth:

A. James Boswell
B. Edward Gibbon
C. Samuel Johnson
D. Edmund Burke
E. Richard Brinsley Sheridan

Choose the correct answer from the following options:

1. C. D, B, A. E
2. C, A, B. E. D
3. A. C, B. D. E

4. B, C. A, D, E

Explanations:
Answer: 1. C. D, B, A. E

- ➤ **Samuel Johnson (1709-1784)**.
- ➤ **Edmund Burke (1729-1797)**.
- ➤ **Edward Gibbon (1737-1794)**.
- ➤ **James Boswell (1740-1795)**.
- ➤ **Richard Brinsley Sheridan (1751-1816)**.

Question 20

Which of the following books were published in the year 1791?

A. Adam Smith's The Wealth of Nations
B. James Boswell's The Life of Samuel Johnson
C. Johnson's Dictionary of the English Language
D. Burke's Thoughts on the Cause of the Present Discontents
E. Paine's The Rights of Man

Choose the Correct answer from the options given below
1. A and C
2. B and E
3. C and D
4. D and E

Explanations:
Answer: 2. B and E
- ➤ *The Life of Samuel Johnson, LL.D. (1791)* by James Boswell.
- ➤ *Rights of Man (1791)* by Thomas Paine.
- ➤ *Thoughts on the Cause of the Present Discontents*, published in **1770**.
- ➤ *The Wealth of Nations,* also known as An Inquiry into the Nature and Causes of the Wealth of Nations, is a seminal work by Adam Smith, the Scottish economist and philosopher. First published in **1776**.
- ➤ *A Dictionary of the English Language*, commonly referred to as Johnson's Dictionary, was written by Samuel Johnson and published in **1755**.

Question 21

Arrange the chronological sequence in which the following works were published:

      A. Reflections on the Revolution in France
      B. Preface to Shakespeare
      C. The Social Contract
      D. Treatise on Human Nature
      E. Enquiry Concerning Human Understanding

Choose the correct answer from the following options:

      1. A, B, C. D. E
      2. C. A, B, E. D
      3. D. E. C. B. A
      4. B. C, A. D. E

Explanations:
Answer: 3. D. E. C. B. A

A Treatise of Human Nature: An Experimental Approach to Moral Subjects (1739–40) is a renowned work by Scottish philosopher David Hume, highly regarded for its influence in the field of philosophy.

An Enquiry Concerning Human Understanding (1748) is an updated version of David Hume's earlier work, *A Treatise of Human Nature* (1739–40).

The Social Contract, also known as On the Social Contract; or, Principles of Political Right (1762), is a French-language book by Jean-Jacques Rousseau.

The Plays of William Shakespeare, **edited by Samuel Johnson and George Steevens, is an 18th-century edition of Shakespeare's dramatic works. Johnson's comprehensive edition, published in 1765,** aimed to determine the original language of the plays and included explanatory notes to aid readers in understanding the texts.

Reflections on the Revolution in France (1790) is a political pamphlet by Edmund Burke, an Irish statesman. It contrasts the French Revolution with the unwritten British Constitution and critiques British supporters and interpreters of the events in France, presenting a thought-provoking analysis.

Question 22

"Discordia Concors" a phrase used by Johnson in his Life of Cowley, implies:

A. A term used to refer to ironic inversion of residual ideology in a text
B. A combination of two philosophically similar discourses
C. A term used to refer to diminishing metaphor
D. A combination of dissimilar images
E. A combination of contradictory ideas and concepts

Choose the most appropriate answer from the options given below:

1. D and E only
2. C and D only
3. A and E only
4. B and D only

Explanations:
Answer: 1. D and E only

Enantiosis, synoeciosis or discordia concors is a rhetorical device in which opposites are juxtaposed so that the contrast between them is striking. Dr. Johnson in his Lives of the Poets (1779) defined discordia concors as

*"But wit, abstracted from its effects upon the hearer, may be more rigorously and philosophically considered as a kind of **"discordia concors;" a combination of dissimilar images,** or discovery of occult resemblances in things apparently unlike. Of wit, thus defined, they have more than enough. The most heterogeneous ideas are yoked by violence together; nature and art are ransacked for illustrations, comparisons, and allusions; their learning instructs, and their subtilty surprises; but the reader commonly thinks his improvement dearly bought, and, though he sometimes admires, is seldom pleased."*

Daniel Defoe (1660-1731)

- **Defoe's life remains largely undetermined**, despite extensive research efforts.
- He was born, lived, and died **in poor circumstances**.
- **Defoe was born in London**, became a soldier, then journalist.
- **One of the greatest Grub Street hacks** of his time.
- **Entered the service of the Whigs** for questionable work.
- **Defoe died in London**, a fugitive in great distress.
- His work can be divided into **political tracts and fiction**.
- Wrote numerous political tracts, many in his journal, **The Review**.
- **The Review began in 1704**, forerunner of *The Tatler*.
- **The Shortest Way with the Dissenters** led to his punishment.
- Defoe's pamphlet **An Enquiry into Occasional Conformity (1698)** was followed by the satirical *Shortest Way With the Dissenters (1703)*, which led to his arrest **for seditious libel in May 1703.**
- **Defoe faced fines and pillory** for controversial political writings.
- Some tracts were written in **vigorous, yet rough, verses**.
- **The True-born Englishman (1701)** is his best-known political tract.
- Defoe's propaganda is marked by **irony and sharp invective**.
- **His fiction works were produced late in life** at speed.
- **Robinson Crusoe (1719)** was Defoe's first major fiction success.
- **Duncan Campbell**, *Memoirs of a Cavalier*, and *Captain Singleton* (1720).
- **Moll Flanders**, *Journal of the Plague Year*, **Colonel Jack (1722)**.
- **Roxana (1724)** and *A New Voyage round the World* (1725).
- His fiction has **flaws due to his rapid writing pace**.
- Novels like **Robinson Crusoe suffer from uneven narrative structure**.
- Defoe's writing style is **plain, even bordering on unpolished**.
- His unpolished style **limits him in other fiction genres**.
- **Robinson Crusoe showcases unmatched realism** and gripping storytelling.
- Defoe's strength lies in **detailed, realistic, matter-of-fact narration**.
- **His use of detail lends credibility** and erases disbelief in readers.
- **Swift, direct narrative style enhances the realism** in his stories.
- **Defoe's contribution to the development of the novel is invaluable.**
- His work influenced **modern realism and literary narrative techniques**.
- **Defoe's legacy endures** through his unique approach to fiction writing.
- Defoe was a prolific and versatile writer, producing more than **three hundred works.**

- ➤ Daniel Defoe's **first** published work was ***An Essay Upon Projects*** in **1697,** and his ***final*** work was ***Roxana*** in 1724.
- ➤ **"The Rise of the Novel: Studies in Defoe, Richardson and Fielding," was by Ian Watt published in 1957.**

Code: (In ProShort Rob Sings the memoir of playge year. Colonel Moll Rocks) 🗨

First Work:
An Essay Upon Projects (1697) (Nonfiction)

Second Work:
The Shortest Way with the Dissenters (1702) (Pamphlets)

Middle Works:
Robinson Crusoe (1719) (Novel)
Captain Singleton (1720) (Novel)
Memoirs of a Cavalier (1720) (Novel)
A Journal of the Plague Year (1722) (Novel)
Colonel Jack (1722) (Novel)

Second Last Work:
Moll Flanders (1722) (Novel)

Last Work:
Roxana: The Fortunate Mistress (1724) (Novel)

The List of His Works:
- ➤ *The Buccaneers and Marooners of America (1684) (Nonfiction)*
- ➤ *An Essay Upon Projects (1697) (Nonfiction)*
- ➤ *The True-Born Englishman: A Satyr (1701) (Pamphlets)*
- ➤ ***The Shortest Way with the Dissenters (1702) (Pamphlets)***
  - o **Full:** *The Shortest Way with the Dissenters; Or, Proposals for the Establishment of the Church.*
  - o It is a **pamphlet** consisting of **twenty-nine pages.**
  - o Prompted to write towards **Dissenters in the wake of the accession of Queen Anne to the throne.**
  - o Written in the same style as the Tory publications that attacked Dissenters.

> - o   It opens with the fable of **the Cock and the Horses**.
> ➢ *The Great Law of Subordination Consider'd (1704) (Pamphlets)*
> ➢ *The Consolidator, or Memoirs of Sundry Transactions from the World in the Moon (1705) (Novel)*

Robinson Crusoe (1719) (Novel)

> ➢ **Full:** *The Life and Strange Surprizing Adventures of Robinson Crusoe, of York, Mariner: Who Lived **Eight and Twenty Years**, All Alone in an Un-inhabited Island on the **Coast of America, Near the Mouth of the Great River of Oroonoque;** Having Been Cast on Shore by Shipwreck, Wherein All the Men Perished but Himself. With an Account, how he was at last as Strangely Deliver'd by Pyrates.*
> ➢ Based part of Robinson Crusoe on the real-life experiences of **Alexander Selkirk**, a Scottish sailor.
> ➢ **Plot Summary:**
> ➢ **Robinson Crusoe** comes from a family with German origins.
> ➢ Crusoe sets sail from **Kingston upon Hull** in 1651.
> ➢ He defies his parents, who wanted a legal career.
> ➢ After a storm wrecks the ship, his desire persists.
> ➢ He sets sail again but is captured by pirates.
> ➢ **Crusoe is enslaved by a Moor after capture**.
> ➢ Two years later, he escapes with a boy, **Xury**.
> ➢ **A Portuguese captain** rescues them off Africa's west coast.
> ➢ Crusoe sells Xury and establishes a plantation in Brazil.
> ➢ He joins an expedition to capture slaves from Africa.
> ➢ **Crusoe's ship is wrecked near the Venezuelan coast**.
> ➢ He names the island **"Island of Despair"** after the wreck.
> ➢ He calculates the island's latitude as 9°22' north.
> ➢ Only Crusoe, a dog, and two cats survive.
> ➢ **Crusoe salvages tools and arms from the wrecked ship**.
> ➢ He builds a home near a cave and starts farming.
> ➢ **Crusoe marks a wooden cross to track time**.
> ➢ He grows barley, rice, dries grapes, and raises goats.
> ➢ He makes pottery, adopts a parrot, and reads the Bible.
> ➢ **Crusoe becomes religious, thanking God for his situation**.
> ➢ He later discovers cannibals who visit the island occasionally.
> ➢ **He initially plans to kill the cannibals but reconsiders**.
> ➢ Crusoe dreams of freeing prisoners to become his servants.
> ➢ He saves a prisoner, names him **Friday**, and teaches him.
> ➢ **Crusoe converts Friday to Christianity and teaches English**.

- ➢ More cannibals arrive, but Crusoe and Friday defeat them.
- ➢ **They rescue two prisoners, one is Friday's father**.
- ➢ The other prisoner, a Spaniard, tells of shipwrecked men.
- ➢ A plan is made to rescue the shipwrecked Spaniards.
- ➢ Before their return, an English ship with mutineers arrives.
- ➢ Crusoe helps the captain retake the ship from mutineers.
- ➢ The mutineers choose to be marooned on the island.
- ➢ **Crusoe returns to England, leaving the mutineers on the island**.
- ➢ *The Farther Adventures of Robinson Crusoe (1719)*
- ➢ *Serious Reflections During the Life and Surprising Adventures of Robinson Crusoe (1720) (Novel)*

- ➢ ***Captain Singleton*** *(1720) (Novel)*
- ➢ ***Memoirs of a Cavalier*** *(1720) (Novel):* Set during the **Thirty Years' War** and the English Civil War.
- ➢ ***A Journal of the Plague Year*** *(1722) (Novel)*
- ➢ ***Colonel Jack*** *(1722) (Novel):* An orphaned boy from a life of poverty and crime to prosperity in the colonies, military

Moll Flanders *(1722) (Novel)*

- ➢ **Full title:** *The Fortunes and Misfortunes of the Famous Moll Flanders, &c. Who Was* **Born in Newgate**, *and During a Life of Continu'd Variety for Threescore Years, Besides her Childhood, was* **Twelve Year a Whore, Five Times a Wife (Whereof Once to her Own Brother), Twelve Year a Thief, Eight Year a Transported Felon in Virginia,** *at Last Grew Rich,* **Liv'd Honest and Died a Penitent.** *Written from Her Own Memorandums.*
- ➢ **Plots:**
- ➢ **Childhood:**
  - o **Moll Flanders** is born in Newgate prison to a convicted mother.
  - o Raised by gypsies until she is taken in by a town nurse.
  - o Adopted by a wealthy family, receives education fit for an upper-class lady.
- ➢ **First Lover and Marriage**
  - o Moll becomes the secret mistress of her adopted brother, expecting marriage.
  - o The younger brother proposes, and she marries him to maintain honor.
  - o After five years, her husband dies, and she leaves their children.
- ➢ **Second Marriage**

- o   Moll marries a draper, living a lavish but unsustainable lifestyle.
- o   Her husband flees from creditors, leaving her to adopt the name "Mrs. Flanders."
- o   Moll is forced to take on a new identity to escape financial ruin.

➢ **An Incestuous Relationship**
- o   Moll marries a Virginia plantation owner, unaware he is her half-brother.
- o   After discovering her mother-in-law is her birth mother, she leaves him.
- o   She returns to England, unable to continue the incestuous relationship.

➢ **A Kept Woman**
- o   Moll becomes the mistress of a wealthy married man in Bath.
- o   She bears his child, but he ends their relationship after finding God.
- o   Moll leaves the child with the man and moves to the country.

➢ **True Love**
- o   Moll falls in love with **Jemy** in Lancashire, and they marry.
- o   Both realize they conned each other and are poor.
- o   Jemy leaves her, and pregnant again, Moll returns to London.

➢ **The Banker**
- o   Moll marries a banker who manages her finances without knowing her past.
- o   Their peaceful life ends when a bad business deal ruins them.
- o   Her husband dies from humiliation, leaving Moll penniless again.

➢ **A Life of Crime**
- o   Moll becomes a thief under the guidance of a midwife and governess.
- o   She enjoys her criminal life but is eventually caught and sent to prison.
- o   A minister helps her repent, changing her death sentence to transportation.

➢ **Reunions**
- o   Moll reunites with Jemy in Newgate, and they both head to Virginia.
- o   She inherits her mother's estate and reunites with her son.
- o   Moll tells Jemy about her incestuous marriage, and they return to England, living in financial security.

➢ **Roxana: The Fortunate Mistress** (1724) (Novel)

- o   Defoe's final novel.
- ➤ **A New Voyage Round the World** (1724) (Nonfiction)
- ➤ **The Political History of the Devil** (1726) (Nonfiction)
- ➤ **The Four Years Voyages of Capt. George Roberts** (1726) (Novel)

Style: In the passage now given note **Defoe's completely unadorned style, the loosely constructed sentences, and the almost laughable attention to the minutest detail:**

I went to work upon this boat the most like a fool that ever man did who had any of his senses awake. I pleased myself with the design, without determining whether I was able to undertake it; not but that the difficulty of launching my boat came often into my head; but I put a stop to my own inquiries into it, by this foolish answer: Let us first make it: I warrant I will find some way or other to get it along when it is done.

This was a most preposterous method; but the eagerness of my fancy prevailed, and to work I went. I felled a cedar-tree, and I question much, whether Solomon ever had such a one for the building of the Temple at Jerusalem; it was five feet ten inches diameter at the lower part next the stump, and four feet eleven inches diameter at the end of twenty-two feet, where it lessened, and then parted into branches. It was not without infinite labour that I felled this tree; I was twenty days hacking and hewing at the bottom, and fourteen more getting the branches and limbs and the vast spreading head of it cut off; after this it cost me a month to shape it and dub it to a proportion, and to something like the bottom of a boat, that it might swim upright as it ought to do. It cost me near three months more to clear the inside, and work it out so as to make an exact boat of it: this I did indeed without fire, by mere mallet and chisel, and by the dint of hard labour, till I had brought it to be a very handsome periagua, and big enough to have carried six-and-twenty men, and consequently big enough to have carried me and all my cargo.

Questions:

Question 23

Which two of the following works are Daniel Defoe's historical narratives?

- A.   History of the Rebellion

    B.   Meditations on a Broomstick
    C.   A Journal of the Plague Year
    D.   Memories of a Cavalier

Choose the correct answer from the options given below:

    1.   (A) and (B) Only
    2.   (B) and(D) Only
    3.   (B) and (C) Only
    4.   (C) and (D) Only

Explanations:
Answer: 4. (C) and (D) Only

Daniel Defoe's historical narratives include A Journal of the Plague Year, which provides a fictionalized account of the Great Plague in London in 1665, and Memories of a Cavalier, which presents a fictional memoir of a Royalist soldier during the English Civil War. Both works delve into historical events and offer vivid portrayals of the time periods they depict. The other options, History of the Rebellion and Meditations on a Broomstick, are not historical narratives by Daniel Defoe.

The other options are

A. The History of the Rebellion by Edward Hyde, 1st Earl of Clarendon and former advisor to Charles I and Charles II, is his account of the Wars of the Three Kingdoms.

B. Meditations on a Broomstick: "Meditations on a Broomstick" is a satirical work by Jonathan Swift, published in 1710, which humorously reflects on the vanity and absurdity of human existence.

Question 24

Arrange the following journals in the chronological order in which they started publication.

    A.   The Tatler
    B.   The Examiner
    C.   The Review
    D.   The Spectator

Choose the correct answer from the options given below
    1.   A, D, C, B

2. B, A, D, C
3. C, A, B, D
4. **C, A, D, B**

Correct Explanations:

The Review was founded by Daniel Defoe in 1704 and it was a political journal. It was published weekly and it primarily supported the Whig Party, although Defoe himself was a Tory. The journal contained news, political commentary, and essays, and it had a significant influence on political opinion during its time.

The Tatler was founded by Richard Steele and Joseph Addison in 1709, and it is generally considered as the first successful English periodical. The journal was published thrice weekly and was aimed at the middle class. It contained a mix of news, gossip, social commentary, and literary criticism, and it helped to establish the essay as a popular form of writing in England.

The Spectator was founded by Joseph Addison and Richard Steele in 1711, and it was a successor to The Tatler. The journal was published daily and it contained essays, poetry, and commentary on social and political issues. The Spectator was hugely popular and influential in its time, and it is often credited with helping to shape the development of the English novel.

The Examiner was a weekly paper founded by Leigh and John Hunt in 1808. The paper was known for its radical political views and support of the Whig party. It was also notable for its literary contributions, publishing the work of writers such as Percy Shelley, John Keats, and William Hazlitt. The paper continued to be published until 1886, and its legacy as an influential publication of the Romantic period in England is still recognized today.

Question 25

Match List I with List II

List I	List II
A. Graham Greene	I. Down and Out in Paris and London
B. Daniel Defoe	II. The Grass is Singing
C. George Orwell	III. Journal of the Plague Year
D. Doris Lessing	IV. A Sort of Life

Choose be correct answer from the options given below:

1. (A)-(IV), (B)-(I), (C)-(II), (D)-(III)
2. (A)-(IV), (B)-(III), (C)-(I), (D)-(II)
3. (A)-(II), (B)-(IV), (C)-(I), (D)-(III)
4. (A)-(III), (B)-(IV), (C)-(I), (D)-(II)

Explanations
Answer: 2. (A)-(IV), (B)-(III), (C)-(I), (D)-(II)

Down and Out in Paris and London, published in 1933, is George Orwell's debut full-length work. It is a memoir divided into two parts that explores the theme of poverty in the cities of Paris and London. The book aimed to shed light on the plight of the poor to a middle- and upper-class readership, exposing the harsh reality of poverty in seemingly prosperous cities.

A Journal of the Plague Year, first published in March 1722, is a book by Daniel Defoe. It serves as an account of one individual's experiences during the Great Plague of London in 1665. The book provides observations and memorials of both public and private occurrences during the epidemic, offering insights into the last major outbreak of the bubonic plague in the city.

A Sort of Life, published in 1971, is the first instalment of Graham Greene's autobiography. The book delves into Greene's personal life and experiences, providing an intimate look into his early years.

The Grass Is Singing, Doris Lessing's inaugural novel published in 1950, is set in Southern Rhodesia (now Zimbabwe) during the 1940s. It explores the complex racial dynamics between white and black communities within the British colony. The story follows a troubled woman's impulsive marriage to an unsuccessful farmer, her subsequent mental decline, her tragic death, and the reactions of the colonial British society to these events.

Samuel Richardson (1689-1761)

- ➤ **Richardson** was born in Derbyshire, son of a joiner.
- ➤ He apprenticed with a London printer, later mastering the trade.

> ➢ Became a master-printer, printing for the **House of Commons**.
> ➢ He was **printer to the King**, known for his gentle nature.
> ➢ His first writing began by composing love letters for women.

Pamela (1740).

> ➢ **At age fifty, Richardson published his first novel.**
> ➢ **Subtitle: Virtue Rewarded**
> ➢ **Pamela** is a series of letters about a virtuous maid.
> ➢ The book became an instant success, with five editions.
> ➢ **Pamela**'s detailed characters marked progress in English novels.
> ➢ Based on a story about a servant and the man who marries, fails to seduce her.
> ➢ After two years a sequel, *Pamela in her Exalted Condition (1742)*.
> ➢ Sought to create a **"male Pamela"** in *Sir Charles Grandison (1753)*.
> ➢ **Ian Watt discussed it in *The Rise of the Novel: Studies in Defoe, Richardson, and Fielding* in 1957.**

Shamela (1741)

> ➢ **In full:** *An Apology for the Life of Mrs. Shamela Andrews.*
> ➢ A novel by Henry Fielding, published under the pseudonym **Conny Keyber** in 1741.
> ➢ In this parody of Samuel Richardson's epistolary novel Pamela
> ➢ **Plots:**
> ➢ Fifteen-year-old maidservant named Pamela Andrews.
> ➢ Her employer, **Mr. B, a wealthy landowner.**
> ➢ Mr. B makes unwanted and inappropriate advances toward her after the death of his mother.
> ➢ Mr. B Kidnaps Pamela.
> ➢ After so many days locked.
> ➢ Mr. B eventually reforms and makes Pamela a sincere proposal of marriage.
> ➢ In the novel's second part, Pamela marries Mr. B and tries to acclimatize to her new position in upper-class society.

Clarissa Harlowe (1749)

> ➢ His second novel had tragic themes.
> ➢ ***Clarissa, in full Clarissa; or, The History of a Young Lady***
> ➢ **Epistolary novel published in 1747–48.**
> ➢ More than a million words.
> ➢ Written in the then fashionable epistolary form.
> ➢ Its main body consists of the letters of **Clarissa Harlowe and her seducer, Lovelace.**.

➢ The villain **Lovelace** causes Clarissa's heartbreak and eventual death.

Sir Charles Grandison (1753)

> ➢ **Sir Charles** was too virtuous, becoming tedious and unrealistic.
> ➢ A hero who is a model of benevolence.
> ➢ **He faces few challenges** that a good heart cannot overcome.
> ➢ His main dilemma is a **"divided love"** between two women.
> ➢ The two women are **Harriet Byron from England** and **Signora Clementina from Italy**.

➢ Richardson's novels reflect his character and personality.

➢ His works are **notable for their immense length** and detail.

➢ Despite length, **plots are simple**, filled with excessive detail.

➢ **Richardson excelled in minute analysis** of character motives and emotions.

➢ His novels often felt **bloodless**, with a prudish tone.

➢ Themes of love-making, **overly moral yet subtly suggestive**.

➢ Characters are either **too virtuous or overtly villainous**.

➢ Lacked humor, with action mostly set indoors, feeling confined.

➢ Readers often **yearn for escape** after prolonged reading.

➢ **Merits include strong character drawing**, especially of women.

➢ His **use of dialogue** advanced the development of the novel.

➢ Richardson significantly contributed to the early **modern English novel**.

Henry Fielding (1707-1754)

➢ **Fielding was born in Somersetshire** and educated at Eton.

➢ He studied law at **Leyden**, but funds stopped him.

➢ Fielding wrote plays to earn a living temporarily.

➢ **His plays had little merit**, not achieving much success.

➢ After marrying, he resumed his **legal studies**.

➢ **Fielding was called to the Bar** and started practicing.

➢ He became **Bow Street magistrate in 1749**, earning a small income.

➢ **Magistrate work** gave him insight into human criminality.

➢ Fielding's **novels benefited from his experiences** as a magistrate.

➢ **He was no Puritan**, indulging in excesses that affected health.

➢ A **voyage to Portugal in 1754** was to improve his health.

➢ **He died in Lisbon** and was buried shortly after.

➢ **Joseph Andrews** (1742) began as a satire on **Pamela**.

➢ The hero **Joseph Andrews** is Pamela's brother and a footman.

- ➢ **Joseph's adventures with Abraham Adams** reveal Fielding's storytelling.
- ➢ Fielding's humor is broad, with insight into human nature.
- ➢ His novels reject the **epistolary method**, focusing on action.
- ➢ **Fielding's prose is lively, humorous, and pithy** throughout.
- ➢ **A Journey from this World to the Next** came in 1743.
- ➢ **Jonathan Wild the Great** (1743) is a satirical biography.
- ➢ The story reflects **Fielding's ironic commentary on morality**.
- ➢ **Fielding reverses moral values**, calling good evil and vice versa.
- ➢ His **intense irony** gives insights into the ruffian mentality.
- ➢ **Lesser writers might fail**, but Fielding's method stays sharp.
- ➢ His **insight into human behavior** offers piercing glimpses.
- ➢ Fielding's works were revolutionary for their style and satire.
- ➢ **Tom Jones** (1749) is Fielding's greatest and most complete novel.
- ➢ It features **greater plot symmetry and deeper human insight**.
- ➢ **Amelia** (1751) is based on Fielding's first wife and himself.
- ➢ **Booth**, the husband, reflects Fielding's own flaws and weaknesses.
- ➢ **Amelia** has power, but lacks the spontaneity of *Tom Jones*.
- ➢ His final work, **Voyage to Lisbon**, is a diary of his journey.
- ➢ It shows **Fielding's resilience**, despite suffering from bodily affliction.

🔔 **Code:**

Shame on Andrew and Jonathan Wild
Because **they blamed The Female Husband**
For **Seducing Tom Jones and Amelia**

📚 **Novels:**

📖 *Shamela* – novella, 1741
📖 *Joseph Andrews* – 1742
📖 *Jonathan Wild, the Great* – 1743
📖 *The Female Husband* – 1746
📖 *The History of Tom Jones, a Foundling* – 1749
📖 *A Journey from this World to the Next* – 1749
📖 *Amelia* – 1751

Novels

- *Shamela – novella, 1741*
  - *An Apology for the Life of Mrs. Shamela Andrews, or simply Shamela*
  - Commonly known, is a **satirical burlesque novella**
  - **Published in April 1741 under Mr. Conny Keyber.**
  - **Attacks the then-popular novel Pamela (1740) by Richardson.**
- *The History of the Adventures of Joseph Andrews and his Friend, Mr. Abraham Adams – 1742*
  - Defined by Fielding as a **"comic epic poem in prose,"**
  - It tells of a good-natured footman's adventures on the road home from London with his friend and mentor, the absent-minded parson Abraham Adams.
  - Described on the title page as **"Written in Imitation of the Manner of Cervantes, author of Don Quixote,"**
  - **Summary**:
  - **Fielding discusses human nature** and control of sexuality.
  - Lady Booby **makes sexual advances toward Joseph** early on.
  - "I have trusted myself with a man alone..."
  - A man tries to **rape Fanny**, Adams prevents it.
  - The Squire **attempts to seduce Fanny** after dinner.
  - The Squire kidnaps Fanny, but **Peter saves her.**
  - **Horatio breaks up with Leonora** for unfaithfulness.
  - **Mr. Wilson's first encounter** was a brief cohabitation.
  - He seduced a girl, "I represented him in so low..."
  - Mr. Wilson's **experiences teach the importance of self-control.**
- *The Life and Death of Jonathan Wild, the Great – 1743 an ironic treatment of Jonathan Wild, a notorious underworld figure of the time.* Published as Volume 3 of Miscellanies
  - **A satirical novel** published in 1743 in Fielding's Miscellanies, third volume.
  - A satiric account of London **underworld boss Jonathan Wild** (1682–1725)
  - Mainly a satire on Britain's first **Prime Minister, Robert Walpole.**
- *The Female Husband or the Surprising History of Mrs. Mary alias Mr. George Hamilton, who was convicted of having married a young woman of Wells*

and lived with her as her husband, taken from her own mouth since her confinement – pamphlet, fictionalized report, 1746

The History of Tom Jones, a Foundling – 1749

- ➢ **A comic novel.**
- ➢ It is a **Bildungsroman and a picaresque novel**.
- ➢ It is the earliest novel mentioned by **W. Somerset Maugham in his 1948 book *Great Novelists and Their Novels* among the ten best novels of the world**.
- ➢ **Coleridge** argued that it has one of the *"three most perfect plots ever planned,"* alongside *Oedipus Tyrannus and The Alchemist*.
- ➢ **Characters**:
- ➢ **Master Thomas "Tom" Jones** – Bastard, ward of Squire Allworthy.
- ➢ **Miss Sophia "Sophy" Western** – Virtuous, beautiful daughter of Squire Western.
- ➢ **Master William Blifil** – Hypocrite and Tom Jones's rival in love.
- ➢ **Squire Allworthy** – Wealthy squire, Tom's guardian of great character.
- ➢ **Squire Western** – Huntsman, simpleton, wants Sophia married to heir.
- ➢ **Miss Bridget Allworthy (later Mrs. Blifil)** – Squire Allworthy's sister and William Blifil's mother.
- ➢ **Lady Bellaston** – Tom's lover, manipulative, tries to sabotage Sophia.
- ➢ **Mrs. Honour Blackmore** – Sophia's maid, egotistical and inconsistent.
- ➢ **Dr. Blifil** – Dies heartbroken after rejection by his brother.
- ➢ **Miss Jenny Jones (later Mrs. Waters),** the Partridges' servant, is a very intelligent woman believed to be Tom's mother.
- ➢ **Mrs. Partridge**, Partridge's extremely ill-natured first wife.
- ➢ **Miss Molly "Moll" Seagrim**, Black George's second daughter and Tom Jones's first lover, has a bastard son, possibly not by Tom.
- ➢ **Summary of the Novel:**
- ➢ Tom Jones is a foundling raised by Allworthy.
- ➢ He incurs Allworthy's displeasure through an affair.
- ➢ Tom falls in love with beautiful Sophia Western.
- ➢ Tutor Thwackum and philosopher Square resent Tom.
- ➢ Blifil, Allworthy's nephew, misrepresents Tom to him.
- ➢ Blifil hopes to marry Sophia, Tom's rival.
- ➢ Tom sets out on adventures with Partridge, a schoolmaster.
- ➢ Some adventures involve Tom's amorous escapades.
- ➢ Sophia escapes a forced marriage with Blifil.
- ➢ She runs away to London with her maid.

- ➤ Blifil's machinations against Tom are eventually exposed.
- ➤ Tom is revealed as Allworthy's sister's son.
- ➤ Sophia forgives Tom for his infidelities.
- ➤ Tom and Sophia's love is restored happily.
- ➤ All ends well for Tom, Sophia, and Allworthy.

A Journey from this World to the Next – 1749
Amelia – 1751

- ➤ A sentimental novel.
- ➤ It was the **fourth and final novel written by Fielding.**
- ➤ **Amelia follows the life of Amelia and Captain William Booth after they are married.**

Questions:

Question 26

Which of the following statements are true in the context of Henry Fielding's Tom Jones (1748)

- A. Tom Jones is comic and moralistic.
- B. Tom and Jones are the main characters of Tom Jones
- C. Tom is caught poaching in neighbor's game preserve.
- D. The History of Tom Jones is the full title of Tom Jones
- E. All of the above

Choose the correct answer from the options given below;
1. E Only
2. **A, C and D Only**
3. A, B, C and D only
4. B, C and D only

Correct Explanations:
Henry Fielding's novel "Tom Jones," which was published in 1749, is considered a classic work of English literature. **The full title of the novel is "The History of Tom Jones, a Foundling,"** which reflects the novel's expansive scope and its emphasis on Tom's journey from his uncertain origins to his eventual place in society.

The novel is known for its comic and picaresque (adventurous) elements, as well as its moralistic tone. It follows the adventures of the eponymous Tom Jones, a good-hearted and lusty young man who is caught up in a variety of romantic entanglements and misadventures.

One of the key incidents in the novel involves Tom being caught poaching on a neighbor's game preserve, which sets off a chain of events that eventually leads to his being disowned by his adoptive father and forced to make his own way in the world.

Question 27

Find the chronological order of the writers in terms of their years of birth:

    A.   Jane Austen
    B.   Henry Fielding
    C.   James M. Barrie
    D.   Richard Doddridge Blackmore
    E.   William Makepeace Thackeray

Choose the correct answer from the options given below:

1.   ABCDE
2.   **BAEDC**
3.   CDABE
4.   DBAEC

Explanations:
1.   Henry Fielding (1707)
2.   Jane Austen (1775)
3.   William Makepeace Thackeray (1811)
4.   Richard Doddridge Blackmore (1825)
5.   James M. Barrie (1860)

Laurence Sterne (1713-1768)

➢ Irish-born English novelist and humorist, author of Tristram Shandy (1759–67).
➢ **Sterne was born in Clonmel**, educated at Cambridge, ordained.

- ➢ **He obtained a living in Yorkshire** in 1740.
- ➢ **Sterne's habits were unclerical** by the standards of the time.
- ➢ **Left his living to publish *Tristram Shandy* in London.**
- ➢ **He toured abroad** before returning to write his second novel.
- ➢ **Sterne died in London** while on book-related business.
- ➢ His novels are ***Tristram Shandy* (1759–67)** and **A Sentimental Journey (1768)**.
- ➢ **Tristram Shandy made him famous**, confirming his worst mannerisms.
- ➢ **Both novels are bundles of episodes and digressions**.
- ➢ **"My uncle Toby"** is his most famous elaborated character.
- ➢ His first long work, a sharp satire of the spiritual courts entitled ***A Political Romance.***
- ➢ Notable Works:

📜 **Code:**
9 Unknown Case of Abuses and Romance
of **Tristram Shandy Sermons** from **France and Italy**

📚 **Works:**

1. *The Unknown World: Verses Occasioned by Hearing a Pass-Bell (1743)*
2. *The Case of Elijah and the Widow of Zerephath (1747)*
3. *The Abuses of Conscience (1750)*
4. *A Political Romance (1759)*
5. *Tristram Shandy vols. 1 and 2 (1759)*
6. *The Sermons of Mr. Yorick vols. 1 and 2 (1760)*
7. *Tristram Shandy vols. 3–6 (1761)*
8. *Tristram Shandy vols. 7 and 8 (1765)*
9. *The Sermons of Mr. Yorick vols. 3 and 4 (1766)*
10. *Tristram Shandy vol. 9 (1767)*
11. *A Sentimental Journey through France and Italy (1768)*
12. *Sermons by the Late Rev. Mr. Sterne vols. 5–7 (1769)*

Tristram Shandy (1759)

- ➢ Episodes blend sentimental and comic experiences.
- ➢ Sterne explores **psychological interplay of sentiment and desire**.
- ➢ **Tristram Shandy's style** marked by digressions and humor.
- ➢ Inspired by **metaphysical poets** and John Locke's philosophy.

- ➤ Arthur Schopenhauer called it an **immortal romance**.
- ➤ **Tristram Shandy** is a precursor to stream of consciousness.
- ➤ **Tristram fails to tell his own life story**.
- ➤ Tristram's **birth delayed until Volume III**.
- ➤ **Characters include** Walter, Uncle Toby, Trim, and Yorick.
- ➤ **Walter's temperament is rational and sarcastic**.
- ➤ **Uncle Toby is gentle and loves humanity**.
- ➤ Tristram discourses on **sex, insults, names, and noses**.
- ➤ **Tristram's life shaped by four mishaps**.
- ➤ **First mishap**: Tristram's procreation disrupted by clock-winding.
- ➤ **Second mishap**: His nose crushed by Dr. Slop's forceps.
- ➤ **Third mishap**: Tristram's name ruined by miscommunication.
- ➤ **His name** brings sorrow, tied to folk etymology.
- ➤ **Tristram's name** doomed him to misfortune.
- ➤ **Fourth mishap**: A window sash caused accidental circumcision.
- ➤ **Domestic misunderstandings drive the novel's humor**.
- ➤ Sterne explores **obstetrics, siege warfare, and philosophy**.
- ➤ **Tristram Shandy's plot is fragmented and nonlinear**.
- ➤ **Yorick reappears** in *A Sentimental Journey*.
- ➤ **Sterne's writing critiques social norms and behaviors**.
- ➤ **Tristram Shandy's characters** explore themes of human folly.

Tobias Smollett (1721-1771)

- ➤ Scotsman, being born in Dumbartonshire.
- ➤ **He apprenticed to a surgeon** and became a surgeon's mate.
- ➤ **Saw much of the world** during his time aboard ship.
- ➤ **Gathered experiences as raw material** for his novels.
- ➤ Smollett became considered as a **'man of letters'**
- ➤ First published work in 1746 was a poem about the Battle of Culloden entitled ***"The Tears of Scotland."***
- ➤ **Published *Roderick Random* in 1748**, achieving great success.
  - o **Settled in London**, where he focused on writing.
  - o **Roderick Random is a "picaresque" novel** featuring a roguish hero.
  - o **The hero roves through lands** with fluctuating fortunes.
  - o **The story lacks symmetry but remains lively throughout**.
  - o **It is often coarse**, but minor characters are captivating.
  - o **Tom Bowling**, the seaman, stands out among minor characters.

> ➢ In 1755 he published an **English translation** of Cervantes' novel *Don Quixote*.

 **Code:**
RoRa PePi FeFa Atom Bomb
Grieve on Complete England Expedition of Humphry Clinker

Novels:

1. *The Adventures of Roderick Random (1748)*
2. *The Adventures of Peregrine Pickle (1751)*
3. *The Adventures of Ferdinand Count Fathom (1753)*
4. *Sir Launcelot Greaves (1762)*
5. *A Complete History of England (1757–1765)*
6. *Travels Through France and Italy (1766)*
7. *The History and Adventures of an Atom (1769)*
8. *The Expedition of Humphry Clinker (1771)*

Question 28

Match List I with List II

LIST I	LIST II
A. David Hume	I. The Decline and Fall of the Roman Empire
B. Edward Gibbon	II. A Complete History of England
C. William Godwin	III. Treatise on Human Nature
D. Tobias Smollett	IV. Enquiry Concerning Political Justice

Choose the correct answer from the options given below:

1. A-III, B-I, C-IV. D-II
2. A-I, B-II. C-III, D-IV
3. A-II, B-III, C-I. D-IV
4. A-IV, B-I, C-II, D-III

Explanations: Challenge
Answer: 1. A-III, B-I, C-IV. D-II

I. The Decline and Fall of the Roman Empire: This is a historical work written by **Edward Gibbon and published in multiple volumes from 1776 to 1789.** It explores the history and reasons behind the fall of the Roman Empire, covering a wide range of topics including politics, religion, military conflicts, and societal changes.

II. A Complete History of England: **A Complete History of England by David Hume, in four volumes, with Smollett adding his own Continuation of the History of England.**

III. Treatise on Human Nature: This is a philosophical work by David Hume, published in 1738. In the treatise, Hume examines the nature of human understanding, perception, and morality. He explores topics such as causality, personal identity, and the relationship between reason and emotion.

IV. Enquiry Concerning Political Justice This is a philosophical work by William Godwin, published in 1793. In the book, Godwin discusses political and social theories, advocating for a society based on reason, justice, and individual freedom. He critiques existing political systems and offers his vision for a more egalitarian and just society.

Sarah Fielding (1710-1768)

- ➢ An English author and translator
- ➢ Her novels were among the earliest English languages.
- ➢ She was the first to examine the interior lives of women and children.
- ➢ Fielding was the younger sister of the novelist Henry Fielding
  - ○ *The Adventures of David Simple*
  - ○ *The Adventures of David Simple, Volume the Last: In Which His History Is Concluded (1753)*
  - ○ *The Governess (1749)*
  - ○ *Greek of Xenophon's Memoirs of Socrates (1762*
- ➢ Other works include collaborating with her friend Jane Collier titled *The Cry: A New Dramatic Fable (1754).*

Charlotte Lennox (1730-1804)

- English novelist whose work, especially *The Female Quixote (1752)*.
- Her Poems on *Several Occasions* was published in 1747.
- *The Life of Harriot Stuart (1751)*.
- *Henrietta (1758)*
- *The Female Quixote (1752)*
    - *The Female Quixote, or, The Adventures of Arabella*
    - Parodying the ideas of Miguel de Cervantes' Don Quixote.
    - It was used as a model by Jane Austen for *Northanger Abbey*.
    - It has been called a burlesque, **"satirical harlequinade,"**
    - Arabella as a coquette who used romance as a tool, Scott Paul Gordon said she *"exercises immense power without any consciousness of doing so."*
    - **Arabella is raised in a remote castle by her father**.
    - She reads French romances, imagining her life equally adventurous.
    - **Her father declares she must marry her cousin Glanville.**
    - **She mistakes fiction for reality and has wild fantasies**.
    - Sir George tries courting her in chivalric, romantic language.
    - **Arabella throws herself into the Thames, mistaking danger.**
    - **A doctor explains reality, and she marries Glanville happily**.

Oliver Goldsmith (1732-1774)

- The son of an Anglo-Irish clergyman, Goldsmith.
- He studied at Trinity College, Dublin,
- He was almost expelled for his involvement in the **Black Dog riot.**
- He often contributed to Ralph Griffiths's Monthly Review.
- Anglo-Irish essayist, poet, novelist, dramatist, and eccentric.
- His essays were collected as *The Citizen of the World in 1762.*
- The prose, *The Citizen of the World or Letters from a Chinese Philosopher (1762).*
    - Chinese traveler in England, Lien Chi.
- The prose, *An Enquiry into the Present State of Polite Learning in Europe*
- The novel *The Vicar of Wakefield (1766),*

- o   Published in two volumes in 1766.
- o   Portrait of village life, is narrated by **Dr. Primrose**, the title character.
- ➢ The Poem ***The Traveller or a Prospect of Society (1764)***
  - o   A philosophical poem.
  - o   The heroic verse of an Augustan style.
- ➢ The poem **The Deserted Village (1770),**
  - o   It is a pastoral elegy.
  - o   Idealizes a rural way of life that was
    - ▪ being destroyed by the displacement of agrarian villagers,
    - ▪ the greed of landlords, and economic and political change.
  - o   **George Crabbe** created a bleak view of the country's poor in his poem *The Village (1783)*.
  - o   The central image of this 430-line poem is the **titular village of Auburn,**
- ➢ The play ***She Stoops to Conquer (1773)***.
- ➢ His work led him into Samuel Johnson's circle.
- ➢ He was a member of **The Club,** a literary dining society founded in 1746, and Johnson and the artist Joshua Reynolds.
- ➢ Johnson helped him sell his novel *The Vicar of Wakefield*.
- ➢ 1764 was the year he cemented his reputation as a poet with ***The Traveller.***
- ➢ Goldsmith died from illness in 1774, at just 43, buried in London's Temple Church.
- ➢ **Johnson** would remember him as a man *'who left scarcely any kind of writing untouched and touched nothing that he did not adorn.'*

The Vicar of Wakefield (1766),

- ➢ Published in two volumes in 1766.
- ➢ Portrait of village life, is narrated by **Dr. Primrose**, the title character.
- ➢ **Dr. Charles Primrose** lives a peaceful country life.
- ➢ He is wealthy through an inheritance investment.
- ➢ **Primrose donates his annual salary** to orphans and veterans.
- ➢ **George's wedding** is called off after Primrose loses money.
- ➢ **The family moves to a humble parish** under Squire Thornhill.
- ➢ **Squire Thornhill is known** as a notorious womanizer.
- ➢ **Sir William Thornhill**, his uncle, is generous and worthy.

- ➤ **Mr. Burchell rescues Sophia**, who is attracted to him.
- ➤ **Mrs. Primrose discourages Sophia's feelings** for Burchell.
- ➤ **Squire Thornhill visits frequently**, charming Olivia and Mrs. Primrose.
- ➤ Olivia falls for Thornhill's **false charm and attention**.
- ➤ **Olivia elopes,** and Burchell is suspected initially.
- ➤ **Dr. Primrose discovers Thornhill's deceitful plan** with Olivia.
- ➤ Thornhill had planned a **mock marriage to deceive Olivia**.
- ➤ **The Primrose house burns down** upon their return.
- ➤ **The family loses their belongings** in the fire.
- ➤ **Squire Thornhill demands rent**, despite the disaster.
- ➤ **Dr. Primrose is imprisoned** for refusing to pay.
- ➤ **Olivia is reported dead**, deepening the tragedy.
- ➤ **Sophia is abducted**, adding to the family's suffering.
- ➤ **George is jailed**, wounded after dueling with Thornhill.
- ➤ **Mr. Burchell arrives** and solves all problems.
- ➤ **Olivia is not dead**, contrary to earlier reports.
- ➤ **Burchell is revealed** as Sir William Thornhill.
- ➤ **Sir William rescues Sophia** from her abduction.
- ➤ **George marries Arabella**, as originally planned.
- ➤ **Sir William marries Sophia**, forming a double wedding.
- ➤ **Squire Thornhill's servant tricks him**, making the marriage valid.
- ➤ **Olivia's marriage to Thornhill is valid**, not a sham.
- ➤ **The Vicar's wealth is restored**, as the merchant is found.

She Stoops to Conquer (1773)

- ➤ A comedy
- ➤ The play is a favorite for study by English literature and theatre classes in the English-speaking world.
- ➤ Initially, the play was titled *Mistakes of a Night,*
- ➤ The events within the play take place in one long night.
- ➤ In 1778, John O'Keeffe wrote a loose sequel, *Tony Lumpkin in Town*.
- ➤ **Charles Marlow** – Educated, brash, nervous around upper-class women.
- ➤ **George Hastings** – Loves Constance, plans to elope with her.
- ➤ **Tony Lumpkin** – Mischievous, uneducated, Mrs. Hardcastle's son.
- ➤ **Mr. Hardcastle** – Father of Kate, mistaken as innkeeper.
- ➤ **Mrs. Hardcastle** – Eccentric, overprotective, hides Tony's inheritance.

- ➤ **Miss Kate Hardcastle** – Mr. Hardcastle's daughter, stooping-to-conquer heroine.
- ➤ **Miss Constance Neville** – Mrs. Hardcastle's niece, loved by Hastings.
- ➤ **Sir Charles Marlow** – Father of Charles, aristocratic gentleman.
- ➤ Mr. Hardcastle plans to marry Kate to Marlow.
- ➤ Mrs. Hardcastle wants Tony to marry Constance Neville.
- ➤ Constance is in love with Hastings, Marlow's friend.
- ➤ Tony tricks Marlow and Hastings into thinking Hardcastle's home is an inn.
- ➤ Kate pretends to be a servant, winning Marlow's heart.
- ➤ Marlow flirts with barmaids but struggles with noblewomen.
- ➤ Tony frees himself from his mother, uniting Constance and Hastings.

Questions:

Question 29

The Deserted Village by Oliver Goldsmith

1. Critiques the rural institutions
2. Advocates urbanism over rural backwardness
3. Reflects upon different views on the human soul
4. **Voices revolt of the individual man against institutions**

CORRECT EXPLANATIONS:

- ➤ The Deserted Village is a poem by Oliver Goldsmith published in 1770.
- ➤ **It is a work of social commentary, and condemns rural depopulation and the pursuit of excessive wealth.**
- ➤ The poem is written in heroic couplets, and describes the decline of a village and the emigration of many of its residents to America.
- ➤ **In the poem, Goldsmith criticises rural depopulation, the moral corruption found in towns, consumerism, enclosure, landscape gardening, avarice, and the pursuit of wealth from international trade.**
- ➤ The poem employs, in the words of one critic, "deliberately precise obscurity", and does not reveal the reason why the village has been deserted.

> The poem was very popular in the eighteenth and nineteenth centuries, but also provoked critical responses, including from other poets such as George Crabbe.

> References to the poem, and particularly its ominous "Ill fares the land" warning, have appeared in a number of other contexts.

Question 30

Which of the following poems is written by Oliver Goldsmith?

1. A Deserted Village
2. A Deserted Villa
3. The Deserted Village
4. A Deserted City

Explanations:
Ans: The Deserted Village

"The Deserted Village" is a poem written by **Oliver Goldsmith, first published in 1770**. The poem is a nostalgic and elegiac portrayal of the **decline of rural life in England** and the displacement of villagers by the enclosure movement.

The poem describes the **village of Auburn,** which has been depopulated and abandoned due to the enclosures that **have forced the peasants off the land.** The village is depicted as a place of rustic simplicity, where the people lived in harmony with nature and each other. Goldsmith contrasts this **idyllic vision of rural life with the depredations of modernity,** which have destroyed the social fabric of the village and left its inhabitants destitute.

Question 31

Dr Primrose is a character in

1. Nicholas Nickleby
2. Adam Bede
3. The Vicar of Wakefield
4. Joseph Andrews

Explanations:
Ans: The Vicar of Wakefield

Dr. Primrose is the protagonist of the novel "The Vicar of Wakefield" written by Oliver Goldsmith. He is a kind-hearted and gentle vicar who lives with his family in the English countryside. He is a deeply religious man who is devoted to his family and his parishioners. Dr. Primrose is portrayed as a man of high moral character who always tries to do what is right. Despite his many trials and tribulations, he remains steadfast in his faith and his love for his family.

Extra Perk:

The protagonist of **Nicholas Nickleby is Nicholas Nickleby** himself, a young man who is trying to support his family after the death of his father. He faces many challenges and obstacles as he tries to find work and navigate the world of 19th-century England.

The protagonist of **Adam Bede is Adam Bede**, a young carpenter who lives in a rural community in England. He is a hardworking, honest man who is respected by his peers. The novel follows his struggles and triumphs as he tries to find love and build a good life for himself.

The protagonist of **Joseph Andrews is Joseph Andrews,** a young footman who is trying to make his way in the world. He is an honest and virtuous man who faces many challenges and temptations as he tries to navigate the social and moral complexities of 18th-century England.

Here are some major protagonists in Victorian Era literature:

- **Jane Eyre** from *Jane Eyre* by Charlotte Bronte
- **Pip** from *Great Expectations* by Charles Dickens
- **Dorothea Brooke** from *Middlemarch* by George Eliot
- **David Copperfield** from *David Copperfield* by Charles Dickens
- **Catherine Earnshaw** from *Wuthering Heights* by Emily Bronte
- **Oliver Twist** from *Oliver Twist* by Charles Dickens
- **Bathsheba Everdene** from *Far From the Madding Crowd* by Thomas Hardy
- **Phineas Finn** from *Phineas Finn* by Anthony Trollope
- **Tess Durbeyfield** from *Tess of the d'Urbervilles* by Thomas Hardy
- **Dr. John Watson** from *Sherlock Holmes* series by Arthur Conan Doyle.

Question 32

Arrange the following poets in accordance with their years of birth.

- A. George Herbert
- B. Edmund Spenser
- C. Philip Sidney
- D. John Donne
- E. Oliver Goldsmith

Choose the correct answer from the options given below:

1. ABDCE
2. **BCDAE**
3. EBADC
4. ADEBC

Explanations:
- ➤ Edmund Spenser (1552/1553 – 1599)
- ➤ Philip Sidney (1554 – 1586)
- ➤ George Herbert (1593 – 1633)
- ➤ John Donne (1572 – 1631)
- ➤ Oliver Goldsmith (c. 1730 – 1774)

Question 33

Who among the following was NOT one of the original members of Johnson's Literary Club?

1. Oliver Goldsmith
2. John Dryden
3. Edmund Burke
4. John Hawkins

Explanations:
Answer: 2. John Dryden

The Club, also known as the Literary Club, is a renowned dining club in London that was established in February 1764. Its founders were artist Joshua Reynolds, essayist **Samuel Johnson, and philosopher-politician**

Edmund Burke. The original nine members included prominent figures such as Reynolds, Johnson, Burke, Christopher Nugent, Topham Beauclerk, Bennet Langton, **Oliver Goldsmith,** Anthony Chamier, and **John Hawkins.** The Club served as a gathering place for intellectuals, writers, and artists, fostering lively discussions and camaraderie among its esteemed members.

Question 34

Match List I with List II

List I (Author)	List II (Work)
A. Ann Radcliff	I. The Deserted Village
B. Oliver Goldsmith	II. The Romance of the Forest
C. Swinburne	III. The Vision of Judgement
D. Lord Byron	IV. The Sisters

Choose the correct answer from the options given below:

1. A - III, B - II, C - I, D - IV
2. A - III, B - IV, C - I, D - II
3. A - II, B - IV, C - III, D - I
4. A - II, B - I, C - IV, D - II

Explanations:
Answer: 4. A - II, B - I, C - IV, D - II

Ann Radcliffe's _The Romance of the Forest,_ published in 1791, melds suspense and mystery with a deep dive into the conflict between pleasure-seeking and virtue. Achieving significant popularity, the novel saw four editions within just three years of its release, cementing Radcliffe's status as a leading romance novelist of her time. The story unfolds with protagonists finding refuge in a dilapidated abbey, uncovering family secrets and navigating threats from both human and supernatural adversaries, all while exploring themes of love, betrayal, and redemption amidst the dark backdrop of the forest.

Oliver Goldsmith's "The Deserted Village," published in 1770, is a pastoral elegy that laments the loss of rural life due to agrarian displacement, landlord greed, and social changes.

<u>Lord Byron's "The Vision of Judgment" (1822)</u> satirizes the heavenly debate over George III's soul with sharp wit in ottava rima.

Algernon Charles Swinburne, an English literary figure, made significant contributions as a poet, playwright, novelist, and critic.

Verse drama
- The Queen Mother (1860)
- Rosamond (1860)
- Chastelard (1865)
- Bothwell (1874)
- Mary Stuart (1881)
- Marino Faliero (1885)
- Locrine (1887)
- **<u>The Sisters (1892)</u>**
- Rosamund, Queen of the Lombards (1899)

Frances Burney (1752-1880)

- Later **Madame d'Arblay,** was an English satirical novelist, diarist, and playwright.
- From 1786 to 1790, she held the post as "Keeper of the Robes"
- The first of her four novels, Evelina (1778), was the most successful.
- Burney anonymously published her first novel, Evelina, in 1778.
- *"My little book, I am told, is now at all the circulating libraries. I have an exceeding odd sensation when I consider that it is now in the power of any and everybody to read what I so carefully hoarded even from my best friends, till this last month or two; and that a work which was so lately lodged, in all privacy, in my bureau, may now be seen by every butcher and baker, cobbler and tinker, throughout the three kingdoms, for the small tribute of threepence."*
- David Garrick and Joshua Reynolds socialized at the Burney household.
- List of Novels
  - *The History of Caroline Evelyn,* (1767)
  - ***Evelina: Or The History of A Young Lady's Entrance into the World, London, (1778)***
  - *Cecilia: Or, Memoirs of an Heiress, London, 1782*
  - *Camilla: Or, A Picture of Youth, London, (1796)*
  - *The Wanderer: Or, Female Difficulties, London: Longmans (1814)*

- o
- ➤ *Evelina (1778)*
  - o **Full**: *Evelina; or, The History of a Young Lady's Entrance into the World.*
  - o *Evelina* pointed the way for the novels of Jane Austen.
  - o **Evelina's grandmother plans to force Belmont's acknowledgment**.
  - o Reverend Villars sends **Evelina to London** to avoid embarrassment.
  - o Evelina **navigates high society** and wins Lord Orville's admiration.
  - o **She fends off advances** from Sir Clement Willoughby.
  - o Evelina helps **a poor poet** and endures vulgar cousins.
  - o A jealous suitor **tries to separate Evelina from Orville**.
  - o **Burney showcases comedy and satire** in Evelina's adventures.
  - o Evelina desires to **reconnect with her estranged father**.
  - o Mrs. Selwyn **arranges a surprise meeting** with Sir John.
  - o **Belmont acknowledges Evelina** after seeing her resemblance to his wife.

Richard Brinsley Sheridan (1751-1816)

- ➤ An Irish satirist, politician, playwright, poet.
- ➤ He was a long-term **owner** of the **London Theatre Royal, Drury Lane**.
- ➤ He is known for his plays such as *The Rivals, The School for Scandal, The Duenna,* and *A Trip to Scarborough*.
- ➤ He was also a Whig MP for 32 years.-------------
- ➤ He is buried at Poets' Corner in Westminster Abbey.
- ➤ In 1775 Sheridan's first play, *The Rivals* was produced at London's Covent Garden Theatre.
- ➤ Sheridan and his father-in-law Thomas Linley the Elder, a successful composer, produced the opera *The Duenna*.
- ➤ *The School for Scandal,* premiered at Drury Lane on 8 May 1777.
- ➤ In 1778 Sheridan wrote *The Camp*.
- ➤ **The Critic (1779)**, an updating of the satirical Restoration play The Rehearsal.

📜 **Code:**

- **Rivals DDay**
- **Scare Scandal**
- **Camp Critic**
- **1st June Pizza**

🗂 **Works:**

1. *The Rivals (1775)*
2. *St Patrick's Day (1775)*
3. *The Duenna (1775)*
4. *A Trip to Scarborough (1777)*
5. *The School for Scandal (1777)*
6. *The Camp (1778)*
7. *The Critic (1779)*
8. *The Glorious First of June (1794)*
9. *Pizarro (1799)*
10. *Clio's Protest (Written 1771, Published 1819)*

The Rivals (1775)

- ➢ **A comedy in five acts.**
- ➢ The Rivals concerns the romantic difficulties of *Lydia Languish*.
- ➢ She is determined to marry for love and into poverty.
- ➢ The aristocratic **Captain Jack Absolute** woos her while **claiming** to be Ensign Beverley.
- ➢ **Mrs. Malaprop**, will not permit her to wed a mere ensign.
- ➢ Lydia will lose half her fortune if she marries without her aunt's permission.
- ➢ Subplot complicates the appearance of **Sir Anthony (Jack's father)**.
- ➢ In the end, Lydia abandons her sentimental notions and **agrees to marry Jack**.

The School for Scandal (1777)

- ➢ The most excellent **comedy of manners** of all time.
- ➢ First performed in London on 8 May **1777 at Drury Lane Theatre**.
- ➢ A perfect example of Restoration literature.
- ➢ Gossip, Marriage, Gender, and Morality themes.

- **Lady Teazle speaks an epilogue to the audience** at the end of the play.
- This humorous epilogue is written by George Colman, the Elder.
- It depicts her as somewhat remorseful of leaving country domesticity for London society.
- An elaborate parody of a well-known speech in **Shakespeare's Othello**.
- **Lady Sneerwell, a wealthy widow,**
- **Snake, one of her hirelings.**
- Lady Sneerwell and Snake discuss her scandalous plots.
- They plan to interfere in the Surface brothers' courtships.
- **Joseph Surface desires Maria**, but she loves Charles.
- Lady Sneerwell and Joseph plot to separate Maria and Charles.
- Rumors spread about Charles and **Lady Teazle**'s supposed affair.
- Joseph meets Lady Sneerwell to discuss their schemes.
- **Maria evades Sir Benjamin's** unwanted advances.
- Mrs. Candour criticizes both tale-bearers and tale-makers.
- Sir Benjamin and Crabtree bring gossip about Sir Oliver.
- They also discuss Charles's worsening financial problems.
- Sir Peter complains about Lady Teazle's extravagant spending.
- He also criticizes Maria for rejecting Joseph Surface.
- Rowley defends Charles and announces Sir Oliver's arrival.
- Sir Oliver wants to test his nephews' true character.
- Oliver requests his arrival remain secret from his nephews.
- Sir Peter argues with Lady Teazle about extravagance.
- He reminds her of her humble country roots.
- Lady Teazle defends herself, citing fashion trends.
- Despite quarrels, Sir Peter still finds her charming.
- At Lady Sneerwell's, gossipers mock absent friends.
- Maria and Lady Teazle arrive; Maria is disgusted.
- Sir Peter's comments disrupt the scandalous gathering.
- Joseph courts Maria again, but she rejects him.
- Lady Teazle flirts with Joseph, who hesitates.
- Joseph doesn't want her, but can't offend her.
- Sir Oliver recalls his old friendship with Sir Peter.
- Rowley plans to test the brothers' true character.
- Sir Oliver will visit them disguised as Stanley.
- Moses explains Charles' financial troubles to Sir Oliver.
- Sir Oliver plans to meet Charles as Mr. Premium.

- ➢ Sir Peter urges Maria to choose Joseph over Charles.
- ➢ Maria refuses, Sir Peter threatens her with authority.
- ➢ Lady Teazle asks Sir Peter for 200 pounds.
- ➢ Sir Peter and Lady Teazle argue, considering separation.
- ➢ Sir Oliver, as Premium, arrives at Charles' house with Moses.
- ➢ Trip, the servant, asks Moses for a loan.
- ➢ Sir Oliver concludes that Charles' house is a temple of dissipation.
- ➢ Charles and his guests prepare to gamble, drinking heavily.
- ➢ Charles toasts to Maria before gambling.
- ➢ Sir Oliver, as Premium, is shocked by the scene.
- ➢ Charles does not recognize his long-lost uncle.
- ➢ Charles asks Premium for credit, expecting future inheritance.
- ➢ Premium dismisses the idea of Oliver dying soon.
- ➢ Charles offers to sell valuables for immediate cash.
- ➢ He admits to selling family silver and his father's library.
- ➢ Charles offers to sell family portraits, angering Sir Oliver.
- ➢ Charles sells family portraits using a family tree gavel.
- ➢ He refuses to sell Sir Oliver's portrait out of respect.
- ➢ Sir Oliver forgives Charles and leaves with Moses.
- ➢ Charles gives a hundred pounds to Mr. Stanley's relief.
- ➢ Sir Oliver learns about Charles' generosity from Rowley.
- ➢ He decides to visit his other nephew, Joseph.
- ➢ Joseph prepares for Lady Teazle's visit, hides behind a screen.
- ➢ Lady Teazle flirts with Joseph, who suggests a faux pas.
- ➢ Lady Teazle hides when Sir Peter unexpectedly arrives.
- ➢ Sir Peter suspects Charles of an affair with Lady Teazle.
- ➢ Joseph defends Charles, acting hypocritically and deceitfully.
- ➢ Sir Peter plans generous maintenance for his wife, Lady Teazle.
- ➢ Joseph is annoyed by Sir Peter's suggestion to pursue Maria.
- ➢ Charles arrives, and Sir Peter hides in the closet.
- ➢ Joseph tells Charles Sir Peter is hiding in the closet.
- ➢ Charles drags Sir Peter out of the closet.
- ➢ Sir Peter expresses regret over suspecting Charles.
- ➢ Joseph continues pretending to be virtuous and trustworthy.
- ➢ Sir Peter dismisses his suspicion of Joseph as a joke.
- ➢ Lady Sneerwell is announced, and Joseph rushes to stop her.
- ➢ Sir Peter tells Charles about the French milliner.
- ➢ Charles insists on seeing the milliner, revealing Lady Teazle.
- ➢ Charles finds Lady Teazle behind the screen, amused.

- Joseph is shocked and tries to explain their situation.
- Lady Teazle refuses to support Joseph's explanation.
- She admits she pursued an affair with Joseph.
- Lady Teazle repents after learning of Sir Peter's generosity.
- Joseph continues pretending innocence, but Lady Teazle denounces him.
- Sir Peter is enraged by Joseph's betrayal and deceit.
- Lady Teazle leaves after confessing, followed by angry Sir Peter.
- Rowley and Sir Oliver visit Joseph unexpectedly.
- Joseph claims he has no money to help Stanley.
- Sir Oliver, disguised as Stanley, becomes furious.
- Sir Oliver declares Charles as his heir.
- Rowley informs Joseph that his uncle has arrived.
- Joseph is resentful but excited to see Sir Oliver.
- At Sir Peter's house, rumors of duels spread.
- Lady Sneerwell hides her involvement in the rumors.
- Sir Oliver arrives and corrects the duel rumors.
- The group is unsure if a sword or bullet caused it.
- Sir Peter arrives, uninjured, and is mocked.
- Sir Peter throws out the gossipers from his house.
- Sir Oliver discusses his nephews' behavior with Sir Peter.
- Sir Peter laments about gossip spreading in the press.
- Sir Oliver leaves for Peter to reconcile with Lady Teazle.
- Rowley and Sir Peter worry about Lady Teazle's feelings.
- Sir Peter agrees to make amends with Lady Teazle.
- Lady Sneerwell and Joseph discuss their ruined plot.
- Joseph hopes Snake's loyalty can salvage the scheme.
- Lady Sneerwell leaves as Joseph expects his uncle.
- Sir Oliver arrives, disguised again as Mr. Stanley.
- Joseph thinks it's Stanley and pushes him out.
- Sir Oliver insists he seeks financial help from Oliver.
- Joseph and Charles both try to dismiss Mr. Stanley.
- Sir Peter, Lady Teazle, Maria, and Rowley enter.
- Sir Oliver reveals his identity to his nephews.
- Sir Oliver decides to leave his fortune to Charles.
- Maria refuses to marry Charles due to rumors.
- Maria hears gossip about Charles and Lady Sneerwell.
- Snake reveals the truth, clearing Charles's name.
- Maria agrees to marry Charles after the truth is revealed.

> ➤ Sir Oliver is pleased with the final resolution.
> ➤ Joseph and Lady Sneerwell's plot is completely exposed.
> ➤ Charles and Maria's marriage is happily secured.
> ➤ Sir Peter and Lady Teazle reconcile after the drama.
> ➤ Lady Teazle delivers a humorous epilogue to the audience.
> ➤ The epilogue humorously parodies a speech from Othello.

Questions

Question 35

Arrange the following plays in the chronological order of publication:

A. All for Love
B. Venice Preserved
C. The School for Scandal
D. The Country Wife

Choose the correct answer from the options given below

1. B, C, A, D
2. D, A, B, C
3. C, 8, D, A
4. A, D, C, B

Explanations:
Answer: 2. D, A, B, C

The chronological order of publication for the given plays is:

> ➤ *The Country Wife (1675)* **by William Wycherley**
> ➤ *All for Love (1677)* **by John Dryden**
> ➤ *Venice Preserved (1682)* **by Thomas Otway**
> ➤ *The School for Scandal (1777)* **by Richard Brinsley Sheridan**

Extra Perk:

"All for Love" is a tragedy play by John Dryden, first performed in 1677.
It is a retelling of the story of Antony and Cleopatra, focusing on the relationship between the two lovers and their tragic endings.

"Venice Preserved" is a tragedy play by Thomas Otway, first performed in 1682. The play revolves around a group of conspirators who plot to overthrow the ruling council of Venice, but their plan is ultimately foiled and they are punished.

"The School for Scandal" is a comedy play by Richard Brinsley Sheridan, first performed in 1777. The play satirizes the manners and morals of the upper classes in 18th-century England, particularly their love of gossip and scandal.

"The Country Wife" is a comedy play by William Wycherley, first performed in 1675. The play follows the exploits of a young man named Horner who pretends to be impotent in order to gain access to the wives of the wealthy men of London, leading to a series of comic misunderstandings and mistaken identities.

Question 36

Arrange the following plays in their chronological order:

    A. The Country Wife
    B. Cymbeline
    C. The Spanish Tragedy
    D. The Rivals

Choose the correct answer from the options given below:

    1. B, A, C, D
    2. B, C, D, A
    3. C, B, A, D
    4. C, A, B, D

Explanations:
Answer: 3. C, B, A, D

The Spanish Tragedy, or Hieronimo is Mad Again is an Elizabethan tragedy written by Thomas Kyd between 1582 and 1592. It initiated the revenge tragedy of his day.

Cymbeline, comedy in five acts by William Shakespeare, one of his later plays, written in 1608–10 and published in the First Folio of 1623 from a careful transcript of an authorial manuscript incorporating a theatrical playbook that had included many authorial stage directions. Set in the pre-Christian Roman world, Cymbeline draws its main theme, that of a wager by a husband on his wife's fidelity, from a story in Giovanni Boccaccio's Decameron.

"The Country Wife" is a Restoration comedy written by William Wycherley in 1675. It follows the story of a man named Horner who pretends to be impotent in order to gain access to the wives of wealthy men.

"The Rivals" is a play written by Richard Brinsley Sheridan in 1775. It is a classic comedy of manners that satirizes the pretensions and foibles of the upper class society of the time. The play follows the story of a young heiress named Lydia Languish who is courted by two men, Jack Absolute and Bob Acres. The play is known for its witty dialogue, memorable characters, and intricate plot. It has been widely performed and adapted over the years and remains a popular work of English drama.

Question 37

Arrange the following plays in their chronological order:

> (A) The Tempest
> (B) All For Love
> (C) Volpone
> (D) The School for Scandal

Choose the correct answer from the options given below :

> 1. (A), (C), (B), (D)
> 2. (C), (B), (A), (D)
> 3. (C), (A), (B), (D)
> 4. (A), (D), (B), (C)

Explanations:
Answer: 3. (C), (A), (B), (D

(C) Volpone - Written by Ben Jonson, it was first performed in **1605** and is a satirical comedy that explores themes of greed, deception, and corruption in Venetian society.

(A) The Tempest - Written by William Shakespeare, it is believed to be one of his last plays and was likely composed around **1610-1611.** It is a complex play that combines elements of romance, comedy, and tragedy, centring around themes of power, magic, and forgiveness.

(B) All For Love - Written by John Dryden, it was first performed in 1677 and is a tragedy based on the story of Antony and Cleopatra. It explores themes of love, loyalty, and the conflict between personal desires and duty.

(D) The School for Scandal - Written by Richard Brinsley Sheridan, it

premiered in 1777 and is a witty comedy of manners that satirizes gossip, hypocrisy, and social conventions of the time. It remains one of the most popular and enduring plays of the 18th century.

Question 38

Which of the playwrights have been correctly matched with their works?

    A.   William Wycherly - The Rivals
    B.   Ben Jonson - Volpone, or the Fox
    C.   William Congreve - The Country Wife
    D.   Aphra Behn - The Dutch Lover
    E.   Richard Sheridan - A School for Scandal

Choose the correct answer from the options given below:

    1.   C, D and E
    2.   B, C and D
    3.   A, C and E
    4.   B, D and E

Explanations:
Ans: B, D and E

Volpone, or the Fox is a comedy written by Ben Jonson and first performed in 1605. The play is set in Venice and revolves around the wealthy and cunning Volpone, who pretends to be dying in order to receive gifts from his wealthy acquaintances. The play is a biting satire of greed and materialism, and explores themes of deception, corruption, and the corrupting influence of wealth.

The Dutch Lover is a Restoration comedy written by Aphra Behn and first performed in 1673. The play is set in Holland and revolves around the romantic entanglements of the wealthy merchant Jeronimo and his love interest, the beautiful and headstrong Lucinda.

A School for Scandal is a comedy of manners written by Richard Brinsley Sheridan and first performed in 1777. The play is set in London and revolves around the scandalous behavior of a group of wealthy aristocrats, who engage in gossip, deceit, and manipulation.

Extra Perk:

The Rivals is a comedy of manners written by Richard Brinsley Sheridan and first performed in 1775. The play is set in Bath, England, and revolves around the romantic pursuits of the wealthy Captain Jack Absolute, who is in love with the beautiful Lydia Languish. The play is known for its witty dialogue, intricate plot, and memorable characters, including the eccentric Mrs. Malaprop.

The Country Wife is a Restoration comedy written by William Wycherley and first performed in 1675. The play is set in London and follows the exploits of the philandering Horner, who feigns impotence in order to gain access to the wives of wealthy men. The play is known for its frank sexual content and bawdy humor, and is considered a classic of English Restoration theatre.

Question 39

Identify the works written by Richard Brinsley Sheridan:

> A. *Richelieu*
> B. *St Patrick's Day*
> C. *The Duenna*
> D. *The Citizen of the World*
> E. *Irene*

Choose the correct answer from the options given below:

> 1. A and B
> 2. C and D
> 3. B and C
> 4. A and E

Explanations
Answer: 3. B and C

***St Patrick's Day*, or, The Scheming Lieutenant is an 18th-century play by Irish playwright and poet Richard Brinsley Sheridan (1751–1816),** first performed on 2 May 1775 at Covent Garden. It is said to have been completed by the author within two days.

The Duenna is a three-act comic opera, mostly composed by Thomas Linley the Elder and his son, Thomas Linley the Younger, to an English-language libretto by Richard Brinsley Sheridan. At the time, it was considered one of the most successful operas ever staged in England, and its admirers included Samuel Johnson, William Hazlitt and George Byron (the latter called it "the best opera ever written").

List of Plays by Richard Brinsley Sheridan

> - *The Rivals*
> - ***St Patrick's Day***
> - ***The Duenna***
> - *A Trip to Scarborough*
> - *The School for Scandal*
> - *The Camp*
> - *The Critic*
> - *The Glorious First of June*
> - *Pizarro*
> - *Clio's Protest* (written 1771, published 1819)

Question 40

Arrange the following writers chronologically in accordance with their years of birth:

A. James Boswell
B. Edward Gibbon
C. Samuel Johnson
D. Edmund Burke
E. Richard Brinsley Sheridan

Choose the correct answer from the following options:

1. C. D, B, A. E
2. C, A, B. E. D
3. A. C, B. D. E
4. B, C. A, D, E

Explanations:
Answer: 1. C. D, B, A. E

Samuel Johnson (1709-1784), known as Dr. Johnson, was an English critic, biographer, essayist, poet, and lexicographer. He is widely regarded as one of the greatest figures of 18th-century life and letters.

Edmund Burke (1729-1797), a British statesman, parliamentary orator, and political thinker, played a prominent role in public life from 1765 to about 1795. He was significant in the history of political theory, championing conservatism in opposition to Jacobinism in his work Reflections on the Revolution in France (1790).

Edward Gibbon (1737-1794), an English rationalist historian and scholar, is best known for his work The History of the Decline and Fall of the Roman Empire (1776–88). This monumental work provides a continuous narrative from the 2nd century CE to the fall of Constantinople in 1453.

James Boswell (1740-1795), a Scottish writer, was a close friend and biographer of Samuel Johnson. His most famous work is The Life of Johnson (1791). The publication of his journals in the 20th century revealed him to be one of the world's greatest diarists.

Richard Brinsley Sheridan (1751-1816), born in Ireland, was a playwright, impresario, orator, and Whig politician. His plays, notably The School for Scandal (1777), occupy an important place in the history of the comedy of manners, bridging the gap between the end of the 17th century and Oscar Wilde in the 19th century.

CHAPTER 2

THE GRAVEYARD POETS OF THE 18TH CENTURY

- The Graveyard Poets were **18th-century pre-Romantic English poets.**
- Their poetry focused on meditations on death and mortality.
- Themes included "skulls, coffins, epitaphs, and worms."
- They moved beyond elegies, rarely sensationalizing death.
- Their poetry expressed feelings of the sublime and uncanny.
- They had an antiquarian interest in ancient English forms.
- Graveyard Poets are seen as precursors to Gothic literature.
- They also influenced the Romantic movement in England.
- The Graveyard School includes a wide variety of authors.
- There's ongoing debate about what defines "graveyard" poetry.
- The core works include Gray's *Elegy* and Parnell's *Night-Piece*.
- Other key poems are Blair's *The Grave* and Young's *Night-Thoughts*.
- The term "Graveyard School" was coined in 1898.
- Many Graveyard Poets were Christian clergymen like Parnell.
- Their poetry often combined aesthetic beauty and moral instruction.
- They explored both religious themes and gothic elements.
- Graveyard poetry was popular in the 18th century.
- **A partial list of Graveyard Poets**
    - Thomas Parnell
    - John Keats
    - Thomas Warton
    - Thomas Percy
    - **Thomas Gray**
    - **Oliver Goldsmith**
    - **William Cowper**
    - **Christopher Smart**
    - James Macpherson
    - **Robert Blair**
    - **William Collins**
    - **Thomas Chatterton**
    - Mark Akenside
    - Joseph Warton

- o   Henry Kirke White
- o   **Edward Young**
- o   David Mallet
- o   William Mason
- o   James Beattie
- o   **James Thomson is also sometimes included as a Graveyard Poet.**

Graveyard Poets
Code 1: *Granite, Gold, Copper, Chrystle*

1. Granite: **Thomas Gray (1716-1771)**
2. Gold: **Oliver Goldsmith (1732-1774)**
3. Copper: **William Cowper (1731-1800)**
4. Chrystle: **Christopher Smart (1722-1771)**

Code 2: *"Robert Young Collins Met James Chatterton on Thomson's Dying Hill"*

1. **Robert** - Robert Blair (1699-1746)
2. **Young** - Edward Young (1683-1765)
3. **Collins** - William Collins (1721-1759)
4. **Met** - James Macpherson (1736-1796)
5. **Chatterton** - Thomas Chatterton (1752-1770)
6. **James** - James Thomson (1700-1748)
7. **Dying Hill** - John Dyer (1699-1757)

Thomas Gray (1716-1771)

- ➤ **Gray was born in London** to a wealthy lawyer.
- ➤ **He owed his education** to his mother's self-denial.
- ➤ **Gray was educated at Eton and Cambridge** universities.
- ➤ **Met Horace Walpole at Cambridge**, toured Italy with him.
- ➤ **Returned to Cambridge**, took his degree, lived elegantly.
- ➤ He was offered **Poet Laureate in 1757, but declined**.
- ➤ **Refused the Laureateship in 1757**, obtained a professorship.
- ➤ **Gray never lectured** despite his Cambridge professorship.
- ➤ **Lived a quiet life**, traveling occasionally and writing sparingly.
- ➤ **Gray had shrinking, fastidious tastes**, avoiding the world's roughness.
- ➤ **His first poem was *Ode on a Distant Prospect*** (1747).

- ➤ **The poem contained gloomy reflections on schoolboys' fate**.
- ➤ *Elegy Written in a Country Churchyard* **appeared** in 1751.
- ➤ **It was familiar yet fresh**, filled with quotable phrases.
- ➤ **The poem's popularity has endured to this day**.
- ➤ **Gray's *Pindaric Odes* (1757)** were criticized for their obscurity.
- ➤ *The Bard* **and** *The Progress of Poesy*, the **two Pindaric Odes** in the book
- ➤ *The Bard* **and** *The Progress of Poesy* **require clarification**.
- ➤ **His odes have splendor and richly adorned language**.
- ➤ **Johnson criticized Gray's work** for its excessive adornment.
- ➤ **Gray's odes have energy and dignity**, despite Johnson's criticism.
- ➤ **Gray's prose includes letters describing his travel experiences**.
- ➤ **His prose style shows vigor and keen observation**.
- ➤ **His descriptions of nature**, like the Lake District, are admirable.
- ➤ **Gray's descriptions were ahead of his time**, in taste.
- ➤ **His slender body of work** is of significant importance.
- ➤ **Gray explored early Norse and Celtic legends** for inspiration.
- ➤ **He expressed genuine sympathy for the poor and oppressed**.
- ➤ **Gray's treatment of nature was innovative for his era**.
- ➤ **He made lasting contributions** in both prose and poetry.
- ➤ **Poems:**
  - ○ *Ode on the Spring (written in 1742)*
  - ○ *On the Death of Richard West (written in 1742)*
  - ○ *Ode on the Death of a Favourite Cat, Drowned in a Tub of Goldfishes (written in 1747)*
    - ▪ A mock-heroic elegy concerning **Horace Walpole's cat.**
    - ▪ **Walpole owned two cats: Zara and Selima.**
    - ▪ *"What female heart can gold despise?*
    - ▪ *What cat's averse to fish?",*
    - ▪ *"a fav'rite has no friend",*
    - ▪ *"[k]now one false step is ne'er retrieved"*
    - ▪ *"nor all that glisters, gold".*
  - ○ *Ode to a Distant Prospect of Eton College (written in 1747 and published anonymously)*
    - ▪ *"where ignorance is bliss, 'tis folly to be wise,"*
    - ▪ *"a mirror in every mind".*
  - ○ *Elegy Written in a Country Churchyard (written between 1745 and 1750)*
  - ○ *The Progress of Poesy: A Pindaric Ode (written between 1751 and 1754)*

- Gray successfully sought **close imitation of the original Pindaric form.**
  - *The Bard: A Pindaric Ode (written between 1755 and 1757)*
  - *The Fatal Sisters: An Ode (written in 1761)*

The Bard. A Pindaric Ode (1757)

- ➤ Set at Edward I's conquest of Wales.
- ➤ Gray was inspired by medieval history and Welsh music.
- ➤ His work influenced poets, painters, and the Celtic Revival.
- ➤ It is considered foundational to Britain's Romantic movement.
- ➤ Edward I's army encounters a Welsh bard near Snowdon.
- ➤ The bard curses Edward and invokes shades of past victims.
- ➤ Cadwallo, Urien, and Mordred are called by the bard.
- ➤ The three weave the Plantagenet line's misfortunes and fate.
- ➤ The bard foretells misery for Edward's descendants.
- ➤ He predicts the return of Welsh rule through the Tudors.
- ➤ The bard also foresees the flowering of British poetry.
- ➤ Spenser, Shakespeare, and Milton are mentioned as poets.
- ➤ The poem blends prophecy, history, and national revival.

Elegy Written In A Country Churchyard (1751)

- ➤ Gray may have been influenced by **Richard West's death** in 1742.
- ➤ It was composed when Gray lived **near Stoke Poges parish church.**
- ➤ He sent it to **Horace Walpole**, who popularized it in London literary circles.
- ➤ The poem is written in a style similar to **odes**.
- ➤ The poem is **written in quatrains**, stanzas of four lines.
- ➤ Each quatrain has **ten syllables per line**.
- ➤ The **rhyme scheme is ABAB**, alternating rhyme patterns.
- ➤ It meditates on **death and remembrance after death**.
- ➤ The narrator reflects on **lives of obscure churchyard rustics**.
- ➤ The final epitaph **soothes the narrator's fear of dying**.
- ➤ Wrote this poem during the **Age of Enlightenment,** a period of intellectual growth.
- ➤ There are **33 stanzas** in the poem.
- ➤ **Each stanza consists of four lines.**
- ➤ In this elegy, ordinary men are mourned.
- ➤ In this poem, Gray discusses death and the lives of the middle class.
- ➤ The **time is evening**, and people have retired.

- The speaker observes the **churchyard and evening sounds**.
- **A bell rings** in the distant church.
- After labor, **shepherds and cattle return home**.
- The setting is **rural with a melancholy mood**.
- **Darkness and silence** prevail, adding gloom.
- Sounds of **hooting owls, buzzing beetles, and bells**.
- Despite the gloom, the **speaker roams the graveyard**.
- The speaker **imagines the lives of the dead**.
- **Gravestones surround** the speaker as he reflects on death.
- The **speaker vividly describes** the churchyard surroundings.
- He highlights both **aural and visual sensations**.
- The focus shifts from **countryside to immediate surroundings**.
- The speaker contrasts **country life with memories**.
- He reflects on **wasted potential and missed opportunities**.
- The speaker contemplates **injustices obscuring individuals in death**.
- **Humans desire remembrance**, discussed near the poem's end.
- A **second speaker recounts the first speaker's death**.
- The poem ends with **the poet's grave and meditation**.
- The poet, though talented, **remains unknown and obscure**.
- His **isolation** kept him from achieving greatness.
- The **final version** includes third-person descriptions of death.
- The **epitaph** reveals the poet's **lack of recognition**.
- The original conclusion **confronts death directly**.
- The final version offers a more **indirect reflection on death**.
- The poem pays tribute to **poor villagers.**
- They may not be famous, but **their character is honest.**
- Written this poem in their honor.
- Death is referred to as an equalizer in the poem.
- All people ought to die.
- Furthermore, no one can escape death.
- We are all equal in death.
- Apart from that, nothing, not even wealth or glory, will bring the dead back to life.
- The dead must be respected, regardless of their financial situation.
- If they had been given a chance, they would have been great men in their lifetime.
- **"Far from the Madding Crowd" (the title of a novel by Thomas Hardy)**

- ➢ **Samuel Johnson also said of Gray that he spoke in "two languages".**
- ➢ **He spoke in the language of "public" and "private"**

The curfew tolls the knell of parting day,
    The lowing herd wind slowly o'er the lea,
The plowman homeward plods his weary way,
    And leaves the world to darkness and to me.
Now fades the glimm'ring landscape on the sight,
    And all the air a solemn stillness holds,
Save where the beetle wheels his droning flight,
    And drowsy tinklings lull the distant folds;
Save that from yonder ivy-mantled tow'r
    The moping owl does to the moon complain
Of such, as wand'ring near her secret bow'r,
    Molest her ancient solitary reign.
Beneath those rugged elms, that yew-tree's shade,
    Where heaves the turf in many a mould'ring heap,
Each in his narrow cell for ever laid,
    The rude forefathers of the hamlet sleep.
The breezy call of incense-breathing Morn,
    The swallow twitt'ring from the straw-built shed,
The cock's shrill clarion, or the echoing horn,
    No more shall rouse them from their lowly bed.
For them no more the blazing hearth shall burn,
    Or busy housewife ply her evening care:
No children run to lisp their sire's return,
    Or climb his knees the envied kiss to share.
Oft did the harvest to their sickle yield,
    Their furrow oft the stubborn glebe has broke;
How jocund did they drive their team afield!
    How bow'd the woods beneath their sturdy stroke!
Let not Ambition mock their useful toil,
    Their homely joys, and destiny obscure;
Nor Grandeur hear with a disdainful smile
    The short and simple annals of the poor.
The boast of heraldry, the pomp of pow'r,
    And all that beauty, all that wealth e'er gave,
Awaits alike th' inevitable hour.

**T*he paths of glory lead but to the grave.*
*Nor you, ye proud, impute to these the fault,***
   If Mem'ry o'er their tomb no trophies raise,
Where thro' the long-drawn aisle and fretted vault
   The pealing anthem swells the note of praise.
Can storied urn or animated bust
   Back to its mansion call the fleeting breath?
Can Honour's voice provoke the silent dust,
   Or Flatt'ry soothe the dull cold ear of Death?
Perhaps in this neglected spot is laid
   Some heart once pregnant with celestial fire;
Hands, that the rod of empire might have sway'd,
   Or wak'd to ecstasy the living lyre.
But Knowledge to their eyes her ample page
   Rich with the spoils of time did ne'er unroll;
Chill Penury repress'd their noble rage,
   And froze the genial current of the soul.
Full many a gem of purest ray serene,
   The dark unfathom'd caves of ocean bear:
Full many a flow'r is born to blush unseen,
   And waste its sweetness on the desert air.
Some village-Hampden, that with dauntless breast
   The little tyrant of his fields withstood;
Some mute inglorious Milton here may rest,
   Some Cromwell guiltless of his country's blood.
Th' applause of list'ning senates to command,
   The threats of pain and ruin to despise,
To scatter plenty o'er a smiling land,
   And read their hist'ry in a nation's eyes,
Their lot forbade: nor circumscrib'd alone
   Their growing virtues, but their crimes confin'd;
Forbade to wade through slaughter to a throne,
   And shut the gates of mercy on mankind,
The struggling pangs of conscious truth to hide,
   To quench the blushes of ingenuous shame,
Or heap the shrine of Luxury and Pride
   With incense kindled at the Muse's flame.
Far from the madding crowd's ignoble strife,
   Their sober wishes never learn'd to stray;

Along the cool sequester'd vale of life
  They kept the noiseless tenor of their way.
Yet ev'n these bones from insult to protect,
  Some frail memorial still erected nigh,
With uncouth rhymes and shapeless sculpture deck'd,
  Implores the passing tribute of a sigh.
Their name, their years, spelt by th' unletter'd muse,
  The place of fame and elegy supply:
And many a holy text around she strews,
  That teach the rustic moralist to die.
For who to dumb Forgetfulness a prey,
  This pleasing anxious being e'er resign'd,
Left the warm precincts of the cheerful day,
  Nor cast one longing, ling'ring look behind?
On some fond breast the parting soul relies,
  Some pious drops the closing eye requires;
Ev'n from the tomb the voice of Nature cries,
  Ev'n in our ashes live their wonted fires.
For thee, who mindful of th' unhonour'd Dead
  Dost in these lines their artless tale relate;
If chance, by lonely contemplation led,
  Some kindred spirit shall inquire thy fate,
Haply some hoary-headed swain may say,
  "Oft have we seen him at the peep of dawn
Brushing with hasty steps the dews away
  To meet the sun upon the upland lawn.
"There at the foot of yonder nodding beech
  That wreathes its old fantastic roots so high,
His listless length at noontide would he stretch,
  And pore upon the brook that babbles by.
"Hard by yon wood, now smiling as in scorn,
  Mutt'ring his wayward fancies he would rove,
Now drooping, woeful wan, like one forlorn,
  Or craz'd with care, or cross'd in hopeless love.
"One morn I miss'd him on the custom'd hill,
  Along the heath and near his fav'rite tree;
Another came; nor yet beside the rill,
  Nor up the lawn, nor at the wood was he;
"The next with dirges due in sad array

> *Slow thro' the church-way path we saw him borne.*
> *Approach and read (for thou canst read) the lay,*
> *Grav'd on the stone beneath yon aged thorn."*
> **THE EPITAPH**
> *Here rests his head upon the lap of Earth*
> *A youth to Fortune and to Fame unknown.*
> *Fair Science frown'd not on his humble birth,*
> *And Melancholy mark'd him for her own.*
> *Large was his bounty, and his soul sincere,*
> *Heav'n did a recompense as largely send:*
> *He gave to Mis'ry all he had, a tear,*
> *He gain'd from Heav'n ('twas all he wish'd) a friend.*
> *No farther seek his merits to disclose,*
> *Or draw his frailties from their dread abode,*
> *(There they alike in trembling hope repose)*
> **The bosom of his Father and his God.**

Questions

Question 41

"The Elegy written in a Country Churchyard" is written in ;

1. **Quatrains of ten syllable lines**
2. Octave and Sestet
3. Heroic couplet
4. Alexandrines

Correct Explanations:

"The Elegy written in a Country Churchyard" is written in quatrains, which are stanzas of four lines. Each line of the quatrain has ten syllables, and the rhyme scheme is ABAB, meaning that the first and third lines rhyme with each other, and the second and fourth lines rhyme with each other. This form is known as heroic quatrains, and it is a common form in English poetry. The use of this form in "The Elegy written in a Country Churchyard" gives the poem a sense of structure and balance, which contributes to its overall effect. Specifically, it is a type of poem known as an elegy, which is a mournful and reflective poem that is often written in honor of someone who has died. The poem was written by the English poet Thomas Gray and was first published in 1751.

Oliver Goldsmith (1732-1774) (Discussed in Chapter 1)

➢ The son of an Anglo-Irish clergyman, Goldsmith.
➢ He studied at Trinity College, Dublin,
➢ He was almost expelled for his involvement in the **Black Dog riot.**
➢ He often contributed to Ralph Griffiths's Monthly Review.
➢ Anglo-Irish essayist, poet, novelist, dramatist, and eccentric.
➢ His essays were collected as ***The Citizen of the World in 1762.***
➢ The prose, ***The Citizen of the World or Letters from a Chinese Philosopher (1762).***
   o Chinese traveler in England, Lien Chi.
➢ The prose, ***An Enquiry into the Present State of Polite Learning in Europe***
➢ The novel ***The Vicar of Wakefield (1766),***
   o Published in two volumes in 1766.
   o Portrait of village life, is narrated by **Dr. Primrose**, the title character.
➢ The Poem ***The Traveller or a Prospect of Society (1764)***
   o A philosophical poem.
   o The heroic verse of an Augustan style.
➢ The poem **The Deserted Village (1770),**
   o It is a pastoral elegy.
   o Idealizes a rural way of life that was
      ▪ being destroyed by the displacement of agrarian villagers,
      ▪ the greed of landlords, and economic and political change.
   o **George Crabbe** created a bleak view of the country's poor in his poem ***The Village (1783).***
   o The central image of this 430-line poem is the **titular village of Auburn,**
➢ The play ***She Stoops to Conquer (1773).***

Question 42

The Deserted Village by Oliver Goldsmith

1. Critiques the rural institutions
2. Advocates urbanism over rural backwardness
3. Reflects upon different views on the human soul
4. **Voices revolt of the individual man against institutions**

CORRECT EXPLANATIONS:

➤ The Deserted Village is a poem by Oliver Goldsmith published in 1770.

➤ **It is a work of social commentary, and condemns rural depopulation and the pursuit of excessive wealth.**

➤ The poem is written in heroic couplets, and describes the decline of a village and the emigration of many of its residents to America.

➤ **In the poem, Goldsmith criticises rural depopulation, the moral corruption found in towns, consumerism, enclosure, landscape gardening, avarice, and the pursuit of wealth from international trade.**

➤ The poem employs, in the words of one critic, "deliberately precise obscurity", and does not reveal the reason why the village has been deserted.

➤ The poem was very popular in the eighteenth and nineteenth centuries, but also provoked critical responses, including from other poets such as George Crabbe.

➤ References to the poem, and particularly its ominous "Ill fares the land" warning, have appeared in a number of other contexts.

Question 43

Which of the following poems is written by Oliver Goldsmith?

1. A Deserted Village
2. A Deserted Villa
3. The Deserted Village
4. A Deserted City

Explanations:

Ans: The Deserted Village

"The Deserted Village" is a poem written by **Oliver Goldsmith, first published in 1770**. The poem is a nostalgic and elegiac portrayal of the

decline of rural life in England and the displacement of villagers by the enclosure movement.

The poem describes the **village of Auburn,** which has been depopulated and abandoned due to the enclosures that **have forced the peasants off the land.** The village is depicted as a place of rustic simplicity, where the people lived in harmony with nature and each other. Goldsmith contrasts this **idyllic vision of rural life with the depredations of modernity,** which have destroyed the social fabric of the village and left its inhabitants destitute.

William Cowper (1731-1800)

- **Cowper wrote** about **joys and sorrows of everyday life**.
- He focused on **rural life and concern for the poor.**
- His style **revolted against 18th-century verse** trends.
- Considered a **forerunner to Burns, Wordsworth, and Coleridge.**
- His **humor often concealed underlying desolation.**
- **"The Castaway" reveals his deeper sense of despair.**
- **In 1767**, Morley Unwin died; Cowper moved to **Olney.**
- Curate **John Newton encouraged Cowper's religious life.**
- Cowper and Newton collaborated on **"Olney Hymns" (1779).**
- Inspired by **Lady Austen**, he wrote **"The Journey of John Gilpin".**
- Her idea also led to **Cowper's long poem "The Task".**
- **"The Task" promoted rural ease**, published in **1785.**
- Cowper moved to **Weston** and began translating **Homer.**
- His health deteriorated, with **occasional mental illness.**
- In **1795**, he moved to **Norfolk** with Mary Unwin.
- After **Mary Unwin's death (1796)**, Cowper **sank into despair.**
- **Robert Southey** edited his works in **15 volumes (1835–1837).**
- Cowper is known as one of the **best letter writers** in English.
- His hymns, like **"God Moves in a Mysterious Way"**, became famous.
- **"The Letters and Prose Writings"** were published in **1979–1980.**
- **List of Poems by William Cowper**
  - *The Snail, 1770*
  - *The Winter Nosegay, 1777*
  - *Olney Hymns, 1778–1779, in collaboration with John Newton*
  - *John Gilpin, 1782*
  - *Epitaph on a Hare, 1782*

- o *Cowper's first independent volume, Poems by William Cowper, of the Inner Temple, Esq., 1782*
- o *The Rose, 1783*
- o *The Task, 1785*
- o *The Morning Dream, 1788*
- o *Homer's Iliad and Odyssey, 1791 (translations from the Greek).*
- o *The Retired Cat, 1791*
- o *To Mary, 1793*
- o *On the Ice Islands Seen Floating in the German Ocean, 1803*
- o *The Castaway*

➢ **The Task (1785)**
- o ***The Task: A Poem, in Six Books.***
- o A poem in blank verse published in 1785.
- o Its six books are called
  - ▪ "The Sofa,"
  - ▪ "The Timepiece,"
  - ▪ "The Garden,"
  - ▪ "The Winter Evening,"
  - ▪ "The Winter Morning Walk,"
  - ▪ "The Winter Walk at Noon."
- o Beginning with a mock-Miltonic passage on the origins of the sofa
- o It develops into a discursive meditation on
  - ▪ the blessings of nature,
  - ▪ the retired life,
  - ▪ religious faith,
  - ▪ attacks on slavery,
  - ▪ blood sports,
  - ▪ fashionable frivolity,
  - ▪ lukewarm clergy,
  - ▪ French despotism among other things.
- o As the poet himself writes,
  - ▪ *...my raptures are not conjur'd up*
  - ▪ *To serve occasions of poetic pomp,*
  - ▪ *But genuine...—* **Book 1, lines 151-5**

Christopher Smart (1722-1771)

➢ **Christopher Smart**, best known for **A Song to David** (1763).

- ➤ The poem praises **David, author of the Psalms.**
- ➤ **Anticipated William Blake** and **John Clare's works.**
- ➤ **Studied at Cambridge**, later became a **hack writer.**
- ➤ Suffered from **religious mania**, confined three times.
- ➤ Smart had **close friendships with Samuel Johnson** and others.
- ➤ He died in **debtor's prison** due to financial struggles.
- ➤ **A Song to David** was **not fully appreciated** until the 19th century.
- ➤ His **"Jubilate Agno"** was published posthumously in **1939.**
- ➤ Known for **contributions to The Midwife and The Student** journals.
- ➤ Wrote **Seaton Prize poems** and the mock epic **The Hilliad.**
- ➤ His works combined **religious and nationalist themes.**
- ➤ **"Jubilate Agno"** was partially written during his asylum confinement.
- ➤ Smart's **vivid imagination** drew critical recognition later.
- ➤ His poetry includes **nature theories** and **English nationalism.**

Robert Blair (1699-1746)

- ➤ **Scottish poet Robert Blair**, known for **The Grave** (1743).
- ➤ Blair was educated in **Edinburgh and Holland.**
- ➤ Ordained in 1731, he served in **Athelstaneford.**
- ➤ **Happily married**, he had **six children.**
- ➤ **The Grave** reflects **mortality through mortuary imagery.**
- ➤ The poem **predates Edward Young's "Night-Thoughts".**
- ➤ It blends **Scottish ghoulishness with sermon-like reflections.**
- ➤ Written in **blank verse**, with **Shakespearean rhythms.**
- ➤ **William Blake illustrated** 12 images for the 1808 edition.
- ➤ Blair was also passionate about **botany and optical experiments.**
- ➤ **The Grave (1743)**
  - o **"The Grave"** is a **blank verse poem** by Robert Blair.
  - o It is Blair's **most renowned work.**
  - o Blair composed **most of the poem before becoming a minister.**
  - o Editor John Johnstone claimed it was written **during student years.**
  - o The poem was later **corrected and expanded** with maturity.
  - o **767 lines long**, it exemplifies **graveyard poetry.**
  - o The poem is part of the **Graveyard School** literary movement.

Edward Young (1683-1765)

- **Edward Young** is remembered for **Night-Thoughts**, written in blank verse.
- The poem reflects **philosophical themes** after several **personal losses**.
- **Night-Thoughts** influenced **Goethe and Edmund Burke**.
- The poem featured **illustrations by William Blake**.
- Young's plays lacked **theatrical sense**, rarely performed.
- **The Revenge** (1721) is considered **his best play**.
- His **Conjectures on Original Composition** (1759) influenced **Romantic thought**.
- *Night-Thoughts (1742-45)*
    - The Complaint: or, Night-Thoughts on Life, Death, & Immortality
    - **Night-Thoughts** is written in **blank verse**.
    - The poem reflects on **death and human frailties**.
    - The adage **"procrastination is the thief of time"** is famous.
    - **Nine nights** reflect the poet's musings on personal loss.
    - **Thomas Stothard** created illustrations for it in **1799**.
    - **James Boswell** praised it as the **grandest poetry** ever.
    - **Night-Thoughts** discusses **life's fleeting opportunities**.
    - **The nine nights are each a poem of their own.** They are:
    - *"Life, Death, and Immortality" (dedicated to Arthur Onslow);*
    - *"Time, Death, Friendship" (dedicated to Spencer Compton);*
    - *"Narcissa" (dedicated to Margaret Bentinck);*
    - *"The Christian Triumph" (dedicated to Philip Yorke);*
    - *"The Relapse" (dedicated to George Lee);*
    - *"The Infidel Reclaim'd" (in two parts, "Glories and Riches"*
    - *"The Nature, Proof, and Importance of Immortality"; dedicated to Henry Pelham);*
    - *"Virtue's Apology; or, The Man of the World Answered" (with no dedication);*
    - *"The Consolation" (dedicated to Thomas Pelham-Holles).*

William Collins (1721-1759) & His Eclogues and His Odes

- **William Collins**, a pre-Romantic poet, mixed **Neoclassical forms** with **Romantic themes**.
- Though his career was brief, **Collins is revered** for his **lyrical odes**.
- Educated at **Winchester College**, he formed a bond with **Joseph Warton**.
- At **17**, he composed his **Persian Eclogues** under **Pope's influence**.
- In **1744**, he published a verse **epistle featuring "Dirge from Cymbeline"**.
- The **pastoral eclogue** genre was renewed in Collins' **Persian Eclogues**.
- His **eclogues** feature exotic settings like **Bagdat, Caucasus, and Circassia**.
- **Persian Eclogues** were re-titled **"Oriental Eclogues"** in 1757.
- Translations of **Oriental Eclogues** appeared in **German** in **1767 and 1770**.
- **Thomas Chatterton** later wrote **African eclogues**, inspired by Collins.
- Scott of Amwell's **Oriental Eclogues (1782)** also honored **Collins' work**.
- **Scott's eclogues** explored **Arabia, Bengal, and China**.
- Collins' **odes** reflected the **renewal of the ode genre** in English poetry.
- His **pindaric odes** sometimes **dispensed with rhyme**.
- **Collins' odes** were influenced by **Thomas Gray and Joseph Warton**.
- **Collins' Odes** were planned to be **published jointly with Warton's**.
- Gray remarked that Collins had a **"fine fancy, modeled on the Antique."**
- Collins was **praised for his imagination**, despite having a **"bad ear"**.
- **Gray** predicted both poets' works would **"last some years"**.
- **Their odes' excess** led to **burlesque parodies** shortly after publication.
- A parody called **"Ode to Horror"** mocked their **stylistic mannerisms**.
- The parody may have been written by **Thomas Warton's brother**.
- Collins' **"Oriental Eclogues"** were set apart by their **exotic locations**.
- His **allegorical and descriptive style** influenced **Romantic poets**.
- Collins had a **short literary career** but left a **lasting impact**.
- **Collins' Persian Eclogues** are examples of the **evolving pastoral tradition**.
- His works reflected **18th-century movements** towards **imagination** in poetry.
- His **Romantic leanings** bridged the gap between **Neoclassical** and **Romantic** poetry.
- **Blended emotions** and **nature imagery** feature heavily in his poems.

- ➤ Despite his struggles, **Collins is regarded as a visionary** among 18th-century poets.

James Macpherson (1736-1796)

- ➤ **James Macpherson** initiated the **Ossianic controversy** in Gaelic studies.
- ➤ His first book, **The Highlander (1758)**, was **undistinguished**.
- ➤ He collected **Gaelic manuscripts** and oral poems with **John Home's** support.
- ➤ Macpherson published **Fragments of Ancient Poetry (1760)**.
- ➤ Followed by **Fingal (1762)** and **Temora (1763)**.
- ➤ He claimed the works were based on **Ossian**, a **3rd-century Gaelic poet**.
- ➤ No **Gaelic manuscripts predate the 10th century**.
- ➤ The authenticity was supported by **Hugh Blair**, doubted by **David Hume**.
- ➤ **Thomas Gray admired** Ossian's work but remained **skeptical**.
- ➤ **Samuel Johnson outright denied** Ossian's authenticity.
- ➤ None of these critics **knew Gaelic**.
- ➤ Macpherson injected a **Romantic mood** into the **Gaelic originals**.
- ➤ Some translations followed **closely**, while others **did not**.
- ➤ His language was **influenced by the Authorized Version of the Bible**.

Thomas Chatterton (1752-1770)

- ➤ English poet whose precocious talents ended in suicide at age 17.
- ➤ Influence on Romantic artists, such as Shelley, Keats, Wordsworth, and Coleridge.
- ➤ **Thomas Chatterton** was fatherless, raised in poverty, and **highly educated**.
- ➤ He **passed off his work** as medieval poetry by **Thomas Rowley**.
- ➤ **Horace Walpole** denounced him for **forging medieval poems**.
- ➤ At **17**, Chatterton sought **political outlets** in London.
- ➤ Despite his talents, **he poisoned himself in despair**.
- ➤ **Romantic poets** were fascinated by **Chatterton's tragic life**.
- ➤ **Alfred de Vigny** wrote a play about Chatterton's **life**.
- ➤ **Henry Wallis's painting**, *The Death of Chatterton*, became famous.
- ➤ Chatterton's first known poem, **"On the Last Epiphany,"** was written at 10.
- ➤ He deceived readers with **his medieval eclogue "Elinoure and Juga."**
- ➤ The **Rowley poems** became separate from Chatterton's **other works**.

- **Thomas Rowley**, Chatterton's imaginary monk, was **taken from a monument.**
- The **Rowley poems** had shortcomings but showed **Chatterton's genius.**
- Chatterton became an **early Romantic pioneer** in **metrics and feeling.**
- In **1767**, Chatterton apprenticed to a **Bristol attorney.**
- He contributed to **Bristol Journal** and **Town and Country Magazine.**
- Chatterton despised **Bristol and his dowdy family.**
- He sent **Rowley's manuscripts** to publisher **James Dodsley**, but was ignored.
- **Horace Walpole**, initially impressed, later **denounced Chatterton's forgeries.**
- Chatterton wrote **noble but bitter lines** against **Walpole.**
- He threatened suicide, forcing **John Lambert** to release him.
- His **comic opera, The Revenge**, earned **some money.**
- The death of a **prospective patron** crushed his **hopes.**
- **"An Excelente Balade of Charitie"** was his **most pathetic Rowley poem.**
- Starving, **Chatterton refused help** and died of **arsenic poisoning.**
- **Rowleians** believed Chatterton was **not the sole author.**
- Many **poets** paid tribute to Chatterton after his death.
- **Coleridge** wrote a **monody** for Chatterton.
- **Wordsworth** called him the **"marvelous boy".**
- **Shelley** gave him a stanza in **"Adonais".**
- **Keats** dedicated **Endymion** to Chatterton.
- **Lord Byron** and **Sir Walter Scott** praised Chatterton.
- **Dante Gabriel Rossetti** added his **praise.**
- In **France**, Chatterton was hailed by the **Romantics.**
- **Alfred de Vigny's play**, *Chatterton*, inspired an **opera.**
- **Chatterton's life** and work continue to **influence Romantic literature.**
- His **tragic death** was idealized by the **Romantic poets.**
- **Chatterton's poems** featured themes of **despair and genius.**
- He contributed significantly to **early Romanticism.**
- **Chatterton's legacy** lives on through **literature and the arts.**

Question 44

Which work of John Keats is dedicated to Thomas Chatterton ?

1. Lamia
2. Endymion

3. Hyperion
4. Ode on a Grecian Urn

Explanations:
Answer: 2. Endymion

Endymion is a poem by John Keats first published in 1818 by Taylor and Hessey of Fleet Street in London. John Keats dedicated this poem to the late poet Thomas Chatterton. The poem begins with the line "A thing of beauty is a joy for ever". Endymion is written in rhyming couplets in iambic pentameter (also known as heroic couplets). Keats based the poem on the Greek myth of Endymion, the shepherd beloved of the moon goddess Selene. The poem elaborates on the original story and renames Selene "Cynthia" (an alternative name for Artemis).

James Thomson (1700-1748) & The Seasons (1726)

- **James Thomson** foreshadowed **Romanticism** in his poetry.
- His works expressed **Newtonian science and England's growth**.
- Best known for **The Seasons, The Castle of Indolence**, and **"Rule, Britannia!"**.
- Educated at **Jedburgh Grammar** and the **University of Edinburgh**.
- **Moved to London** in 1725 and worked as a **tutor**.
- Published **The Seasons**: Winter (1726), Summer (1727), Spring (1728).
- The **full poem**, including Autumn, was published in **1730**.
- Believed **poets and scientists** must **serve God through nature**.
- Wrote **"Rule, Britannia!"** for **Alfred, a Masque (1740)**.
- Authored the ambitious **five-part poem Liberty (1735-36)**.
- Wrote **The Castle of Indolence (1748)**, an allegory in **Spenserian stanzas**.
- **The Seasons** was the **first sustained nature poem** in English.
- It concluded with a **"Hymn to Nature"**.
- The poem's novelty lay in its **non-narrative structure**.
- Thomson's audacity lay in **unifying the poem without a plot**.
- The **complete edition of The Seasons** included **Autumn (1730)**.
- Influenced by **Milton's Latin vocabulary** and word order.
- Extended **blank verse** for **description and meditation**.
- **Critic Raymond Havens** found Thomson's style **pompous**.

- ➤ Thomson avoided **simple, direct, and natural speech**.
- ➤ His **poetic style** featured **complex and contorted language**.
- ➤ **The Seasons** had a significant **impact on English poetry**.

John Dyer (1699-1757) & Grongar Hill (1726)

- ➤ **John Dyer** is chiefly remembered for **"Grongar Hill"** (1726).
- ➤ **"Grongar Hill"** is a **meditative poem** in the style of **Pope's "Windsor-Forest"**.
- ➤ Dyer describes **Welsh countryside** with **classical landscape references**.
- ➤ The poem begins a reflection on **human life**: "A little rule, a little sway...".
- ➤ Dyer's longest poem, **The Fleece** (1757), mimics **Virgil's Georgics**.
- ➤ **The Fleece** is a blank-verse poem about **tending sheep**.
- ➤ Dyer also wrote **The Ruins of Rome** (1740), mixing description and reflection.
- ➤ **Grongar Hill** is a **loco-descriptive** poem about a **Welsh landscape**.
- ➤ Published during the **Augustan period**, it's a **Romantic precursor**.
- ➤ The poem sparked debate on **artistic standards and personal experience**.
- ➤ First published in **Miscellaneous Poems** by **Richard Savage** in 1726.
- ➤ Written in **irregular pindaric lines**, but the poetic diction was conventional.
- ➤ The second version is **unencumbered**, using **swift-moving, rhythmic lines**.
- ➤ The poem features phrases like **"mossy Cells"** and **"grassy Bed"**.
- ➤ Descriptions include **"watry Face"**, **"bristly Sides"**, and **"rugged Cliffs"**.
- ➤ Dyer refined the poem with **four-stressed rhyming couplets**.
- ➤ Influenced by **Milton's "L'Allegro"** and **Marvell's "Appleton House"**.
- ➤ Geoffrey Tillotson linked the poem to **Milton's syntax** style.
- ➤ The meter is similar to **Marvell's "Upon the Hill"** and **"Cooper's Hill"**.
- ➤ **Grongar Hill** is considered part of the **prospect poem tradition**.
- ➤ Dyer mined **freshness and simplicity** from his earlier, more elaborate work.
- ➤ His style reflects the **natural beauty of the Vale of Towy**.

- ➤ The poem's **reflection on life** adds depth to its landscape portrayal.
- ➤ **"The Fleece"** (1757) is about the **sheep industry** in England.
- ➤ **The Fleece** attempts to elevate the **rural profession** to epic status.
- ➤ **"The Ruins of Rome"** reflects on the **impermanence of civilizations**.
- ➤ Dyer's **Romantic qualities** emerged through his **natural descriptions**.
- ➤ His **classical references** give his poems a **Neoclassical foundation**.
- ➤ **Grongar Hill's second version** moved away from **poetic conventions**.
- ➤ The poem uses the **natural world** to reflect on **human experience**.
- ➤ Dyer's **pastoral themes** align him with **early Romantic poetry**.
- ➤ His works combine **Neoclassical form** with **Romantic themes**.
- ➤ **The Fleece** was an attempt to **modernize Virgil's agricultural epics**.
- ➤ **Grongar Hill's significance** lies in its influence on **later poets**.
- ➤ Dyer's works are celebrated for their **meditative, descriptive style**.

William Blake (1757-1827)

- ➤ **William Blake** was born in **London**, son of a **City hosier**.
- ➤ **Began as an artist** at age **ten**, poet at **twelve**.
- ➤ **Apprenticed to an engraver** by his **father**.
- ➤ Blake had **visions** and hovered near **insanity** throughout life.
- ➤ His **mental peculiarities** are evident in **his art and poems**.
- ➤ Blake's **wild, fantastic engravings** occupied him all his life.
- ➤ He gained **neither money nor fame** during his lifetime.
- ➤ Blake died **poor but serene** in his **birth city**.
- ➤ His notable works include **Poetical Sketches** (1783).
- ➤ Other major works: **Songs of Innocence** (1789) and **Experience** (1794).
- ➤ His works are filled with **visions, simplicity, and obscurity**.
- ➤ Blake's **genius is undoubted** but marked by **wayward tendencies**.
- ➤ His poetry was often **charming yet mystifying** in style.
- ➤ He lived modestly, with **simple desires and fulfillment**.
- ➤ **Engravings and poems** were his **life's occupation**.
- ➤ Despite his **unbalanced mind**, Blake's **artistic influence endures**.
- ➤ **Blake saw visions** from childhood, starting at **age four**.
- ➤ At **nine**, he saw a **tree filled with angels**.

- ➤ His parents noticed **he was different** but didn't force school.
- ➤ **Blake learned to read and write** at home.
- ➤ At **age ten**, he wanted to become a **painter**.
- ➤ He attended **drawing school** at his **parents' encouragement.**
- ➤ At **twelve**, Blake began **writing poetry.**
- ➤ At **fourteen**, Blake apprenticed with an **engraver.**
- ➤ Art school was **too costly** for his family.
- ➤ As an apprentice, he **sketched tombs at Westminster Abbey.**
- ➤ The Gothic styles there **influenced his future work.**
- ➤ After his apprenticeship, he briefly **studied at the Royal Academy.**
- ➤ In **1782**, Blake married **Catherine Boucher**, an **illiterate woman.**
- ➤ Blake taught her **reading, writing, and draftsmanship.**
- ➤ Catherine helped Blake **print his illuminated poetry.**
- ➤ In **1784**, Blake opened a **print shop** with **James Parker.**
- ➤ The print shop venture **failed**, leaving him to engrave for a living.
- ➤ Blake trained his younger brother **Robert in art and engraving.**
- ➤ Robert died in **1787**, and Blake saw his **spirit rise.**
- ➤ Blake claimed Robert taught him the **illuminated printing method.**
- ➤ His first printed work, **Poetical Sketches** (1783), was **apprentice verses.**
- ➤ **Songs of Innocence** (1789) and **Songs of Experience** (1794) became famous.
- ➤ Some interpret **Songs of Innocence** as **children's literature** with deeper meaning.
- ➤ Blake's poems were **illustrated in an illuminated manuscript style.**
- ➤ **Blake opposed 18th-century conventions**, preferring **imagination over reason.**
- ➤ He associated with **radicals like Thomas Paine** and **Mary Wollstonecraft.**
- ➤ In his poem, Blake declared, **"I must create a system...".**
- ➤ Works like **"The French Revolution"** and **"America, a Prophecy"** critiqued tyranny.
- ➤ **The Book of Urizen** (1794) addressed **theological oppression.**
- ➤ In **The Marriage of Heaven and Hell**, Blake **satirized church and state.**
- ➤ In **1800**, Blake moved to **Felpham**, supported by **William Hayley.**
- ➤ Blake taught himself **Greek, Latin, Hebrew, and Italian** in Felpham.
- ➤ There, he experienced **spiritual insights** for his visionary works.

- ➤ His epics like **Milton** and **Jerusalem** envision the **triumph of spirit over reason**.
- ➤ Blake believed **ordinary people could understand** his poetry.
- ➤ In **1808**, he exhibited his **watercolors at the Royal Academy**.
- ➤ Some praised his work, others deemed his paintings **"hideous"**.
- ➤ **Blake's poetry was not well-known**, but **Coleridge** called him a **"man of Genius."**
- ➤ **Wordsworth** admired his work, and **Lamb shared his poems**.
- ➤ **Robert Southey**, despite thinking Blake insane, appreciated **his poetry**.
- ➤ Blake's final years were spent in **poverty** but cheered by **"the Ancients."**
- ➤ In **1818**, he met **John Linnell**, who **supported him financially**.
- ➤ **Linnell commissioned Blake** to illustrate **Dante's Divine Comedy**.
- ➤ Blake worked on **Dante's illustrations** until his **death in 1827**.
- ➤ His illuminated works included **hand-painted watercolor illustrations**.
- ➤ **Catherine** was devoted to Blake, helping with his **art and printing**.
- ➤ Blake's work often **focused on spiritual and visionary themes**.
- ➤ His paintings and engravings depicted **otherworldly, imaginative scenes**.
- ➤ Blake opposed **rigid neoclassical conventions** in both art and poetry.
- ➤ **Blake's Romantic ideals** influenced **later artists and poets**.
- ➤ His **visionary epics** were unlike traditional poetry in **plot or meter**.
- ➤ Despite his lack of fame, **Blake remained true** to his unique vision.
- ➤ Blake's **opposition to political tyranny** fueled his artistic expression.
- ➤ His work **satirized oppressive societal structures**, including religion.
- ➤ **Blake's spiritual experiences** profoundly influenced his creativity.
- ➤ The **Romantic movement** was significantly impacted by Blake's ideas.
- ➤ His illuminated manuscripts merged **visual art and poetry**.
- ➤ Blake's **legacy grew posthumously**, recognized for his unique genius.
- ➤ He combined **mysticism, mythology, and political critique** in his work.

- ➤ Blake's works emphasized the **power of imagination and inner vision**.
- ➤ His **deeply symbolic art and poetry** left a lasting influence.
- ➤ **Blake's unorthodox life and work** represent the **spirit of artistic freedom**.
- ➤ **Notable Works:**
    - o *"A Vision of the Last Judgment"*
    - o *"Auguries of Innocence"*
    - o *"Jerusalem: The Emanation of the Giant Albion"*
    - o *"London" "Milton"*
    - o *"Songs of Experience"*
    - o *"Songs of Innocence"*
    - o *"The Everlasting Gospel"*
    - o *"The First Book of Urizen"*
    - o *"The Tyger"*
    - o *"Vala or The Four Zoas"*
    - o *"Visions of the Daughters of Albion"*

Songs of Innocence and of Experience

- ➤ **Songs of Innocence and Experience** is **Blake's illustrated poem collection**.
- ➤ First printed and illuminated by **Blake in 1789**.
- ➤ In **1794**, Blake bound these with **new poems**.
- ➤ **Blake's illustrations** featured **mythical subjects like Oberon and Puck**.
- ➤ **"Innocence" and "Experience"** represent two **states of human consciousness**.
- ➤ The collection reinterprets **Milton's "Paradise" and "Fall"**.
- ➤ **Innocence** symbolizes the **"unfallen world,"** **Experience** the "fallen world".
- ➤ **Blake's dualism** contrasts childhood and the **fallen adult world**.
- ➤ **Childhood** is a state of **innocence, not original sin**.
- ➤ This innocence **is affected by the fallen world**.
- ➤ **Experience** reflects **social, political corruption**, and lost innocence.
- ➤ The poems examine **fear, inhibition, and societal oppression**.
- ➤ Blake critiques the **Church, State, and ruling classes**.
- ➤ **Romanticism's themes** of innocence and experience are explored here.

> The collection shows **perception's transformation from innocence to experience**.

Songs of Innocence

> Songs of Innocence was originally a complete work first printed in 1789.
> It is a conceptual collection of 19 poems engraved with artwork.
> This collection mainly shows a happy, innocent perception of pastoral harmony.
> The Chimney Sweeper" and "The Little Black Boy," subtly shows the dangers of this naïve and vulnerable state.
> The poems are each listed below:
> - *Introduction*
> - *The Shepherd*
> - *The Echoing Green*
> - ***The Lamb***
> - ***The Little Black Boy***
> - *The Blossom*
> - ***The Chimney Sweeper***
> - ***The Little Boy Lost***
> - ***The Little Boy Found***
> - *Laughing Song*
> - *A Cradle Song*
> - *The Divine Image*
> - ***Holy Thursday***
> - *Night*
> - *Spring*
> - *Nurse's Song*
> - ***Infant Joy***
> - *A Dream*
> - *On Another's Sorrow*

Songs of Experience

> Songs of Experience is a poetry collection of 26 poems.
> The poems were published in 1794.
> Some of the poems, such as **"The Little Girl Lost" and "The Little Girl Found,"**
> The poems are listed below:
> - *Introduction*

- *Earth's Answer*
- *The Clod and the Pebble*
- ***Holy Thursday***
- ***The Little Girl Lost***
- ***The Little Girl Found***
- ***The Chimney Sweeper***
- *Nurse's Song*
- ***The Sick Rose***
- *The Fly*
- *The Angel*
- ***The Tyger***
- *My Pretty Rose Tree*
- *Ah! Sun-flower*
- *The Lilly*
- *The Garden of Love*
- *The Little Vagabond*
- ***London***
- *The Human Abstract*
- *Infant Sorrow*
- ***A Poison Tree***
- ***A Little Boy Lost***
- ***A Little Girl Lost***
- *To Tirzah*
- ***The School Boy***
- *The Voice of the Ancient Bard*

The Lamb

- ➤ Published in Songs of Innocence in 1789.
- ➤ It is the counterpart poem to Blake's poem: "The Tyger" in Songs of Experience.
- ➤ The poem is about **Christianity**.
- ➤ Used name of **Jesus Christ, also called "The Lamb of God"** in the Gospel of John 1:29 and 36 and throughout John's Book of Revelation (or Revelations) at the end of the New Testament.
  - *Little Lamb who made thee?*
  - *Dost thou know who made thee?*

The Little Black Boy

- ➤ Included in Songs of Innocence in 1789.

- ➤ Published when **slavery was still legal,** and the campaign for **the abolition of slavery was still young**.
- ➤ Blake speaks of "black bodies" and a "sunburnt face" in the fourth stanza
- ➤ The black boy says that he will "shade him [the English boy] from the heat" this implies that the English boy's pale skin is not used to the heat (derived from God's love)..

The Chimney Sweeper

- ➤ **Published in two parts, Songs of Innocence (1789) and Experience (1794)**.
- ➤ The poem critiques **child labor in 18th-19th century England**.
- ➤ **Boys as young as four** were sold as **chimney sweepers**.
- ➤ These children lived **oppressed, diminutive lives, socially accepted**.
- ➤ They were often **unfed, poorly clothed, and mistreated**.
- ➤ Many **died from falls or diseases** caused by soot exposure.
- ➤ In **"Songs of Innocence"**, a child dreams of **angelic rescue**.
- ➤ The angel takes **sweepers from coffins to sunny meadows**.
- ➤ In **"Songs of Experience"**, a **child is abandoned in the snow**.
- ➤ His parents are at **church or possibly with God** after death.

The Tyger

- ➤ **"The Tyger"** was published in **1794 in "Songs of Experience"**.
- ➤ It rose to prominence in the **Romantic period**.
- ➤ The poem is one of the most **anthologized in English literature**.
- ➤ It has been subject to **literary criticism and musical adaptations**.
- ➤ **"The Tyger"** explores Christian religious themes of **creation**.
- ➤ It questions **God's intentions in creating the tiger** and lamb.
- ➤ **"The Tyger"** is the **sister poem to "The Lamb"**.
- ➤ **Beauty and ferocity** are contrasted, requiring understanding of both.
- ➤ **Songs of Experience** contrasts **Songs of Innocence**, reflecting duality.
- ➤ Blake argues that **human struggles** arise from **contrasting concepts**.
- ➤ **Truth lies in resolving the contradictions** between innocence and experience.
- ➤ **Experience** is seen as a **necessary part of life**, not evil.
- ➤ Blake believed in resolving, not battling, **existence's contraries**.

- ➤ According to **Kazin**, "The Tyger" reflects **triumphant human awareness**.
- ➤ The poem is a **hymn to pure being and existence.**

London

- ➤ **"London"** was published in **Songs of Experience (1794)** by **William Blake**.
- ➤ It lacks a **corresponding poem** in **Songs of Innocence**.
- ➤ Blake writes of **London as a resident**, not a visitor.
- ➤ The poems explore **"Two Contrary States of the Human Soul"**.
- ➤ **Songs of Innocence** focuses on **love, childhood, and nature**.
- ➤ Critics suggest the poems reflect **modernity's effects** on society.
- ➤ Themes include **industrial conditions, child labor, prostitution,** and **poverty**.
- ➤ **"London" reflects Blake's feelings** towards oppressive society.
- ➤ England in the **1800s became oppressive** due to **French Revolution fears**.
- ➤ Laws restricted **individual freedoms** during this period.
- ➤ Blake initially loved **London**, praising its **beauty and prosperity**.
- ➤ Post-revolution, **Blake saw London as dark and oppressive**.
- ➤ He offers **social criticism of 18th-century England** through this poem.
- ➤ An **acrostic** spelling "Hear" can be found in the **third stanza**.
- ➤ This acrostic is **foreshadowed by the last word** of the second stanza.
- ➤ The poem reflects **London's transformation and societal decay**.

 Do You Know?
"London" by Samuel Johnson (1738)
A **satirical imitation** of Juvenal's Third Satire in heroic couplets.
 "London" by William Blake (1794)
Critiques **oppression and industrialization** in society.
 "London, 1802" by William Wordsworth
Opens with: **"MILTON! thou shouldst be living at this hour."**
Wordsworth **laments England's decline** and praises Milton.
 "London" (novel) by Edward Rutherfurd
Spans **2,000 years** of London's history, following multiple families.

A Poison Tree

- ➤ **"A Poison Tree"** was published in **1794** in *Songs of Experience*.
- ➤ It describes **repressed anger** leading to **murder**.
- ➤ Themes include **indignation, revenge**, and **the fallen state of mankind**.
- ➤ The poem follows a **trochaic beat** and has **four stanzas**.
- ➤ **First-person perspective** shifts after the first stanza with **"And."**
- ➤ Originally, Blake intended to **end the poem at line 4**.
- ➤ There are **manuscript differences**, such as "Mirth at the Errors of a Foe."
- ➤ The poem suggests **acting on anger** reduces **vengeance**.
- ➤ It reflects **British views on anger** after the **French Revolution**.
- ➤ Anger was debated as either **motivating or blinding** reason.
- ➤ Blake believed **anger should be expressed**, but cautiously.
- ➤ Poisoning appears in **many of Blake's poems**.
- ➤ The **poisoner** in the poem resembles **Jehovah, Urizen, and Satan**.
- ➤ **Victim ingests poison** through reading or other actions.
- ➤ The victim's **individuality** is lost, replaced by the **poisoner's influence**.
- ➤ The **poisoned reason** is forced onto the victim.
- ➤ **Dominance** is vital in this world; **trust is absent**.
- ➤ There is no **reciprocal interaction** due to mistrust.
- ➤ The poem critiques how **anger destroys relationships**.
- ➤ **Blake and Coleridge** were wary of anger **seizing control**.
- ➤ The poem highlights the dangers of **unchecked emotion**.
- ➤ **"A Poison Tree"** reflects Blake's vision of a **distrustful society**.

Questions:

Question 45

Match List I and List II List I

List I Author	List II Work
A. John Keats	I. Alastor
B. Willam Wordsworth	II Songs of Experience
C. PB Shelley	III. Comic
D. William Blake	IV. The Excursion

Choose the correct answer from the options given below:

1. A – Ill, B – I, C – IV, D – II
2. A – III, B – IV, C – 1, D – II
3. A – I, B – IV, C – III, D – II
4. A – IV, B – II, C – I, D – Ill

Explanations:
Answer: 2. A – III, B – IV, C – 1, D – II

"Alastor" is a poem by Percy Bysshe Shelley, published in 1816. It is a Gothic poem about a young poet's search for the ideal woman.

"The Excursion" is a long poem by William Wordsworth, published in 1814. It is part of Wordsworth's larger work "The Prelude" and tells the story of a group of travelers who discuss nature, humanity, and the role of art in society.

"Songs of Experience" is a collection of poems by William Blake, published in 1794. It is a companion volume to "Songs of Innocence" and explores the darker side of human experience, including themes of oppression, corruption, and mortality.

"Comic" is indeed a poem by John Keats, published in 1817. It is a satirical poem that mocks the futility of human ambition and the transience of earthly pleasures.

Question 46

Name the poet who has composed the following poems:

    A. The Divine Image
    B. The Holy Thursday
    C. The Little Boy Lost
    D. The Little Boy Found

Choose the correct answer from the options given below:

    1. William Shakespeare
    2. William Blake
    3. William Collins
    4. Samuel Johnson

Explanations:

Answer: 2. William Blake

Songs of Innocence and of Experience (1795)

William Blake's "Songs of Innocence and of Experience" is a compilation of illustrated poems that explores contrasting states of the human soul. Initially, Blake created and presented "Songs of Innocence" and "Songs of Experience" as distinct collections. It wasn't until 1795 that he merged these works into a single volume, aptly named "Songs of Innocence and of Experience Shewing the Two Contrary States of the Human Soul." Despite this unification, Blake maintained the practice of publishing the collections separately as well.

"The Divine Image" is a poem Songs of Innocence (1789), not to be confused with "A Divine Image" from Songs of Experience (1794). It was later included in Songs of Innocence and of Experience (1794).

The poems are listed below:

> - Introduction
> - Earth's Answer
> - The Clod and the Pebble
> - **Holy Thursday**
> - The Little Girl Lost
> - The Little Girl Found
> - The Chimney Sweeper
> - Nurse's Song
> - The Sick Rose
> - The Fly
> - The Angel
> - The Tyger
> - My Pretty Rose Tree
> - Ah! Sun-flower
> - The Lilly
> - The Garden of Love
> - The Little Vagabond
> - London
> - The Human Abstract
> - Infant Sorrow
> - A Poison Tree

> ➢ **A Little Boy Lost**
> ➢ A Little Girl Lost
> ➢ To Tirzah
> ➢ The School Boy
> ➢ The Voice of the Ancient Bard

Question 47

Who said about Northrop Frye that "he did not lock Iterature into an ivory tower, instead he emphasized its centrality to the development of a civilised humane society"?

1. Philp Wheelwright
2. Margaret Atwood
3. Ernest Jones
4. Richard Chase

Explanations:
Answer: 2. Margaret Atwood

Herman Northrop Frye, born on July 14, 1912, and passing on January 23, 1991, was a Canadian luminary in literary criticism and theory, regarded as one of the 20th century's pivotal figures in the field.

Frye's international acclaim skyrocketed with the publication o**f "Fearful Symmetry" in 1947**, a work that significantly altered the understanding of William Blake's poetry. His enduring legacy, however, is largely founded on his groundbreaking literary criticism theory presented in **"Anatomy of Criticism" (1957),** a seminal text in literary theory of the twentieth century. Upon its release, Harold Bloom praised Frye, stating that "Anatomy established Frye as 'the foremost living student of Western literature.'" Over his extensive career, Frye's influence extended beyond literary circles, affecting cultural and social critique, for which he was widely honored and celebrated. Reflecting on his impact, **Margaret Atwood, who was once his student,** remarked in The Globe and Mail, _**"He did not lock literature into an ivory tower: instead he emphasized its centrality to the development of a civilized and humane society."**_

Robert Burns (1759-1796)

- Also known familiarly as Rabbie Burns
- Robert Burns was a **Scottish poet and lyricist.**
- He is widely regarded as the **national poet of Scotland**.
- He is the best known of the poets who have written in the Scots language.
- Much of his writing is in a "light Scots dialect" of English.
- He also wrote in standard English, and his political or civil commentary is often blunt.
- He is regarded as a pioneer of the Romantic movement.
- After death, he **inspired the founders of liberalism and socialism**.
- He became a **cultural icon in Scotland** and globally.
- His life became a **national charismatic cult** by the 19th century.
- His influence remains **strong on Scottish literature** today.
- **"Auld Lang Syne"** is often sung at **Hogmanay** celebrations.
- **"Scots Wha Hae"** was an **unofficial national anthem** for Scotland.
- Other famous **poems and songs** by **Robert Burns** remain globally known today.
    - *"Scots Wha Hae"*
    - ***"Auld Lang Syne"***
    - ***"A Red, Red Rose,"***
    - *"A Man's a Man for A' That,"*
    - ***"To a Louse,"***
    - ***"To a Mouse,"***
    - *"The Battle of Sherramuir,"*
    - *"Tam o' Shanter."*
    - *"Ae Fond Kiss."*

Auld Lang Syne

- "Auld Lang Syne" is a popular song, particularly in English-speaking countries.
- Sung to bid farewell to the old year at midnight on New Year's Eve.
- The text is a Scots-language.
- By extension, it is also often heard at funerals, graduations, and as a farewell.

Should Old Acquaintance be forgot,
and never thought upon;
The flames of Love extinguished,
and fully past and gone:
Is thy sweet Heart now grown so cold,
that loving Breast of thine;
That thou canst never once reflect
On old long syne.

Tam o' Shanter

- ➤ Tam o' Shanter is a narrative in 1790 while living in Dumfries.
- ➤ First published in 1791,
- ➤ 228 (or 224) lines,
- ➤ It is one of Burns' longer poems and employs a mixture of Scots and English.
- ➤ The poem describes **Tam, a drunk farmer in Ayr**.
- ➤ **Tam's wife** waits angrily for him at home.
- ➤ After a night out, **Tam rides home on Meg**.
- ➤ He sees a **haunted church lit up** during a storm.
- ➤ **Witches and warlocks** are dancing, and **the Devil plays bagpipes**.
- ➤ Tam watches, **amazed by gruesome objects** in the church.
- ➤ He sees a witch in a **short dress and shouts**.
- ➤ The **music stops**, and the creatures chase after Tam.
- ➤ **Tam flees** towards the **River Doon** on Meg's horse.
- ➤ The creatures can't cross **running streams**, so they chase.
- ➤ A witch **grabs Meg's tail** just before they cross the bridge.
- ➤ **Tam and Meg escape**, but **Meg loses her tail**.

A Red, Red Rose

- ➤ "A Red, Red Rose" is a 1794 song in Scots by Robert Burns
- ➤ It is based on traditional sources.
- ➤ The song is also referred to by the title "(Oh) My Love is Like a Red, Red Rose"
- ➤ It is often published as a poem.
- ➤ Many composers have set Burns' lyrics to music,
- ➤ It gained worldwide popularity set to the traditional tune "Low Down in the Broom"

My luve is like a red red rose
That's newly sprung in June;
O my Luve's like the melodie

That's sweetly play'd in tune;
As fair art thou, my bonnie lass,
So deep in luve am I;
And I will luve thee still, my dear,
Till a' the seas gang dry;
Till a' the seas gang dry, my dear,
And the rocks melt wi' the sun;
I will luve thee still, my dear,
While the sands o' life shall run.

And fare thee weel, my only Luve
And fare thee weel, a while!
And I will come again, my Luve,
Tho' it were ten thousand mile.

Questions:

Question 48

Robert Burns was born in

1. Scotland
2. England
3. Ireland
4. America

Explanations:
Ans: Scotland

Robert Burns was a Scottish poet and lyricist who lived in the late 18th century. He is widely **regarded as the national poet of Scotland** and is celebrated for his works, which reflect the Scottish people and culture.

Some of his most famous works include:

➢ *Auld Lang Syne*
➢ *Tam o' Shanter*
➢ *To a Mouse*
➢ *To a Louse*

> ➤ *A Red, Red Rose*
> ➤ *Scots Wha Hae*
> ➤ *Address to a Haggis*
> ➤ *The Battle of Sherramuir*
> ➤ *My Heart's in the Highlands*

In addition to his literary works, Burns was also a collector and editor of traditional Scottish songs and ballads, and his work helped to preserve and **popularize the Scottish musical heritage.**

Extra Perk:

The Irish national poet is William Butler Yeats. He was born in Dublin, Ireland in 1865 and went on to become one of the most famous and influential poets of the 20th century. Yeats was also a playwright, essayist, and Nobel laureate, and his works are known for their rich symbolism, intricate language, and exploration of Irish mythology, history, and culture.

Throughout his career, **Yeats was deeply involved in the Irish cultural and political movements of his time.** He was a founding member of the Irish Literary Revival, a movement dedicated to promoting the Irish language, literature, and culture. He was also an active participant in the Irish nationalist movement, and his works often reflect his political and social views.

Some of Yeats' most famous works include "The Lake Isle of Innisfree," "The Second Coming," "Easter 1916," "Sailing to Byzantium," and "The Tower."

Question 49

Who has composed "A Red Red Rose"?

1. Joanna Ballie
2. Robert Burns
3. William Wordsworth
4. Samuel Taylor Coleridge

Explanations:
Answer: 2. Robert Burns

<u>"A Red, Red Rose," crafted by the Scottish poet Robert Burns in 1794,</u> is a song that draws from traditional sources and has become known worldwide, particularly when set to the melody "Low Down in the Broom." Though originally a song in Scots, it is commonly presented as a poem under the title "(Oh) My Love is Like a Red, Red Rose," and has inspired numerous musical adaptations through the years.

Robert Burns, born on 25 January 1759 and passing on 21 July 1796, affectionately known as Rabbie Burns, is celebrated as **Scotland's national poet** and enjoys international acclaim.

Beyond his original works, Burns was dedicated to preserving Scottish folk songs, often enhancing or modifying them. His legacy includes the universally sung **"Auld Lang Syne"** at New Year's celebrations, and **"Scots Wha Hae,"** which has been considered an unofficial anthem of Scotland. Other notable works that continue to resonate globally include **"A Man's a Man for A' That," "To a Louse," "To a Mouse," "The Battle of Sherramuir," "Tam o' Shanter," and "Ae Fond Kiss,"** affirming Burns's lasting influence on poetry and song.

Joanna Baillie, born on 11 September 1762 and passing away on 23 February 1851, was a notable Scottish poet and playwright. Her prominent works include the "**Plays on the Passions**" series, spanning **three volumes from 1798 to 1812, and "Fugitive Verses" published in 1840.**

George Crabbe (1754-1832)

- ➤ **George Crabbe** was an **English poet, surgeon, and clergyman.**
- ➤ Known for **realistic narratives** of **middle and working-class life.**
- ➤ In the **1770s**, Crabbe began his career as a **doctor's apprentice.**
- ➤ Later, he became a **surgeon** and eventually a **poet.**
- ➤ In **1780**, he moved to **London** to make a **living as a poet.**
- ➤ After **financial difficulties**, Crabbe reached out to **Edmund Burke.**
- ➤ Burke was **impressed** and **helped him publish his work.**
- ➤ They became **close friends**, and Burke **supported Crabbe's career.**
- ➤ **Burke introduced Crabbe** to **London's literary society.**
- ➤ **Crabbe became Chaplain** to the **Duke of Rutland.**

- ➤ He remained a **clergyman** for the rest of his life.
- ➤ **Crabbe befriended** literary figures like **Sir Walter Scott** and **Wordsworth**.
- ➤ **Lord Byron** called him **"nature's sternest painter, yet the best"**.
- ➤ Crabbe's poetry was **unsentimental**, using **heroic couplets**.
- ➤ **Frank Whitehead** considered Crabbe a **major, undervalued poet**.
- ➤ **Crabbe's work** is notable for its **depiction of provincial life**.
- ➤ His literary career was **greatly supported by Edmund Burke**.
- ➤ Crabbe's works include
    - ○ *The Village (1783)*
    - ○ *Poems (1807)*
    - ○ *The Borough (1810)*
    - ○ *His poetry collections Tales (1812) and Tales of the Hall (1819)*

John Dennis (1657-1734)

- ➤ **John Dennis** was an **English critic and dramatist**.
- ➤ He emphasized the **importance of passion in poetry**.
- ➤ Educated at **Harrow School** and the **University of Cambridge**.
- ➤ **Dennis met leading literary figures** after settling in London.
- ➤ Although a **prolific dramatist**, he was **never very successful**.
- ➤ His notable works include **"The Usefulness of the Stage" (1698)**.
- ➤ Other important works are **"The Advancement and Reformation of Modern Poetry" (1701)**.
- ➤ **Dennis prioritized passion** over **decorum and polish** in art.
- ➤ **John Milton** was Dennis's **idol among English poets**.
- ➤ Dennis had **enthusiasm for the sublime**, a new concept.
- ➤ His **quarrel with Pope** arose due to differences in **poetry style**.
- ➤ **Pope ridiculed Dennis** in his **"Essay on Criticism"**.
- ➤ Dennis responded with **"Reflections Critical and Satyrical" (1711)**.
- ➤ He launched **personal attacks** on Pope, calling him **a hunch-back'd toad**.
- ➤ Despite reconciliation attempts, **the quarrel continued** until Dennis's death.
- ➤ **Dennis figured prominently** in Pope's **mock-epic, The Dunciad (1728)**.
- ➤ Dennis defended **drama against Jeremy Collier's 1698 condemnation**.

GOTHIC FICTION

- **Gothic fiction** is a **literary aesthetic of fear and haunting**.
- The term **references Gothic architecture** from the **Middle Ages**.
- The first Gothic novel was **"The Castle of Otranto" (1764)**.
- Early contributors include **Clara Reeve and Ann Radcliffe**.
- **Gothic themes** influenced **19th-century Romantic poets and novelists**.
- Authors like **Mary Shelley and Walter Scott** used Gothic motifs.
- The **Victorian period** saw Gothic novels by **Dickens and the Brontës**.
- **Edgar Allan Poe** and **Nathaniel Hawthorne** used Gothic elements.
- **"Dracula" by Bram Stoker** remains a **classic Gothic novel**.
- **"Fragment of a Novel" is an unfinished 1819 vampire horror story written by Lord Byron.**
- The story, also known as "A Fragment" and "The Burial: A Fragment", was one of the first in English to feature a vampire theme.
- **Richard Marsh's "The Beetle"** was another notable Gothic work.
- **Stevenson's "Strange Case of Dr. Jekyll and Mr. Hyde"** is well-known.
- **20th-century Gothic authors** include **Daphne du Maurier and Stephen King**.
- **Shirley Jackson** contributed to the Gothic genre with **psychological horror**.
- **Anne Rice** is known for **Gothic vampire literature**.
- **Toni Morrison** incorporated **Gothic elements in her novels**.
- **Gothic fiction** continues to influence **modern horror and literature**.

Code 1: Pole on Wall of Castle, There Lives Shallow Frank with Old English Baron Clara

1. Horace Walpole – Castle of Otranto (1765)
2. Mary Shelley – Frankenstein
3. Clara Reeve – The Old English Baron (1778)

Code 2: I Turned The Old Manor House Into Beckford Vathek

1. Charlotte Turner Smith – The Old Manor House (1793)
2. William Thomas Beckford – Vathek (1786)

Code 3: Lewis the Monk Stands on the Cliff of Udolpho

1. Gregory Lewis – The Monk (1796)
2. Anne Radcliffe – The Mysteries of Udolpho (1794)

Code 4: Caleb Wins Gold

1. William Godwin – Caleb Williams (1794

Code 5: Mature Melmoth

1. Charles Robert Maturin – Melmoth the Wanderer (1820)

Horace Walpole (1717-1797) & Castle of Otranto (1765)

- **Horace Walpole** was an **English writer, connoisseur, and collector.**
- Known for **"The Castle of Otranto" (1764)**, the first **Gothic novel.**
- He was a **prolific letter writer** and built **Strawberry Hill.**
- Youngest son of **Prime Minister Robert Walpole.**
- Educated at **Eton and King's College, Cambridge.**
- In **1739**, he toured **France and Italy** with **Thomas Gray.**
- They quarreled during the trip but later **reconciled.**
- Walpole admired **Gray's poetry** throughout his life.
- After returning in **1741**, he entered **Parliament.**
- His **Parliament career** was undistinguished but attended regularly.
- In **1791**, he inherited the **peerage from his nephew.**
- He remained **unmarried**, and his **earldom became extinct** upon death.
- **Walpole's literary output** included **romance and Gothic fiction.**
- **The Castle of Otranto** restored **romance to contemporary fiction.**
- He also wrote **"The Mysterious Mother"** (1768), a tragedy on **incest.**
- Authored **"Historic Doubts on the Life of Richard III"** (1768).
- Wrote on **art history**, including **"Anecdotes of Painting in England".**
- Walpole's works influenced the **Gothic novel genre** greatly.

Castle of Otranto (1765)

- **First published in 1764**, it is **the first Gothic novel.**
- **Walpole added "Gothic"** to the subtitle in **the second edition.**
- Set in a **haunted castle**, it merged **medievalism and terror.**
- The novel influenced **modern-day gothic books, films, and music.**
- Walpole was inspired by **a nightmare** at **Strawberry Hill House.**
- The novel started a **popular literary genre** in the late **18th century.**
- Influential Gothic authors include **Radcliffe, Shelley, and Poe.**
- **"The Castle of Otranto"** tells the story of **Manfred and his family.**
- **Manfred's son Conrad** dies after being **crushed by a giant helmet.**
- **An ancient prophecy** warns of the **castle's fate.**

- Manfred, fearing the prophecy, **plans to marry Isabella**.
- **Manfred's wife Hippolita** is seen as unable to provide a strong heir.
- Isabella **escapes with the help of Theodore**, a peasant.
- **Manfred orders Theodore's death**, but **Jerome recognizes Theodore**.
- Jerome identifies Theodore as **his son** and **begs for his life**.
- **Knights arrive**, revealing **Fredric's claim to the castle**.
- **Manfred and the knights** race to **find Isabella**.
- **Theodore is freed** by **Manfred's daughter, Matilda**.
- Theodore **finds Isabella**, hides her in **a cave**.
- Theodore fights a knight, who is **Isabella's father**.
- **Frederic falls in love with Matilda**, and they **make a deal**.
- Frederic **backs out of the deal** after **a ghostly warning**.
- **Manfred mistakes Matilda** for Isabella and **stabs her**.
- **Theodore is revealed** as the **true prince of Otranto**.
- Matilda dies, leaving **Manfred to repent** for his actions.
- A **giant ghost appears**, declaring **the prophecy fulfilled**.
- **The castle walls** are **shattered by the ghostly figure**.
- **Manfred abdicates** the principality and **retires**.
- **The novel** ends with Theodore as the **rightful prince**.
- **The Castle of Otranto** established many Gothic **tropes**.
- **Its themes** of fate, **guilt, and the supernatural** are prominent.

Mary Shelley (1797-1851)

- **Mary Shelley** was an **English novelist** known **worldwide**.
- Best known for **"Frankenstein: or, The Modern Prometheus"** **(1818)**.
- Daughter of **philosopher William Godwin** and **Mary Wollstonecraft**.
- Shelley grew up in an **intellectually vibrant household**.
- Shelley's mother died **days after her birth**.
- Raised by her father, **encouraged to follow anarchist beliefs**.
- She had a **troubled relationship with her stepmother**, Mary Clairmont.
- At **16**, she eloped to **Italy with Percy Bysshe Shelley**.
- **They married** in 1816 after **Shelley's wife died**.
- **Only one of their children** survived into adulthood.
- **Frankenstein** was inspired by a **ghost-writing contest** in 1816.

- ➢ The novel is often called the **first science-fiction work.**
- ➢ **Influenced by Luigi Galvani**, it addresses **power and destruction.**
- ➢ **"Frankenstein" tells the story** of **Victor Frankenstein** and his creation.
- ➢ It was an **instant success** and remains iconic today.
- ➢ After **Percy Shelley's death in 1822**, she returned to **London.**
- ➢ She became a **novelist, biographer**, and **travel writer.**
- ➢ Shelley also **edited and promoted her husband's writings.**
- ➢ **Her work** continues to influence **literature and popular culture.**
- ➢ Shelley remains a **pioneering figure in Gothic and sci-fi genres.**
- ➢ **Frankenstein's myth** continues to inspire films, books, and discussions.
- ➢ Shelley's **legacy** lives on through **her writings and influence.**
- ➢ **Notable Works:**
  - o *"Falkner"*
  - o ***"Frankenstein; or, The Modern Prometheus"***
  - o *"History of a Six Weeks' Tour"*
  - o *"Lodore" "Selected Letters of Mary Wollstonecraft Shelley"*
  - o *"The Fortunes of Perkin Warbeck"*
  - o *"The Journals of Mary Shelley, 1814-1844"*
  - o ***"The Last Man"***
  - o *"Valperga"*

Frankenstein (1818)

Background:
- ➢ **Mary Shelley** devised **Frankenstein in 1816** at **Lake Geneva.**
- ➢ She stayed with **Lord Byron**, **Polidori**, Claire Clairmont, and **Percy Shelley.**
- ➢ **Byron suggested** the group **write ghost stories.**
- ➢ Scientists were exploring **corpse regeneration through electricity.**
- ➢ **Victor Frankenstein's experiment** leads to **tragic consequences.**
- ➢ **The creature** turns malign after **societal rejection.**
- ➢ **Frankenstein has been adapted** in **numerous films and theatre plays.**
- ➢ The novel contains **Gothic and Romantic elements.**
- ➢ **Brian Aldiss** considers **Frankenstein the first true sci-fi story.**
- ➢ The **novel influenced** the **horror genre in literature and film.**
- ➢ **Frankenstein's legacy** continues to inspire **horror and sci-fi genres.**

Summary of the Novel:

- **Robert Walton writes letters** to his sister about his expedition.
- **Walton's ship** becomes trapped in **ice** near the **North Pole**.
- Walton **rescues Victor Frankenstein**, weakened from traveling.
- Victor recounts his **life in Geneva** and **university studies**.
- **Victor discovers the secret of life** after studying **natural philosophy**.
- **Victor creates a monster** from body parts in his **apartment**.
- Horrified by his creation, **Victor falls ill** and is **nursed by Henry**.
- **Victor receives news** of his **brother William's murder**.
- He sees the monster and believes it **killed William**.
- **Justine Moritz is accused** and **executed** for the crime.
- **Victor feels guilty** for the **deaths of his loved ones**.
- **Victor meets the monster** on a glacier, seeking understanding.
- The monster confesses to **William's murder** out of **revenge**.
- The monster asks Victor to **create a female companion** for him.
- **Victor reluctantly agrees** and begins working on the second monster.
- **Victor destroys the female monster**, fearing the consequences.
- The monster swears **revenge** and vows to be at **Victor's wedding**.
- **Victor dumps the remains** of the creature into a lake.
- Victor is **arrested** for a murder and **shown Henry's dead body**.
- **Victor falls ill** and is imprisoned until his recovery.
- After **returning to Geneva**, Victor **marries Elizabeth**.
- He fears the monster's warning and **sends Elizabeth away**.
- **Elizabeth is killed** by the monster on their **wedding night**.
- **Victor's father dies of grief** soon after Elizabeth's death.
- **Victor vows revenge** and chases the monster to the **Arctic**.
- The two engage in a **dogsled chase**, but the **ice breaks**.
- **Walton finds Victor** and nurses him as he tells his story.
- **Victor dies** from illness, unable to continue his revenge.
- Walton discovers the **monster weeping over Victor's body**.
- The monster tells Walton of **his suffering and remorse**.
- **The monster departs** to the **northernmost ice to die.**

Clara Reeve (1729-1807) and The Old English Baron (1778)

- English novelist best known for the Gothic novel *The Old English Baron (1777)*.
- She also wrote an innovative history of prose fiction, *The Progress of Romance (1785)*.
- After her **father's death** in 1755, **Reeve lived with family.**
- She later **moved to her own house** in **Ipswich.**
- Her first work was **translating "Argenis" as "The Phoenix" (1772).**
- **She was saddened** by the poor **reception of her translation.**
- Reeve called it the **"best book" but "worst received."**
- Reeve published at least **24 volumes over a 33-year** career as an author.
- They included five novels, of which only
  - *The Champion of Virtue*
  - *The Old English Baron (1777)* became well known.
- The latter was written in imitation of *The Castle of Otranto* or as a rival to it.
- The two have often been printed together.
- The first edition, entitled **The Old English Baron, was dedicated to the daughter of Samuel Richardson,** who is said to have helped Reeve revise and correct it.
- It would have a noticeable influence on Mary Shelley's *Frankenstein (1818).*
- Reeve also wrote **an epistolary novel,** *The School for Widows (1791).*
- Followed by *Plans of Education (1792).*
- Her innovative history of prose fiction, *The Progress of Romance (1785)*
- It upholds explicitly the tradition of female literary history heralded by Elizabeth Rowe **(1674–1737) and Susannah Dobson (died 1795).**
- One story in work, "*The History of Charoba, Queen of Egypt,*" inspired Walter Savage Landor's first significant piece, Gebir.

The Old English Baron (1778)

- **The Old English Baron** is an **early Gothic novel** by **Clara Reeve.**
- It was first **published in 1778** under this title.

> ➢ Originally appeared **anonymously in 1777** as **The Champion of Virtue**.
> ➢ **Mrs. Bridgen, Samuel Richardson's daughter**, edited the novel.
> ➢ The **revision only corrected typographical errors**, nothing major.
> ➢ The story follows **Sir Philip Harclay's return** to **medieval England**.
> ➢ He finds his friend, **Arthur Lord Lovel, dead**.
> ➢ Arthur's cousin, **Walter Lord Lovel**, took over the estate.
> ➢ Walter **sold the castle** to the **baron, Fitz-Owen**.
> ➢ Edmund Twyford, **a peasant's son**, lives with Fitz-Owen's family.
> ➢ Sir Philip likes Edmund, noticing his **resemblance to Arthur**.
> ➢ **Sir Philip offers Edmund** to join his family, but he refuses.
> ➢ **Edmund stays with the baron**, but Sir Philip promises future help.
> ➢ The narrative **skips forward four years**.
> ➢ Edmund's **superior nature** causes **jealousy** from the baron's nephews.
> ➢ **William, the younger son**, is Edmund's **staunch ally**.
> ➢ Edmund is **in love with Lady Emma**, the baron's daughter.

Charlotte Turner Smith (1749-1806) & The Old Manor House (1793)

> ➢ **Charlotte Smith** was an **English Romantic novelist and poet**.
> ➢ She **revived the English sonnet** and influenced **Gothic fiction**.
> ➢ Smith wrote **political novels of sensibility** and **ten novels**.
> ➢ She saw herself mainly as a **poet**.
> ➢ Her **Elegiac Sonnets** turned the sonnet into **woeful sentiment**.
> ➢ Smith left her husband and wrote to **support her children**.
> ➢ Her **legal struggles as a woman** influenced her writing.
> ➢ Early novels showed **sentimentality**, later ones praised the **French Revolution**.
> ➢ By 1803, she was **destitute** due to waning interest.
> ➢ Smith sold her **book collection** to pay debts.
> ➢ She **died in 1806**, barely able to **hold a pen**.
> ➢ Largely forgotten by the **mid-19th century**, but later appreciated.
> ➢ She is now seen as a **significant Romantic writer**.

The Old Manor House (1793)

- **The Old Manor House** was **first published in 1793** by **Charlotte Smith**.
- The plot centers on **Orlando Somerive** and **Monimia Morysine's love story**.
- The novel **blends Gothic, sentimental,** and **political narrative techniques**.
- It critiques **war injustices** and **property laws**.
- **Depicts the American Revolution,** commenting on **the French Revolution**.
- **Considered the best** of Smith's **ten novels**.
- Praised for **deep characterization**, plot, and nature descriptions.
- Written during the **violent French Revolution**, between **1792-1793**.
- Smith supported the **French political goals**.
- **The Old Manor House** softened **political ideas** amid anti-French sentiment.
- Expressed similar ideals as **Smith's earlier work Desmond (1792)**.

Anne Radcliffe (1764-1823) & The Mysteries of Udolpho (1794)

- **Ann Radcliffe** was a **pioneer of Gothic fiction**.
- She explained **supernatural elements,** gaining Gothic fiction **respectability**.
- Radcliffe was **highly admired**, known as the **"mighty enchantress."**
- **Her popularity** extended through the **19th century**.
- Interest in Radcliffe **revived in the early 21st century**.
- **Radcliffe published five novels** during her lifetime.
- **Gaston de Blondeville** was **published posthumously in 1826**.
- She earned **£500 for** *The Mysteries of Udolpho (1794)*.
- *The Italian (1797)* earned her **£800**, making her highly paid.
- *Romance of the Forest (1791)* was her **first successful novel**.
- Radcliffe **lived a retired life** and never visited her novels' settings.
- **Her only journey** abroad was in **1794**.
- **A Journey Made in the Summer of 1794** described this trip.
- **Jane Austen parodied The Mysteries of Udolpho in Northanger Abbey.**
- **The Italian** was written in response to **Lewis's The Monk.**

The Mysteries of Udolpho (1794)

- **The Mysteries of Udolpho** was **published in 1794** in **four volumes**.
- The novel tells the story of **Emily St. Aubert**.
- **Emily faces misadventures** including the death of **her parents**.
- The novel contains **supernatural terrors** in a **gloomy castle**.
- The villain is an **Italian brigand** named **Signor Montoni**.
- **Emily is the archetypal Gothic heroine**, facing terror and persecution.
- **Jane Austen parodied** *Udolpho* in her novel **Northanger Abbey**.
- The novel features **psychological terror**, **crumbling castles**, and villains.
- Only about **one-third** of the novel is set in **Castle Udolpho**.
- Radcliffe added **descriptions of exotic landscapes** in **France and Italy**.
- She relied on **travel books** but made **several anachronisms**.
- The novel is set in **1584** in **France and Italy**.
- Emily investigates the **relationship between her father** and **Marchioness de Villeroi**.
- **Emily and her father** share a close bond and **love of nature**.
- They journey from **Gascony** to **Roussillon**, encountering **Valancourt**.
- **Emily and Valancourt** fall in love during the journey.
- **Emily's father dies**, leaving her **orphaned and destitute**.
- She is forced to live with her **aunt, Madame Cheron**.
- **Madame Cheron marries Montoni**, a **dubious nobleman**.
- **Montoni forces Emily** to marry **Count Morano**.
- **Emily rejects Morano**, still loving **Valancourt**.
- **Montoni brings Emily** and her aunt to **Castle Udolpho**.
- Montoni tries to force **his wife to sign over her properties**.
- **Madame Cheron dies** from **illness caused by Montoni's harshness**.
- **Many frightening events** happen in the **castle**, but are coincidental.
- **Emily escapes** with the help of **Du Pont** and her **servants**.
- **Emily learns** that **Valancourt** has **lost his wealth**.
- Despite this, **Emily regains control** of her **aunt's estate**.
- **Emily and Valancourt** are reunited at the novel's end.
- The novel blends **Gothic romance**, **sentimentality**, and **psychological terror**.
- **The Mysteries of Udolpho** is considered a **quintessential Gothic novel**.

Mathew Gregory Lewis (1775-1818) & The Monk (1796)

> - **Matthew Gregory Lewis** was an **English Gothic horror novelist.**
> - He is **nicknamed "Monk" Lewis** after his novel **The Monk.**
> - Lewis was also a **diplomat, politician**, and **Jamaican estate owner.**
> - **The Monk** was written when **Lewis was 19 years old.**
> - The novel was influenced by **Ann Radcliffe** and **German Gothic literature.**
> - **The Monk** emphasized **horror, violence**, and **eroticism**, rather than romance.
> - It was **avidly read**, but also **universally condemned.**
> - **The Castle Spectre** (1797) was a **successful musical drama.**
> - Lewis' other work was **Journal of a West India Proprietor (1834).**
> - His journal reflected **humane and liberal attitudes.**

The Monk (1796)

> - **The Monk: A Romance** is a **Gothic novel** by **Matthew Gregory Lewis.**
> - Published in **1796**, it was **written early in Lewis's career.**
> - **Lewis claimed to have written it in ten weeks.**
> - **Published before he turned twenty**, it's a **male Gothic novel.**
> - The novel is **known for horror**, not romance, and **scandalous plotlines.**
> - **Ambrosio, a monk**, is led into **depravity by Matilda.**
> - **Matilda disguises herself as a man** to enter the **monastery.**
> - **Ambrosio sells his soul** to the devil to **escape torture.**
> - He is **eventually thrown to his death** by the devil.
> - The book is a **prime example of male Gothic literature.**
> - It has been **adapted for stage** and **screen many times.**
> - **The Monk's scandalous nature** made it an **influential Gothic novel.**

William Thomas Beckford (1760-1844) & Vathek (1786)

> - **William Beckford** was an **eccentric English author** of **Vathek (1786).**

- **Byron and Mallarmé** acknowledged his **genius** as a writer.
- Beckford is also known for building **Fonthill Abbey**.
- **Vathek** is considered a **masterpiece of fantastic Gothic invention**.
- **The final image in Vathek** has sustained **Beckford's literary reputation**.
- He also wrote **travel accounts** and **parodies of Gothic novels**.
- His **journal, Life at Fonthill (1807–22)**, was also **published**.

Vathek (1786)

- **Vathek** is also titled **"An Arabian Tale"** or **"The History of the Caliph Vathek."**
- **William Beckford** wrote **the Gothic novel Vathek** in **French**.
- It was **translated into English by Reverend Samuel Henley**.
- Published anonymously as **"An Arabian Tale"** in **1786**.
- The **first French edition** of Vathek was published in **December 1786**.
- Some 20th-century editions include **"The Episodes of Vathek."**
- **Episodes were published separately** long after **Beckford's death**.
- **Vathek** is loosely based on **Abbasid caliph al-Wathiq (842–847 AD)**.
- The story owes little to **anything outside Beckford's imagination**.
- **Caliph Vathek**, encouraged by his **mother, seeks forbidden sorcery**.
- **Vathek outrages his subjects**, including **vizier Morakanabad**.
- **A Giaour tempts Vathek** with the treasures of **Subterranean Fire**.
- **Vathek abjures the Prophet** and commits many **crimes**.
- **He seeks entry** into the **Palace of Subterranean Fire**.
- **Vathek desires Nouronihar**, the **Emir's daughter**, despite her engagement.
- **Nouronihar is tempted** by Vathek's promises of **power and treasure**.
- The two travel to **Istakhar** to access the **Palace of Eblis**.
- **Eblis' domain offers immense power**, but it's **not what they expected**.
- The promised **rewards turn out to be deceptive and dangerous**.

William Godwin (1756-1836) & Caleb Williams (1794)

- ➢ **William Godwin** was a **social philosopher** and **religious dissenter**.
- ➢ He **anticipated the Romantic movement** with **ideas of personal freedom**.
- ➢ Godwin's **liberalism was based on reason** and **individual sovereignty**.
- ➢ He believed in **man's future perfectibility** and **cultural determinism**.
- ➢ His key work, **Political Justice (1793)**, rejects **conventional government**.
- ➢ Godwin advocated for **small self-subsisting communities**.
- ➢ He argued **social institutions fail** by imposing **preconceived ideas**.
- ➢ His works laid foundations for **communism** and **anarchy**.
- ➢ He believed property should be held in **sacred trust** for those in need.
- ➢ Godwin viewed **co-operation as an evil**, leading to **anarchic doctrines**.
- ➢ He married **Mary Wollstonecraft** and was **Mary Shelley's father**.
- ➢ ***Maria: or, The Wrongs of Woman*** is Mary Wollstonecraft's unfinished novelistic sequel to her revolutionary political treatise A Vindication of the Rights of Woman (1792). **The Wrongs of Woman was published posthumously in 1798** by her husband, William Godwin, and is often considered her most radical feminist work.
- ➢ Other works include
  - ○ *The Enquirer (1797)*
  - ○ *Of Population (1820).*
  - ○ *Thoughts on Man: His Nature, Production, and Discoveries (1831);*
  - ○ *Things as They Are; or, The Adventures of Caleb Williams (1794).*

Things as They Are; or, The Adventures of Caleb Williams (1794)

- ● **Caleb Williams (1794)** is a **three-volume novel by William Godwin**.
- ● It calls for an **end to the abuse of power**.

- ➤ **Godwin shows how legal institutions destroy individuals' lives**.
- ➤ The novel reflects **"things as they are" in society**.
- ➤ A preface was **removed due to alarming booksellers**.
- ➤ It **popularized ideas from Godwin's Political Justice (1793)**.
- ➤ **Caleb Williams**, a **poor orphan**, becomes a servant of **Ferdinando Falkland**.
- ➤ **Falkland's sudden fits of rage** cause Caleb to **grow suspicious**.
- ➤ **Mr. Collins explains** Falkland's **long-standing conflict** with **Barnabas Tyrrel**.
- ➤ **Tyrrel's tyrannical behavior** leads to **Emily Melvile's death**.
- ➤ **Falkland's heroic actions** earn him respect but **Tyrrel's murder** follows.
- ➤ **Caleb investigates the murder**, suspecting **Falkland's involvement**.
- ➤ **Falkland confesses** but **forces Caleb** to remain silent **under threat**.
- ➤ **Falkland falsely accuses Caleb** of **stealing money**.
- ➤ **Caleb flees** but is **later captured** and tried **fraudulently**.
- ➤ **Caleb escapes prison** with help from **Falkland's servant**.
- ➤ **Caleb joins a band of criminals**, debates **moral questions** with them.
- ➤ **Jones betrays Caleb** to the authorities, forcing him **to flee again**.
- ➤ **Caleb is arrested** while attempting to **leave for Ireland**.
- ➤ **He bribes captors** but is **relentlessly pursued by Jones**.
- ➤ **Caleb publishes criminal stories** while **evading capture**.
- ➤ **Caleb is eventually betrayed**, captured, and **brought to court**.
- ➤ **Falkland requests Caleb** to declare his accusations **unfounded**.
- ➤ **Falkland sends Caleb money** to bribe him **to remain silent**.
- ➤ **Caleb confronts Falkland**, accusing him in **an emotional court scene**.
- ➤ **Falkland dies** shortly after **Caleb's public accusations**, leaving Caleb regretful.

Charles Robert Maturin (1782-1824) & Melmoth the Wanderer (1820)

- ➤ **Charles Robert Maturin** was an **Irish clergyman, dramatist, and Gothic author**.
- ➤ He is known as **"the last of the Goths"**.
- ➤ His **best-known work** is **Melmoth the Wanderer (1820)**.

- ➢ **Melmoth** is considered the **last of classic Gothic romances**.
- ➢ **Maturin** was educated at **Trinity College**, ordained in **1803**.
- ➢ His early works **pioneered Romantic Irish national tales**.
- ➢ His first **popular success was the tragedy Bertram (1816)**.
- ➢ **Bertram** starred **Edmund Kean** but exhausted Maturin's gains.
- ➢ His masterpiece, **Melmoth**, is about **an Irish Faust-like figure**.
- ➢ **Melmoth** was admired by many **British writers and in France**.
- ➢ **Oscar Wilde** adopted **"Sebastian Melmoth"** as his pseudonym in exile.

Melmoth the Wanderer (1820)

- ➢ The novel's titular character is a scholar.
- ➢ **He sold his soul to the devil in exchange for 150 extra years of life.**
- ➢ He earched the world for someone who would take over the pact.
- ➢ It is kind of reminiscent of the Wandering Jew.
- ➢ The novel is composed of a series of nested stories.
- ➢ It gradually reveals **the story of Melmoth's life**.
- ➢ The novel offers social commentary on early 19th-century England.
- ➢ It denounces Roman Catholicism in favor of the virtues of Protestantism.

Questions:

Question 50

Match List - I with List - II.

List - I (Novel)	List - II (Subtitle)
A. The Castle of Otranto	I. A Pure Woman
B. Tess of the d' Urbervilles	II. The Modern Prometheus
C. Frankenstein	III. A Novel without A Hero
D. Vanity Fair	IV. A Gothic Story

Choose the correct answer from the options given below :

1. (A)-(IV), (B)-(I), (C)-(II), (D)-(III)
2. (A)-(I), (B)-(II), (C)-(III), (D)-(IV)
3. (A)-(II), (B)-(I), (C)-(IV), (D)-(III)

4. (A)-(III), (B)-(IV), (C)-(II), (D)-(I)

Explanations:
Answer: 1. (A)-(IV), (B)-(I), (C)-(II), (D)-(III)

"The Castle of Otranto," written by Horace Walpole and initially released anonymously in 1764, with the first editions dated the following year, is regarded as the pioneering Gothic novel in English literature. **In the second edition, Walpole applied the word 'Gothic' to the novel in the subtitle – A Gothic Story**.

"Tess of the d'Urbervilles: A Pure Woman," authored by Thomas Hardy, first made its appearance through a serialized, edited version in The Graphic, a British illustrated newspaper, in 1891.

Frankenstein; or, The Modern Prometheus is an 1818 novel written by English author Mary Shelley. In Mary Shelley's "Frankenstein," Captain Robert Walton recounts the tragic tale of Victor Frankenstein, a young scientist who discovers the secret to creating life.

"Vanity Fair: A Novel without A Hero," a novel by William Makepeace Thackeray published from 1847 to 1848, marks his first work released under his real name, drawing inspiration from John Bunyan's allegory Pilgrim's Progress to explore the moral corruption at the heart of early 19th-century English society.

Question 51

In the 1985 essay, "Three Women's Texts and a critique of Imperialism", Gayatri Spivak shows the development of the white liberal feminist subject. Which are the texts referred in the title of the essay ?

    A.   The Wide Sargasso Sea by Jean Rhys
    B.   Jane Eyre by Charolotte Bronte
    C.   Frankenstein by Mary Shelley
    D.   Pride and Prejudice by Jane Austen
    E.   The Mill on the Floss by George Eliot

Choose the correct answer from the options given below :

(1) A, B and D only
(2) C, D and A only
(3) A, B and C only
(4) E, B and D only

Explanations:
Answer: (3) A, B and C only

"Three Women's Texts and a Critique of Imperialism" is an essay by Gayatri Spivak that analyzes three works by women and the role of women in imperialist society:

1. **Jane Eyre: By Charlotte Brontë**
2. **Wide Sargasso Sea: By Jean Rhys**
3. **Frankenstein: By Mary Shelley**

In the essay, Spivak focuses on the "imperialist narrativization of history" in the works and how contemporary Anglo-American feminist literary criticism privileges it. She also highlights the importance of "childbearing and soul-making" for feminist individualism in the age of imperialism.

Question 52

Who is the author of the pandemic fiction *The Last Man*?

1. Mary Shelley
2. Jose Saramago
3. Ahmad Ali
4. Gabriel Garcia Marquez

Explanations:
Answer: 1. Mary Shelley

"Mary Shelley's "The Last Man," an apocalyptic and dystopian novel published in 1826, imagines a late 21st-century Europe devastated by a global bubonic plague pandemic, leading humanity to the brink of extinction. The narrative weaves in allegorical references to her late husband, Percy Bysshe Shelley, and their friend Lord Byron, both of whom had passed away prior to the novel's release.

Arrange the following texts chronologically on the basis of the date of publication:

> A. Frankenstein by Mary Shelley
> B. A Room of One's Own by Virginia Woolf
> C. Maria by Mary Wollstonecraft
> D. The Female Eunuch by Germaine Greer
> E. The Return of the Soldier by Rebecca West

Choose the correct answer from the options given below

1. C,B,A,D,E
2. C,A,E, D,B
3. C,B,E,A,D
4. A,E,B,C,D

Explanations:
Answer: 2. C,A,E, D,B

Maria: or, The Wrongs of Woman is Mary Wollstonecraft's unfinished novelistic sequel to her revolutionary political treatise A Vindication of the Rights of Woman (1792). **The Wrongs of Woman was published posthumously in 1798** by her husband, William Godwin, and is often considered her most radical feminist work.

***Frankenstein; or, The Modern Prometheus*, Gothic horror novel by Mary Wollstonecraft Shelley that was first published in 1818.** The epistolary story follows a scientific genius who brings to life a terrifying monster that torments its creator.

***The Return of the Soldier* is the debut novel of English novelist Rebecca West, first published in 1918.**

***A Room of One's Own*, essay by Virginia Woolf, published in 1929.** The work was based on two lectures given by the author in 1928 at Newnham College and Girton College, the first two colleges for women at Cambridge.

***The Female Eunuch* is a 1970 book by Germaine Greer** that became an international bestseller and an important text in the feminist movement.

Match List I with List II

LIST I	LIST II
A. David Hume	I. The Decline and Fall of the Roman Empire
B. Edward Gibbon	II. A Complete History of England
C. William Godwin	III. Treatise on Human Nature
D. Tobias Smollett	IV. Enquiry Concerning Political Justice

Choose the correct answer from the options given below:

1. A-III, B-I, C-IV. D-II
2. A-I, B-II. C-III, D-IV
3. A-II, B-III, C-I. D-IV
4. A-IV, B-I, C-II, D-III

Explanations: Challenge
Answer: 1. A-III, B-I, C-IV. D-II

I. The Decline and Fall of the Roman Empire: This is a historical work written by **Edward Gibbon and published in multiple volumes from 1776 to 1789.**

II. A Complete History of England: **A Complete History of England by David Hume, in four volumes, with Smollett adding his own Continuation of the History of England.**

III. Treatise on Human Nature: This is a philosophical work by David Hume, published in 1738..

IV. Enquiry Concerning Political Justice This is a philosophical work by William Godwin, published in 1793.

Walter Scott (1771-1832)

Life and Career:

- ➤ **Sir Walter Scott** was a **Scottish novelist, poet, and historian**.
- ➤ He is **known for classic works** like **Ivanhoe and Rob Roy**.
- ➤ Other famous novels include **Waverley and Old Mortality**.
- ➤ His narrative poems include **The Lady of the Lake and Marmion**.
- ➤ Scott had **a huge influence on European and American literature**.
- ➤ He balanced **writing with his legal career** as **Clerk of Session**.
- ➤ Scott was **active in Edinburgh's Tory establishment** and **Highland Society**.
- ➤ He served as **president of the Royal Society of Edinburgh (1820-1832)**.
- ➤ Also a **vice president of the Society of Antiquaries of Scotland**.
- ➤ His **historical knowledge** helped him establish the **historical novel genre**.
- ➤ Scott was a major figure in **European Romanticism**.
- ➤ He became a **baronet in 1820**, titled "**of Abbotsford**".
- ➤ His **title became extinct** when his son died in **1847**.
- ➤ Scott's novels are **still considered classics in Scottish literature**.
- ➤ He was also **a legal administrator and judge by profession**.

Novels:

- ➤ **The Waverley Novels is the title given to the long series of Scott novels released from 1814 to 1832.**
- ➤ It takes its name from **Waverley's first novel**.
- ➤ The following is a chronological list of the entire series:
    - o **1814: Waverley**
    - o *1815: Guy Mannering*
    - o *1816: The Antiquary*
    - o *1816: The Black Dwarf and Old Mortality or The Tale of Old Mortality – the 1st installment from the subset series, Tales of My Landlord*
    - o *1817: Rob Roy*
    - o *1818: The Heart of Mid-Lothian – the 2nd installment from the subset series, Tales of My Landlord*
    - o *1819: The Bride of Lammermoor and A Legend of Montrose or A Legend of the Wars of Montrose – the 3rd installment from the subset series, Tales of My Landlord*
    - o *1820: Ivanhoe*

- o *1820: The Monastery*
- o *1820: The Abbot*
- o ***1821: Kenilworth***
- o *1822: The Pirate*
- o *1822: The Fortunes of Nigel*
- o *1822: Peveril of the Peak*
- o *1823: Quentin Durward*
- o *1824: St. Ronan's Well or Saint Ronan's Well*
- o *1824: Redgauntlet*
- o *1825: The Betrothed and The Talisman – a subset series, Tales of the Crusaders*
- o *1826: Woodstock*
- o *1827: Chronicles of the Canongate — containing two short stories ("The Highland Widow" and "The Two Drovers") and a novel (The Surgeon's Daughter)*
- o *1828: The Fair Maid of Perth – the 2nd installment from the subset series, Chronicles of the Canongate*
- o *1829: Anne of Geierstein*
- o *1832: Count Robert of Paris and Castle Dangerous – the 4th installment from the subset series, Tales of My Landlord*

- **Other novels:**
  - ➢ *1831–1832: The Siege of Malta – a finished novel published posthumously in 2008*
  - ➢ *1832: Bizarro – an unfinished novel (or novella) published posthumously in 2008*

Poetry

- ➢ Many of the short poems or songs released by Scott.
- ➢ They were initially not separate pieces but parts of longer poems interspersed throughout his novels, tales, and dramas.
  - o *1796: The Chase, and William and Helen: Two Ballads, translated from the German of Gottfried Augustus Bürger*
  - o *1800: Glenfinlas*
  - o ***1802–1803: Minstrelsy of the Scottish Border***
  - o ***1805: The Lay of the Last Minstrel***
  - o ***1806: Ballads and Lyrical Pieces***
  - o ***1808: Marmion:: A Tale of Flodden Field***
  - o ***1810: The Lady of the Lake***
  - o *1811: The Vision of Don Roderick*

- *1813: The Bridal of Triermain*
- *1813: Rokeby*
- ***1815: The Field of Waterloo***
- *1815: The Lord of the Isles*
- *1817: Harold the Dauntless*
- *1825: Bonnie Dundee*

Waverley (1814)

- **Waverley** is a **historical novel** published anonymously in **1814**.
- It is **Scott's first prose fiction** venture after being **a famous poet**.
- Considered one of the **first historical novels** in Western tradition.
- Scott published his later works as **"by the author of Waverley."**
- His novels from this period are known as **the Waverley Novels**.
- The novel was **well-received by critics** and readers in the **early 19th century**.
- **Waverley** remains favored by **modern critics**.
- Scott was granted a **baronetcy in 1818**, becoming **Sir Walter Scott**.
- It was an **open secret** he was **"the author of Waverley."**
- Scott **admitted authorship** publicly at a **dinner in 1827**.
- **Edward Waverley** is an English gentleman who joins the **army**.
- He visits Scottish friends and enjoys their **hospitality**.
- Amid the **Jacobite uprising**, he faces loyalty challenges and conflict.
- **Waverley** falls in love with two women and chooses one.
- His **honor and friendships** save him after the rebellion's defeat.

Guy Mannering (1815)

- **Guy Mannering** is the second of Scott's **Waverley novels**.
- It was **published anonymously in 1815** and quickly sold out.
- Scott initially intended it to be a **supernatural story**.
- **The book's first edition sold out** on its **release day**.
- **Harry Bertram** is kidnapped by **smuggler Dirk Hatteraick**, taken to Holland.
- Raised unaware of his identity, **he becomes Vanbeest Brown**.
- Bertram falls for **Julia Mannering**, leading to a deadly duel.
- **His gypsy nurse** Meg Merrilies recognizes him and saves him.
- **Bertram regains his estates** and marries Julia after the rescue.

The Antiquary (1816)

- **The Antiquary** (1816) is the third of **Walter Scott's Waverley novels**.
- The novel features an **amateur historian and archaeologist** as the hero.
- The love interest centers on **Lovel and Isabella Wardour**.
- **Scott regarded this novel** as his personal favorite.
- Critic **H.J.C. Grierson** praised its blend of **truth and poetry**.
- The novel documents **Scottish life during the 1790s**.
- It explores **how the past influences the present**.
- The story's **setting spans July and August 1794**.
- It combines **comedy, melodrama, and moments of pathos**.
- **Scott intended to depict Scottish manners** and historical life.
- The novel has a **predominantly comic tone** throughout.
- **Themes include romance, history, and social commentary**.

The Heart of Mid-Lothian (1818)

- **The Heart of Mid-Lothian** is the **seventh of Scott's Waverley novels**.
- Published on **25 July 1818** in four volumes.
- Released under **"Tales of My Landlord, 2nd series"**.
- The author was named **"Jedediah Cleishbotham"** as a pseudonym.
- The action takes place between **September 1736 and May 1737**.
- Set in motion by **the Porteous Riots in Edinburgh**.
- A **working-class girl embarks on an epic journey**.
- She seeks a **royal commutation for her sister's death sentence**.
- The sister is accused of **murdering her newborn baby**.
- Despite some negative reviews, it's considered Scott's **best novel**.

Ivanhoe (1820)

- **Ivanhoe: A Romance** was published in **three volumes in 1819**.
- It marked Scott's shift to **English medieval settings**.
- **Ivanhoe** became **one of Scott's most influential novels**.
- Set in **1194**, during Richard I's return from the **Third Crusade**.
- **Richard's power** was usurped by his brother **John**.
- Scott drew on **Robert Henry's The History of Great Britain**.

- ➢ Sources also include **Sharon Turner's The History of the Anglo-Saxons.**
- ➢ **David Hume's The History of England** inspired Richard's portrayal.
- ➢ Scott used **Chaucer's Canterbury Tales** for medieval England depiction.
- ➢ **Shakespeare's King John** influenced **Richard's brother John.**
- ➢ **Merchant of Venice** inspired Scott's **Jewish characters.**
- ➢ **Joseph Ritson's Robin Hood** shaped Robin Hood's **representation.**
- ➢ **Ivanhoe**, son of Cedric, a Saxon nobleman, is disinherited.
- ➢ Cedric plans to marry **Rowena** to **Athelstane** for Saxon restoration.
- ➢ **Ivanhoe's love for Rowena** disrupts Cedric's dynastic ambitions.
- ➢ Ivanhoe joins the **Third Crusade**, gaining **Richard the Lionheart's favor.**
- ➢ **Prince John** plots to depose Richard, imprisoned in Austria.
- ➢ Ivanhoe, disguised as a pilgrim, visits his **father's house.**
- ➢ He saves **Isaac the Jew** from an ambush on his journey.
- ➢ At Ashby tournament, **Ivanhoe** vanquishes John's supporters with **Richard's help.**
- ➢ Ivanhoe is **wounded**, nursed by Isaac's daughter, **Rebecca.**
- ➢ **Bois-Guilbert** and **de Bracy** plot to abduct **Rowena and others.**
- ➢ **Locksley (Robin Hood)** and Richard rescue captives from **Torquilstone Castle.**
- ➢ Rebecca is taken by **Bois-Guilbert** to the **Preceptory of Templestowe.**

Kenilworth (1821)

- ➢ **Kenilworth** is a historical romance by **Sir Walter Scott.**
- ➢ Published on **13 January 1821**, part of the **Waverley novels.**
- ➢ Set in **1575**, leading to **Queen Elizabeth's reception** at Kenilworth.
- ➢ **Earl of Leicester** is complicit in his wife **Amy Robsart's murder.**
- ➢ The murder occurred at **Cumnor** before the Queen's elaborate visit.
- ➢ Amy Robsart secretly marries the Earl of Leicester.
- ➢ Leicester hides the marriage to protect his court position.
- ➢ Amy flees her father's house and is kept a prisoner.
- ➢ Edmund Tressilian suspects Varney abducted Amy.
- ➢ Tressilian accuses Varney of unlawful seduction before the Queen.
- ➢ Varney claims Amy is his wife to defend Leicester.
- ➢ The Queen orders Varney to present Amy at Kenilworth.
- ➢ Amy refuses, and Varney plots to make her ill.

> ➤ Amy escapes with Wayland Smith's help to Kenilworth.
> ➤ Amy appeals to the Queen but can't reveal her marriage.
> ➤ The Queen dismisses Amy as mad and returns her to Varney.
> ➤ Varney convinces Leicester of Amy's affair with Tressilian.
> ➤ Leicester orders Varney to kill Amy at Cumnor Place.
> ➤ Amy dies in an engineered accident; Varney poisons himself.
> ➤ Tressilian dies in Virginia, and Leicester returns to favor.

Question 55

Which of the following is not included in the positive evils of Scott as a novelist?

1. His great haste in the composition of his stories
2. His haphazard financial methods which tended to over production
3. Haste in the construction of. his plots
4. He had sensitive ear for rhythm and melody

Explanations:
Answer: 4. He had sensitive ear for rhythm and melody

The correct answer is option 4: "He had sensitive ear for rhythm and melody." This option does not reflect one of the criticisms often attributed to Sir Walter Scott as a novelist. Instead, it contrasts with the critiques regarding his approach to novel writing, which include:

His great haste in the composition of his stories: Scott's rapid pace in writing is cited as a detriment, contributing to a lack of depth and polish in his narratives.

His haphazard financial methods which tended to overproduction: Scott's financial strategies, driven by immediate need or opportunity, led to an excessive output of work, possibly at the expense of quality.

Haste in the construction of his plots: Similar to his overall speed in writing, Scott's plots are often seen as hastily assembled and carelessly developed, reflecting a lack of thorough planning and refinement.

CHAPTER 3

ROMANTIC AGE (1798-1815)

The French Revolution (1789–1799)

- **French Revolution**: Period of **ideological, political**, and **social upheaval**.
- Absolute **monarchy** shifted to **Enlightenment**-based **republicanism** and **citizenship**.
- **Violent turmoil: Reign of Terror, executions**, and **warfare**.
- Revolution opposed **king's power** and **elite privileges**.
- Fought for **liberty, equality**, and **fraternity**.
- Resulted in **loss of freedom, dictatorship**, and **nationalism**.
- Motivated by **hatred of tradition** and creating a **new order**.
- Citizens' identities were **redefined** under **state control**.
- **Resistance crushed: 18,000 - 40,000** executions.
- **Governance instability**: Republics, dictatorships, monarchies, empires
- Subsequent **events** caused by the Revolution include:
    - **The Napoleonic wars**.
    - **The restoration of the monarchy**.
    - Two other revolutions as modern France took shape.
- **Counter-enlightenment** and **romantic movement** emerged in **Germany**.
- **German reunification** as defense against **future Napoleon** threats.
- **French ideas** influenced **Marxist** and **Bolshevik** revolutions.
- **Bolsheviks** replicated **French executions** by **government organs**.
- **Not all** French people supported the **Revolution's vision**.
- Too many **monarchists** for a republic, too many **Republicans** for monarchy.
- Emphasized **citizenship rights**, not subjects of a **ruler**.
- **Nation belongs** to its **citizens**, not the **ruler**.
- Revolution promoted **nationalism** as a **political concept**.
- No **dominant vision** of **governance** emerged in **France**.

Thomas Paine (1736-1809)

- Pamphleteer, **controversialist**, and **international revolutionary**.
- **Common Sense** (1776): Influenced **American independence** from **Britain**.
- **Rights of Man** (1791–2): Popular in **British reform** movement.
- Active in the **French Revolution**, member of **National Convention**.
- Key figure in **welfare** and **educational responsibility** ideas.
- **Age of Reason**: Popular **deist text**, influential in **19th century**.
- Paine was **vilified** and **dismissed** in his lifetime.
- His ideas still command **interest** and **enthusiasm worldwide**.
- Many see him as crucial to **modern political thought**.

Common Sense:

- **Thomas Paine** advocated **independence** from **Great Britain** in 1776.
- Written in **clear, persuasive prose** for **common people**.
- **Published anonymously** on **January 10, 1776** during the Revolution.
- **Argued for independence** using **Protestant beliefs** and **American identity**.
- Structured like a **sermon**, it sparked **intellectual consideration**.

The American Crisis:

- Series published from **1776 to 1783** during the Revolution.
- Aimed to **inspire** colonists and **recharge revolutionary** cause.
- Written in **ordinary language**, promoting **liberal philosophy**.
- Paine claimed war had **God's support** against Britain.
- Famously begins: "**These are the times that try men's souls.**"

The Age of Reason:

- **Challenges institutional religion** and questions **Bible's legitimacy**.
- Published in **three parts** from **1794 to 1807**.
- Paine critiques **Christian Church's corruption** and political power.
- Promotes **reason over revelation**, rejecting **miracles** and divinity.
- Argues for **natural religion** and a **creator-god's existence**.

Edmund Burke (1729-1797) & Reflections on the Revolution in France (1790)

- **Edmund Burke** was born in **Dublin** on **12 January 1729**.
- He studied at **Trinity College, Dublin**, then pursued **law**.
- Burke **abandoned law** and focused on **literary and political career**.
- Became **member of parliament** in **1765**.
- Involved in debates about **limits to king's power**.
- Advocated for **parliamentary control** over **royal patronage**.
- Opposed **Stamp Act (1765)**, criticizing **British policy's inflexibility**.
- Called for **pragmatism** in dealing with **colonial opposition**.
- Believed in **government as a cooperative relationship**.
- Advocated **adapting to change** while preserving **traditional values**.
- Showed interest in **Indian governmental corruption** reforms.
- Proposed **independent commissioners** to govern **India**.
- Burke's bill to **reform Indian governance** was **defeated**.
- Initiated **impeachment proceedings** against **Warren Hastings**.
- Criticized the **French Revolution** in **Reflections on the Revolution**.
- Fought against **mob rule**, fearing **societal destruction**.
- Promoted **British values** of **continuity, tradition, rank**, and **property**.
- Opposed the **Revolution** till the **end of his life**.
- Retired from **parliament** in **1794**.
- Son's death clouded his **later years**.
- Continued to **write** and defend his **arguments**.
- Burke emphasized **constitutional conventions** and **political parties**.
- Argued for **MP independence** once **elected**.
- Regarded as a **founder** of **British Conservative tradition**.

A Vindication of Natural Society (1756):

- **Edmund Burke** published **satire** on **Bolingbroke's deism** in 1756.
- Critiqued **civil society and government**, not **religion**.
- Burke argued that **Bolingbroke's logic** applied to **all institutions**.
- Some readers **misunderstood Burke's satire** as a serious argument.
- Burke clarified his **satire** in the **second edition** (1757).
- Considered by **William Godwin** as **first philosophical anarchism**.
- Work explored **miseries from artificial society** and **government**.

> ➢ **Irony** in the text **challenged artificial societal norms.**

Reflections on the Revolution in France (1790):

- Burke's view of the **French Revolution** changed by **1789.**
- Initially praised as a **wonderful spectacle** but soon changed.
- Burke felt the revolution **discarded laws, morals, and tradition.**
- The revolution threatened **European stability** and **security.**
- Dismissed it as based on immature **rights of man.**
- Criticized comparison to England's **Glorious Revolution** of 1688.
- Valued **tradition** over France's destruction of **state and religion.**
- Paine's **Declaration of Rights** mocked Burke's praise for **Marie Antoinette.**

Question 56

Who among the following was NOT one of the original members of Johnson's Literary Club?

1. Oliver Goldsmith
2. John Dryden
3. Edmund Burke
4. John Hawkins

Explanations:
Answer: 2. John Dryden

The Club, also known as the Literary Club, is a renowned dining club in London that was established in February 1764. Its founders were artist Joshua Reynolds, essayist **Samuel Johnson, and philosopher-politician Edmund Burke.** The original nine members included prominent figures such as Reynolds, Johnson, Burke, Christopher Nugent, Topham Beauclerk, Bennet Langton, **Oliver Goldsmith,** Anthony Chamier, and **John Hawkins.** The Club served as a gathering place for intellectuals, writers, and artists, fostering lively discussions and camaraderie among its esteemed members.

Question 57

In which year was Edmund Burke's Enquiry into the Origin of Our Ideas of the Sublime and the Beautiful published?

1. 1742
2. 1744
3. 1750
4. 1757

Explanations:
Answer: 4. 1757

List of Major Works by Edmund Burke:

- A Vindication of Natural Society (1756)
- **A Philosophical Enquiry into the Origin of Our Ideas of the Sublime and Beautiful (1757)**
- Thoughts on the Cause of the Present Discontents (1770)
- On American Taxation (1774)
- Reflections on the Revolution in France (1790)
- Letter to a Member of the National Assembly (1791)
- An Appeal from the New to the Old Whigs (1791)
- Thoughts and Details on Scarcity (1795)
- Letters on a Regicide Peace (1795–97)
- Letter to a Noble Lord (1796)

Question 58

Arrange the following writers chronologically in accordance with their years of birth:

A. James Boswell
B. Edward Gibbon
C. Samuel Johnson
D. Edmund Burke
E. Richard Brinsley Sheridan

Choose the correct answer from the following options:

1. C. D, B, A. E
2. C, A, B. E. D
3. A. C, B. D. E
4. B, C. A, D, E

Explanations:
Answer: 1. C. D, B, A. E

Samuel Johnson (1709-1784)
Edmund Burke (1729-1797)
Edward Gibbon (1737-1794)
James Boswell (1740-1795)
Richard Brinsley Sheridan (1751-1816)

Which of the following books were published in the year 1791?

    A. Adam Smith's The Wealth of Nations
    B. James Boswell's The Life of Samuel Johnson
    C. Johnson's Dictionary of the English Language
    D. Burke's Thoughts on the Cause of the Present Discontents
    E. Paine's The Rights of Man

Choose the Correct answer from the options given below
    1. A and C
    2. B and E
    3. C and D
    4. D and E

Explanations:
Answer: 2. B and E

The Life of Samuel Johnson, LL.D. (1791) by James Boswell.
Rights of Man (1791) by Thomas Paine is a seminal book comprising 31 articles.
Thoughts on the Cause of the Present Discontents, originally published in 1770, is a political pamphlet by Edmund Burke.
The Wealth of Nations, also known as An Inquiry into the Nature and Causes of the Wealth of Nations, is a seminal work by Adam Smith.
A Dictionary of the English Language, commonly referred to as Johnson's Dictionary, was written by Samuel Johnson and published in 1755.

Mary Wollstonecraft (1759-1797) & A Vindication of the Rights of Woman (1792)

- ➢ **Mary Wollstonecraft** advocated for **educational and social equality** for women.
- ➢ Her classic work, **A Vindication of the Rights of Woman** (1792).
- ➢ Wollstonecraft's experiences as a **teacher** shaped her feminist views.
- ➢ Published **Thoughts on the Education of Daughters** in **1787**.
- ➢ Worked as a **translator** for publisher **Joseph Johnson** in 1788.
- ➢ Published her novel **Mary: A Fiction** in the same year.
- ➢ **A Vindication of the Rights of Woman** urged **equal education**.
- ➢ Observed the **French Revolution** and lived in **Paris** (1792).
- ➢ Lived with **Captain Gilbert Imlay**, had a daughter **Fanny**.
- ➢ Attempted **suicide** after the breakdown of the **Imlay relationship**.
- ➢ Returned to **London** and joined a **radical group** of thinkers.
- ➢ Began a relationship with **William Godwin** in **1796**.
- ➢ Married **Godwin** in **1797** while pregnant with her second daughter.
- ➢ **Died 11 days** after the birth of **Mary Wollstonecraft Shelley**.
- ➢ Notable work: **Letters from Sweden, Norway, and Denmark** (1796).
- ➢ Posthumous novel: **Maria; or, The Wrongs of Woman** (1798).

A Vindication of the Rights of Woman (1792)

- ➢ **A Vindication of the Rights of Woman** is early **feminist philosophy**.
- ➢ Wollstonecraft critiques **educational theorists** opposing **women's rational education**.
- ➢ Argues women's education should match their **societal roles**.
- ➢ Women are essential as **mothers** and **companions** to husbands.
- ➢ **Women deserve the same rights** as **men**, says Wollstonecraft.
- ➢ Treating women as **property** undermines **society's moral foundation**.
- ➢ Entered debate in **1790** with **A Vindication of the Rights of Men**.
- ➢ **Rights of Men** responds to Burke's **Reflections on the Revolution**.
- ➢ Burke criticized **British thinkers' support** for the French Revolution.
- ➢ Saw French Revolution as analogous to **English Civil War**.
- ➢ **Charles I's execution** made French Revolution seem illegitimate.
- ➢ Burke argued **citizens can't revolt** against **government**.
- ➢ Believed **civilization results from social-political consensus**.

> ➢ Burke feared challenging traditions would cause **anarchy**.
> ➢ Wollstonecraft argued rights aren't based on **tradition**.
> ➢ Rights should be based on **reason and justice**, not tradition.

A Vindication of the Rights of Woman **was written by Mary Wollstonecraft. Who wrote** *A Vindication of the Rights of Man*

1. J.S. Mill
2. Thomas Paine
3. John Braine
4. Amis Kingsley

Explanations:
Answer: 2. Thomas Paine

"A Vindication of the Rights of Men," penned by 18th-century British author and advocate for women's rights Mary Wollstonecraft in 1790, stands as a critical examination of aristocracy while championing the principles of republicanism. This pamphlet, responding directly to **Edmund Burke's "Reflections on the Revolution in France,"** initiates a pamphlet war by critiquing Burke's support for constitutional monarchy, aristocracy, and the Church of England, marking Wollstonecraft's entry into political debate.

In 1792, Wollstonecraft furthered her philosophical and feminist discourse with "A Vindication of the Rights of Woman: with Strictures on Political and Moral Subjects," among the pioneering texts in feminist philosophy.

In "Rights of Man" (1791), Paine articulates a defense of the French Revolution and the concept that political revolution is justified to protect a population's natural rights, countering Edmund Burke's criticisms in "Reflections on the Revolution in France."

Which among the following are not true about Feminist Movement?

A. Mary Wollstonecrafts A Vindication of the Rights of Woman challenges the notion that women exist only to please men.

B. Issue of women's suffrage dominated international feminism for more than fifty years:

C. The Female Eunuch was witten and published by an African writer named Sarah Millin.

D. Kate Millet's Sexual Politics broadened the term politics' to include all "power-structured relationships"

E. The second wave of feminism was led by Generation Xers.

Choose the correct answer from the options given below.

1. A and B only
2. B and C only
3 C and E only
4. D and E only

Explanations:
Answer: 3 C and E only

___***A Vindication of the Rights of Woman: with Strictures on Political and Moral Subjects***___ (1792), written by British philosopher and women's rights advocate Mary Wollstonecraft (1759–1797), is one of the earliest works of feminist philosophy. She argues that women ought to have an education commensurate with their position in society, claiming that women are essential to the nation because they educate its children and because they could be "companions" to their husbands, rather than mere wives. ___**Instead of viewing women as ornaments to society or property to be traded in marriage, Wollstonecraft maintains that they are human beings deserving of the same fundamental rights as men**___.

Women's suffrage is the right of women to vote in elections. At the beginning of the 18th century, some people sought to change voting laws to allow women to vote. Liberal political parties would go on to grant women the right to vote, increasing the number of those parties' potential constituencies.

"The Female Eunuch," authored by Germaine Greer in 1970, emerged as a groundbreaking and bestselling work within the feminist discourse. Greer articulates that women are sexually repressed by the conventional dynamics of suburban life and consumer culture, leading to a loss of vitality akin to being eunuchs. First released in London in October 1970, the book garnered mixed reviews yet achieved significant commercial success, exhausting its second print run by March 1971. It has since been translated into eleven different languages, cementing its status as a pivotal feminist text. **In 1999, Greer expanded on her initial arguments with a sequel titled "The Whole Woman."**

"Sexual Politics," authored by Kate Millett and originating from her PhD dissertation at Columbia University, made its debut in 1970, published by Doubleday. This groundbreaking work is celebrated as **a foundational text in feminist literature and stands as a cornerstone of radical feminism.** It played a pivotal role in defining the goals of the **second-wave feminist movement.** Millett's analysis critically examines how male dominance is embedded within the fabric of 20th-century Western art and literature, highlighting the perpetuation of patriarchal norms and societal heteronormativity. She **contends that the power dynamics favoring men over women stem from societal constructs**, challenging the notion that such dominance is rooted in biological determinism.

Second-wave feminism was a period of feminist activity that began in the early 1960s and lasted roughly two decades, ending with the feminist sex wars in the early 1980s and being replaced by third-wave feminism in the early 1990s.Some important events laid the **groundwork for the second wave, specifically the work of French writer Simone de Beauvoir** in the 1940s where she examined the notion of women being perceived as "other" in the patriarchal society. The term **"intersectionality"** was not coined until 1989 by Kimberlé Crenshaw at the end of the second wave.

Question 62

Arrange the following texts chronologically on the basis of the date of publication:

> A. Frankenstein by Mary Shelley
> B. A Room of One's Own by Virginia Woolf
> C. Maria by Mary Wollstonecraft
> D. The Female Eunuch by Germaine Greer
> E. The Return of the Soldier by Rebecca West

Choose the correct answer from the options given below

1. C,B,A,D,E
2. C,A,E, D,B
3. C,B,E,A,D
4. A,E,B,C,D

Explanations:
Answer: 2. C,A,E, D,B

Maria: or, The Wrongs of Woman is Mary Wollstonecraft's unfinished novelistic sequel to her revolutionary political treatise A Vindication of the Rights of Woman (1792). **The Wrongs of Woman was published posthumously in 1798** by her husband, William Godwin, and is often considered her most radical feminist work.

Frankenstein; or, The Modern Prometheus, Gothic horror novel by Mary Wollstonecraft Shelley that was first published in 1818.

The Return of the Soldier is the debut novel of English novelist Rebecca West, first published in 1918.

A Room of One's Own, essay by Virginia Woolf, published in 1929.

The Female Eunuch is a 1970 book by Germaine Greer that became an international bestseller and an important text in the feminist movement..

Periodical Writing

The Examiner (1808–1886)
- ➢ **The Examiner** was a **weekly paper** founded in **1808**.
- ➢ Founded by **Leigh and John Hunt**, focused on **politics**.
- ➢ Sub-titled "**A Sunday paper** on politics and theatricals."
- ➢ Featured writers like **Byron, Shelley, Keats**, and **Hazlitt**.

Edinburgh Review (1802-1929)
- ➢ **Edinburgh Review** was a prominent **intellectual and cultural magazine**.
- ➢ It promoted **Romanticism** and **Whig politics** in its publications.
- ➢ Notoriously **critical** of some significant **Romantic poetry**.

> Founded on **10 October 1802** by **Jeffrey, Smith, Brougham, Horner**.
> Known for **attacking the Lake Poets**, especially **Wordsworth**.

Quarterly Review (1809-1967)

> **The Quarterly Review** was founded in **March 1809** by **John Murray**.
> The periodical **ceased publication** in **1967**.
> Known as **The London Quarterly Review** in **American edition**.
> **William Gifford** appointed as first editor by **George Canning**.
> Contributors included **Robert Southey** and **Sir Walter Scott**.
> Other notable contributors: **Ugo Foscolo, Charles Maturin**, and **Charles Lamb**.

Blackwood's Magazine (1817-1980)

> **Blackwood's Magazine** was a British **magazine** published from **1817 to 1980**.
> Founded by **William Blackwood**, initially called **Edinburgh Monthly Magazine**.
> First issue appeared in **April 1817** under **Pringle** and **Cleghorn**.
> Principal writer **John Wilson** used the pseudonym **Christopher North**.
> Published works of **radicals** like **Shelley** and **Coleridge**.
> Supported **Wordsworth**, parodied **Byronmania**, and criticized **Cockney School**.
> Published early **feminist essays** by **American John Neal**.

The London Magazine (1732*)

> **The London Magazine** has had six versions since **1732**.
> **Resurrected in 1820** by Baldwin, Craddock & Joy, edited by **John Scott**.
> Published **poems** by **Wordsworth, Shelley, Clare**, and **Keats**.
> **De Quincey's Confessions of an English Opium-Eater** appeared in 1821.
> Scott began a **literary feud** with **Blackwood's Magazine**.
> **Lockhart's criticism** of the **Cockney School** sparked conflict.
> The feud led to a **fatal duel** in **1821**.
> **Scott lost his life** in a duel with **J.H. Christie**.

- ➤ Continued under editor **John Taylor**, featuring **Lamb, Hazlitt**, and **Hood**.
- ➤ **Lamb's Essays of Elia** began publication in **1820**.
- ➤ **Taylor's editing** led contributors to abandon the **magazine** in **1829**.

The Westminster Review (1824-1914)
- ➤ **The Westminster Review** was a **quarterly British publication**.
- ➤ Established in **1823** as the **Philosophical Radicals' organ**.
- ➤ Published from **1824 to 1914**, driven by **James Mill**.
- ➤ **John Chapman** acquired the journal in **1851**.
- ➤ The then-unknown **Mary Ann Evans** (George Eliot) gathered authors.
- ➤ Authors included **Francis Newman, Harriet Martineau**, and **Herbert Spencer**.
- ➤ These authors lived in **The Economist's offices**.
- ➤ Supported the **flagship of free thought** and **reform**.
- ➤ Joined by **John Stuart Mill, William B. Carpenter**, and others.
- ➤ **Thomas Huxley**, future naturalist, later joined the group.
- ➤ Group met to discuss **free thought** and **reform** ideas.

William Wordsworth (1770-1850)

Life:

- ➤ **Wordsworth** was born at **Cockermouth**, outside the **Lake District**.
- ➤ His father, a **lawyer**, died when William was **thirteen**.
- ➤ Left a modest sum, but **money was unavailable** immediately.
- ➤ William depended on **two uncles** for his **education**.
- ➤ Attended **Hawkshead School**, near **Lake Windermere**.
- ➤ In **1787**, Wordsworth entered **St. John's College, Cambridge**.
- ➤ His university work was **undistinguished** and **uninspiring**.
- ➤ Graduated in **1791** without a **fixed career** in view.
- ➤ Spent a few months in **London** after graduation.
- ➤ Crossed to **France** in **1791**, staying at **Orléans and Blois**.
- ➤ Became enthusiastic about the **French Revolution**.
- ➤ He chronicled this enthusiasm in the lines:
    - ○ *Bliss was it in that dawn to be alive,*
    - ○ *But to be young was very heaven.*
- ➤ Returned to **Paris** in **1792** after the **September massacres**.
- ➤ Horrified by the **political violence**, faith in **Revolution** shaken.

- ➢ Considered becoming a **Girondin**, or moderate **Republican**.
- ➢ His allowance was stopped, forcing him back to **England**.
- ➢ Settled with **Dorothy**, his lifelong companion, in **Dorset**.
- ➢ Moved to **Alfoxden** to live near **Coleridge**.
- ➢ Their **walks inspired** the **Lyrical Ballads**.
- ➢ After visiting **Germany** in **1798**, settled in **Lake District**.
- ➢ Lived at **Dove Cottage, Grasmere**, from **1802**.
- ➢ Moved to **Allan Bank, Grasmere Parsonage**, and finally **Rydal Mount**.
- ➢ **Rydal Mount** was Wordsworth's home from **1813** until death.
- ➢ Became **Distributor of Stamps** for **Westmorland**.
- ➢ This position secured him financially from **poverty**.
- ➢ His life became a model of **domesticity** and simplicity.
- ➢ **Wife and sister** zealously preserved his **poetry**.
- ➢ Wordsworth's passion was for **traveling and exploring**.
- ➢ Explored most **accessible parts** of the **Continent**.
- ➢ Visited **Scotland** several times, meeting **Scott** in **1831**.
- ➢ Saw **Scott** when he was in **mental decline**.
- ➢ Wordsworth's poetry initially received with **derision**.
- ➢ Later, **recognition** and appreciation for his poetry grew.
- ➢ **Oxford** awarded him a **D.C.L. degree** in **1839**.
- ➢ In **1842**, awarded a **£300 pension** by the Crown.
- ➢ Became **Poet Laureate** after **Southey's** death in **1843**.
- ➢ His **early ideals** shifted towards **conservatism**.
- ➢ Opposed the **Reform Bill**, rejecting early revolutionary causes.
- ➢ He wasn't the **"lost leader"** lamented by **Browning**.
- ➢ Continued to believe in his **poetic immortality**.
- ➢ Never wavered in faith in his **own abilities**.
- ➢ Saw his belief in his **powers triumphantly justified**.
- ➢ **Gigantic egoism** was richly and justly **rewarded**.
- ➢ His relationship with **Dorothy** shaped his **personal life**.
- ➢ Wordsworth's circle included **Coleridge** and **radical thinkers**.
- ➢ His poetic output, from **Lyrical Ballads** to **later works**.
- ➢ Experienced major **shifts in political and social views**.
- ➢ His poetic recognition aligned with **British Romanticism**.

His Literary Career:

- ➢ **Wordsworth's earliest verses** were **imitations of Pope**.

- His **university poems** were **The Evening Walk** and **Descriptive Sketches** (1793).
- These poems showed **little originality** but a **nature-focused style**.
- **Lyrical Ballads** (1798) was a joint effort with **Coleridge**.
- It marked the **prelude to the Romantic Movement**.
- Wordsworth had the **larger share** in **Lyrical Ballads**.
- Some poems, like **The Thorn**, were criticized as **trivial**.
- Others, like **Simon Lee**, showed **adequate expression**.
- **Tintern Abbey** is considered one of his **greatest works**.
- During his **Germany visit**, Wordsworth composed **Lucy Gray** and **Nutting**.
- His **two-volume poetry** collection (1807) was **critically attacked**.
- Despite criticism, appreciation for **Wordsworth** grew steadily.
- In **Germany**, he planned **The Prelude**, completed in **1805**.
- **The Prelude** deals with **Wordsworth's education and early ideals**.
- It was intended as an **introduction to The Recluse**.
- **The Excursion** (1814) was the **second part** of **The Recluse**.
- **The Excursion** is a **huge poem of nine books**.
- Much of **The Excursion** is **dull and prosaic**.
- **The Prelude** has some of **Wordsworth's best blank verse**.
- Further parts of **The Recluse** would likely show **decline**.
- After **The Excursion**, Wordsworth's **poetical power declined**.
- His later volumes include **The White Doe of Rylstone** (1815).
- Published **The Waggoner** and **Peter Bell** in **1819**.
- **Yarrow Revisited** appeared in **1835**, and **The Borderers** in **1842**.
- These later works show **increasing decline** in **poetic merit**.
- Occasionally, there were **flashes of the old spirit**.
- **Ettrick Shepherd's death** poem shows his **diminished fire**.
- His later poems became **more garrulous and less inspired**.
- **Lyrical Ballads** is a major milestone in **Romantic literature**.
- Wordsworth's **productivity remained high** despite **waning inspiration**.
- **The Prelude** remained **unpublished during his lifetime**.
- **The Recluse**, his planned **blank-verse epic**, remained unfinished.
- His later works mark **increasing verbosity** and **diminished brilliance**.
- **The Excursion** is **inferior** to **The Prelude**.
- **The Recluse** would have likely **continued Wordsworth's decline**.
- **Tintern Abbey** and **Lucy Gray** represent his **great poetic moments**.

- **Coleridge and Wordsworth's collaboration** changed literary history.
- The **Romantic Movement** gained momentum with **Lyrical Ballads.**
- Wordsworth's early works showed **genius despite initial criticism.**
- **His best poetry** is often **nature-centered and introspective.**
- **The White Doe** marked his **declining poetic phase.**
- **Yarrow Revisited** showed a **flash of Wordsworth's earlier inspiration.**
- **The Ettrick Shepherd poem** had a **touch of his former spirit.**
- His works declined in **stature but maintained high output.**
- **Wordsworth's legacy** remains **influential despite later decline.**

Features of His Poetry:

- **Wordsworth's poetry** shows both **inequality** and **limitations.**
- **Matthew Arnold** ends Wordsworth's best work at **1808.**
- **The Excursion** is **long, meditative,** and often **prosaic.**
- Wordsworth struggled to **recognize his limitations** as a poet.
- He lacked a **sense of humor**, dramatic power, and narrative gift.
- His drama **The Borderers** was only a **partial success.**
- Narrative poems like **Ruth** aren't considered **his best work.**
- **Wordsworth's egoism** was almost **heroic** due to his genius.
- His **self-esteem** was nurtured by domestic **admiration.**
- His best poems, like **The Prelude**, reflect his **personal experiences.**
- He lacks a **purely lyrical gift**, unlike **Burns** or **Shelley.**
- Wordsworth excels at **reflective, analytic moods** in nature.
- "My heart leaps up when I behold a rainbow in the sky."
- His lyrical gift is **reflective rather than passionate.**
- **Lucy poems** illustrate his **intimate yet restrained emotions.**
- "She dwelt among the untrodden ways beside the springs of Dove."
- His lyrical mood shines in his **sonnets**, ranking among **the best.**
- Wordsworth's treatment of **nature** is his **greatest poetic strength.**
- He wrote with his **eye steadily fixed on the object.**
- "The cattle are grazing, their heads never raising."
- **Resolution and Independence** demonstrates **his keen observation** of nature.
- "There was a roaring in the wind all night."
- Nature gives him **joy**, which is **his most appealing charm.**
- Wordsworth seeks to understand the **deep joy** in **nature's beauty.**
- "The soul that rises with us...cometh from afar."

Major Works:

- ***Lyrical Ballads, with a Few Other Poems (1798)***
  - *"Simon Lee"*
  - *"We are Seven"*
  - *"Lines Written in Early Spring"*
  - *"Expostulation and Reply"*
  - *"The Tables Turned"*
  - *"The Thorn"*
  - *"Lines Composed A Few Miles above Tintern Abbey"*
- ***Lyrical Ballads, with Other Poems (1800)***
  - *Preface to the Lyrical Ballads*
  - *"Strange fits of passion have I known."*
  - *"She Dwelt among the Untrodden Ways"*
  - *"Three years she grew"*
  - *"A Slumber Did my Spirit Seal"*
  - *"I travelled among unknown men."*
  - *"Lucy Gray"*
  - *"The Two April Mornings"*
  - *"Nutting"*
  - *"The Ruined Cottage"*
  - *"Michael"*
  - *"The Kitten at Play"*
- ***Poems, in Two Volumes (1807)***
  - *"Resolution and Independence"*
  - *"I Wandered Lonely as a Cloud," Also known as "Daffodils."*
  - *"My Heart Leaps Up"*
  - *"Ode: Intimations of Immortality"*
  - *"Ode to Duty"*
  - *"The Solitary Reaper"*
  - *"Elegiac Stanzas"*
  - *"Composed upon Westminster Bridge, September 3, 1802"*
  - *"London, 1802"*
  - *"The World Is Too Much with Us"*
- ***"French Revolution" (1810)***
- *Guide to the Lakes (1810)*
- *"To the Cuckoo"*
- ***The Excursion (1814)***
- *Laodamia (1815, 1845)*
- *The White Doe of Rylstone (1815)*

> ***Peter Bell (1819)***
> *Ecclesiastical Sonnets (1822)*
> **The Prelude (1850)**

Lyrical Ballads, with a Few Other Poems (1798)

> Considered to have marked the **beginning of the English Romantic movement**.
> Most of the poems in the 1798 edition were written by Wordsworth.
> Coleridge contributed only four verses to the collection:
>   1. ***The Rime of the Ancyent Marinere (Coleridge)***
>   2. ***The Foster-Mother's Tale (Coleridge)***
>   3. ***The Nightingale, a Conversational Poem (Coleridge)***
>   4. ***The Dungeon (Coleridge)***

Poems by Wordsworth are:

1. *Lines left upon a Seat in a Yew-tree which stands near the Lake of Esthwaite*
2. *The Female Vagrant*
3. *Goody Blake and Harry Gill*
4. *Lines written at a small distance from my House, and sent by my little Boy to the Person to whom they are addressed*
5. ***Simon Lee,** the old Huntsman*
6. *Anecdote for Fathers*
7. ***We are seven***
8. *Lines written in early spring*
9. **The Thorn**
10. *The last of the Flock*
11. **The Mad Mother**
12. **The Idiot Boy**
13. *Lines written near Richmond, upon the Thames, at Evening*
14. *Expostulation and Reply*
15. **The Tables turned; an Evening Scene, on the same subject**
16. *Old Man travelling*
17. *The Complaint of a forsaken Indian Woman*
18. **The Convict (This was removed from 1800 Editions)**

Lines written a few miles above Tintern Abbey

> **Full title:** *Lines are Composed a Few Miles above Tintern Abbey, on Revisiting the Banks of the Wye during a Tour, in July 13, 1798*
> Wordsworth wrote it after a walking tour **with his sister** in this section of the **Welsh Borders**.

- ➢ *"Five years have past; five summers, with the length*
  - o *Of five long winters! and again I hear"*
- ➢ *"Of vagrant dwellers in the houseless woods,*
  - o *Or of some Hermit's cave, where by his fire*
  - o *The Hermit sits alone."*
- ➢ *"O sylvan Wye! thou wanderer thro' the woods,*
  - o *How often has my spirit turned to thee!"*
- ➢ **Five years** have passed since the speaker's last **visit**.
- ➢ The speaker recalls the **"steep and lofty cliffs."**
- ➢ The **"dark sycamore"** tree offers him **deep seclusion**.
- ➢ He observes **cottage grounds, orchards,** and **rising smoke**.
- ➢ Imagines **hermits** or **vagrant dwellers** in the **woods**.
- ➢ **Memories** of the woods brought him **sensations sweet**.
- ➢ Memory influenced his **deeds of kindness** and **love**.
- ➢ The woods lifted **burdens** and offered **spiritual peace**.
- ➢ He doubts the effect, but turns to the **memory**.
- ➢ The **past experience** lingers, evoking **bittersweet joy**.
- ➢ Recent experiences will bring him **future happiness**.
- ➢ The poet is different from his **youthful self**.
- ➢ **Nature shaped** his youthful **passions, appetites,** and **love**.
- ➢ He no longer **misses** his **boyhood connection** with nature.
- ➢ Now sees nature with a **reflective, mature perspective**.
- ➢ Nature reveals the **"still, sad music of humanity."**
- ➢ Senses a **subtle energy** in the **sun, ocean, air**.
- ➢ Believes this **spirit pervades** all **things and thoughts**.
- ➢ **Mountains, pastures, and forests** still anchor his **thoughts**.
- ➢ **Nature protects** his **innermost being** and purest thoughts.
- ➢ He would still be joyful, even without these **understandings**.
- ➢ His sister reflects his **younger self** through her **voice**.
- ➢ He prays to nature for **continued understanding**.
- ➢ **Nature never betrays** those who **love her**.
- ➢ Nature leads from **joy to joy** and **faith**.
- ➢ A mind filled with **spirit** repels **evil tongues** and **judgments**.
- ➢ The **moon** and **wind** will later **comfort his sister**.
- ➢ She will recall his love for **nature** in times of need.
- ➢ The memory of their shared **love for the woods** remains.
- ➢ Nature became **dearer** because **his sister shared** the experience.

Lyrical Ballads, with Other Poems (1800)

- Included additional **poems and a preface detailing the pair's avowed poetical principles**.
- The poem *The Convict (Wordsworth)* was in the 1798 edition, but Wordsworth omitted it from the 1800 edition, replacing it with **Coleridge's "Love."**

Preface to Lyrical Ballads (1800)

- Essay published in **January 1801**, often called **"1800 Edition"**.
- **Lyrical Ballads** collection expanded in **third edition** (1802).
- Regarded as the **de facto manifesto** of **Romanticism**.
- **Wordsworth** and **Coleridge** created it through **intellectual conversations**.
- **Lyrical Ballads** contains four poems by **Coleridge**, rest by **Wordsworth**.
- **Coleridge** wanted a **Preface** to clarify their **poetic style**.
- He criticized **"artificiality"** and **"aristocratic taste"** in poetry.
- **Wordsworth's and Coleridge's** poetry deemed more **accurate and lasting**.
- **Coleridge** conceived the **Preface** but **never wrote it**.
- **Wordsworth** wrote the **Preface** for the **1800 edition**.
- Wordsworth **refined** the **Preface** in the **1802 edition**.
- **Coleridge** disagreed with the **Preface**, shown in **Biographia Literaria**.
- Expressed differences through **letters** and **essays** later on.
- Differences between **Wordsworth and Coleridge** don't fully **clash**.
- The manifesto includes **four guidelines.**
  - Poetry is best **suited to ordinary life.** He uses the common man's language.
  - Poetry is best **written in everyday language**.
  - **Feelings are more important than plot or action.**
  - ***"Poetry is the spontaneous overflow of emotion"*** that ***"takes its origin from emotion, recollected in tranquility."***
- Wordsworth **rejected** the **style** of **18th-century poetry**.
- He ormed an understandable art form for the **"ordinary man."**
- Wordsworth remarks that ***"personifications of abstract ideas** rarely occur in these volumes; and are utterly rejected, as an ordinary device to elevate the style, and raise it above prose"* (Preface, 9).
- The author explains **why and how he chooses his poems' subjects.**

- **Wordsworth** believes **emotional truths** and **nature** reveal ordinary lives.
- He prefers **rural life** for its **simplicity and naturalness.**
- **Wordsworth** favors a **unified population** with **shared experiences.**
- **Natural truths** are absent in rapidly expanding **urban cities.**
- He makes **ordinary experiences** seem more **extraordinary and lasting.**
- **Wordsworth's literature** reflects **people's simplicity** and **life's depth.**
- **Nature illustrates permanence** and **unchanging truths**, inspiring his work.
- **Urban life** lacks the **permanence** that **nature provides.**
- Wordsworth expresses poetry must derive from the "**spontaneous overflow of powerful feelings; it takes its origin from emotion recollected in tranquility."**
- A poem must r**eminisce emotion or passion**, not simply record observations.
- The poet must **describe real-life experiences with ordinary language.**
- The poet must "*throw over them a certain colouring of the imagination, whereby **ordinary things should be presented to the mind in an unusual aspect.*"
- **Poet's imagination** creates new worlds connecting to **reality.**
- Poet observes something that **provokes emotion.**
- Then contemplates the emotion in **tranquillity and reflection.**
- Poet may recall related **observations** or **past experiences.**
- Contemplation is **personal**, meant only for the **poet.**
- **Reflection's tranquillity fades**, preparing for **expression.**
- Poet distils thoughts, **eliminating some, keeping others.**
- Poetry becomes a **universal expression** of original emotion.
- Poet is ready to **write** and share with an **audience.**
- Poetry doesn't come from **classical models** or **supernatural inspiration.**
- **Ordinary experience** and reflection are essential to **poetry.**
- **Wordsworth examines** his views on **poetry and prose.**
- Rejects past distinctions between **heroic** and **higher art.**
- He aims to reveal both as sharing the fundamental characteristics of *"the language of men."*

- As Wordsworth facilitates the art of poetry into "*a man speaking to men,*" he effectively removes the lines diverging prose from poetry.
- He sees both as different from **science**, as he understands it, because science is a relatively new field that focuses on the facts.
- Wordsworth considers the use of **most meters produces a forced type of "verse"** rather than the *"naked,"* more **straightforward poetry that shares truths with prose**.
- Wordsworth exemplifies that he chooses to write poetry with a proper and natural *"Poetic Diction"* rather than prose.
- At the end of the Preface, Wordsworth writes, "*They both speak by and to the same organs ... their affections are kindred, and almost identical, not necessarily differing even in degree.*"
- The Preface concludes with the statement that the essential principle of his art, made up of imagination and sentiment, will employ the exact natural language of meter or prose regardless of whether he writes in prose or verse.

"I Wandered Lonely as a Cloud," Also known as "Daffodils."

- The poem was inspired by **Wordsworth's daffodil encounter** in 1802.
- **Wordsworth and Dorothy** found a **"long belt" of daffodils**.
- Written between **1804 and 1807**, first published **in 1807**.
- Revised version published in **1815**.
- The poem has **four six-line stanzas** with **ABABCC rhyme scheme**.
- Each line is in **iambic tetrameter**.
- The speaker wanders like a **cloud over hills** and valleys.
- He encounters a **field of daffodils beside a lake**.
- The **fluttering daffodils** stretched endlessly along the **shore**.
- The **daffodils' joy** surpassed the **lake's dancing waves**.
- The poet couldn't help but feel **happy among the flowers**.
- He stared but didn't realize the **scene's lasting impact**.
- The memory brings joy when he feels **"vacant" or "pensive"**.
- The memory flashes upon his **"inward eye"** in solitude.
- His heart fills with pleasure, **dancing with daffodils**.
- The poem captures **joy from nature's beauty** and solitude.

I wandered lonely as a cloud
That floats on high o'er vales and hills,
When all at once I saw a crowd,

A host, of golden daffodils;
Beside the lake, beneath the trees,
Fluttering and dancing in the breeze.

Continuous as the stars that shine
And twinkle on the milky way,
They stretched in never-ending line
Along the margin of a bay:
Ten thousand saw I at a glance,
Tossing their heads in sprightly dance.

The waves beside them danced; but they
Out-did the sparkling waves in glee:
A poet could not but be gay,
In such a jocund company:
I gazed—and gazed—but little thought
What wealth the show to me had brought:

For oft, when on my couch I lie
In vacant or in pensive mood,
They flash upon that inward eye
Which is the bliss of solitude;
And then my heart with pleasure fills,
And dances with the daffodils.

"Ode: Intimations of Immortality"

- ➤ **Full**: "*Ode: Intimations of Immortality from Recollections of Early Childhood*"
- ➤ Completed in 1804 and published in ***Poems in Two Volumes (1807)***
- ➤ The poem was completed in **two parts**, starting in **1802**.
- ➤ First four stanzas were written about **childhood** in 1802.
- ➤ Completed on **27 March 1802**, shared with **Coleridge**.
- ➤ **Coleridge's response** was his poem **"Dejection: An Ode"**.
- ➤ Wordsworth added **seven stanzas** in **early 1804**.
- ➤ First printed as **"Ode"** in **1807**, revised in **1815**.
- ➤ Now known as **"Ode: Intimations of Immortality"**.
- ➤ The poem is an **irregular Pindaric ode** in **11 stanzas**.
- ➤ Combines **Coleridge's influence**, biblical, and **elegiac traditions**.
- ➤ Split into three movements: discusses **death and youth** first.

- Next stanzas explain how **age clouds divine sight**.
- Final stanzas express **hope through divine memory**.
- **Pre-existence** connects **children** to the divine in **nature**.
- As children mature, they **lose divine vision**.
- **Psychological development** also seen in **The Prelude**.
- **Wordsworth's "best philosopher" praise** drew **Coleridge's criticism**.
- Important Phrases and Lines:
  - ***"apparelled in celestial light"***
  - ***"the things I have seen I can see no more"***
  - *"something that is gone"*
  - *"Where is it now, the glory and the dream?"*
  - *"a sleep and a forgetting"*
  - ***"Heaven lies about us in our infancy!"***
  - *"some little plan or chart"*
  - *"a wedding or a festival"*
  - *"a mourning or a funeral"*
  - *"earthly freight"*
  - *"the gladness of the May"*
  - *"primal sympathy"*
  - *"a philosophic mind"*
  - ***"thoughts that do often lie too deep for tears"***

"London, 1802"

- **Wordsworth** castigates **England's stagnation** and **selfishness** in "London, 1802."
- Composed in **1802**, published in **Poems in Two Volumes** (1807).
- Speaker addresses **John Milton's soul**, asking for his return.
- **England** is described as **stagnant and selfish**.
- **Milton** could give **"manners, virtue, freedom, power"** to England.
- Milton's soul was like a **star**, his voice **pure** like the sea.
- Milton lived with **"cheerful godliness"** and accepted the **"lowest duties."**
- This is one of Wordsworth's excellent **early 1800s sonnets**.
- **Sonnets** are fourteen-line poems written in **iambic pentameter**.
- "London, 1802" takes the form of a **Petrarchan sonnet**.
- **Petrarchan sonnets** have an **octave** and a **sestet** structure.
- The **octave** follows the rhyme scheme **ABBAABBA**.
- The **sestet** follows a **variable rhyme scheme, BCCDBD** here.

- ➢ The poem begins with a **dramatic cry: "Milton!"**
- ➢ **Octave** lists vices, ruining the current era's **institutions**.
- ➢ Institutions like the **altar**, **sword**, and **pen** lost "inward happiness."
- ➢ Milton is seen as a specifically **English poet**.
- ➢ In the **sestet**, Milton's virtues could **correct England's waywardness**.
- ➢ **Milton's soul** stood apart, bright as a **star**.
- ➢ His voice was as powerful as the **sea**.
- ➢ Milton acted with **moral perfection** but remained **humble**.
- ➢ These virtues were lacking in **Wordsworth's contemporaries**.
- ➢ Wordsworth's poetry emphasizes **goodness** and **morality**.
- ➢ His ideas aimed to communicate **natural morality** to readers.
- ➢ Wordsworth's **angry moral sonnets** came from this **ethical impulse**.

Milton! thou shouldst be living at this hour:
England hath need of thee: she is a fen
Of stagnant waters: altar, sword, and pen,
Fireside, the heroic wealth of hall and bower,
Have forfeited their ancient English dower
Of inward happiness. We are selfish men;
Oh! raise us up, return to us again;
And give us manners, virtue, freedom, power.
Thy soul was like a Star, and dwelt apart:
Thou hadst a voice whose sound was like the sea:
Pure as the naked heavens, majestic, free,
So didst thou travel on life's common way,
In cheerful godliness; and yet thy heart
The lowliest duties on herself did lay.

> **Do You Know?**
> "London" by Samuel Johnson (1738): A **satirical imitation** of Juvenal's Third Satire in heroic couplets.
>
> "London" by William Blake (1794): Critiques **oppression and industrialization** in society.
>
> "London, 1802" by William Wordsworth
> Opens with: **"MILTON! thou shouldst be living at this hour."**
> Wordsworth **laments England's decline** and praises Milton.
>
> "London" (novel) by Edward Rutherfurd: Spans **2,000 years** of London's history, following multiple families.

The World Is Too Much with Us

- **Wordsworth criticizes** materialism during the **First Industrial Revolution.**
- Composed circa **1802**, first published in **Poems in Two Volumes (1807).**
- The poem is a **14-line Italian sonnet** in **iambic pentameter.**
- The speaker condemns the modern age's **loss of connection** to **nature.**
- **"Getting and spending, we lay waste our powers."**
- "We have given our hearts away, a **sordid boon!"**
- Humanity is **"out of tune"** with nature's wonders.
- Even when the sea **"bares her bosom to the moon,"** people are indifferent.
- The speaker wishes to be a **pagan** for a **different vision** of the world.
- He imagines ancient gods rising from **"this pleasant lea."**
- **Proteus rising from the sea** and **Triton blowing his horn.**
- The poem is an **excellent example** of Wordsworth's early sonnets.
- A **Petrarchan sonnet** follows the **form of Italian poet Petrarch.**
- A **Petrarchan sonnet** consists of an **octave** and a **sestet.**
- The octave raises a question; the **sestet answers or comments.**
- The rhyme scheme for the **octave** is **ABBAABBA.**

- ➢ The rhyme scheme for the **sestet** is **CDCDCD**.
- ➢ **Octave** proposes an idea; **sestet** offers a resolution or critique.
- ➢ The speaker laments the **detachment from nature** and spirituality.
- ➢ **Nature's beauty** no longer stirs the **modern human spirit**.

The Prelude (1850)

- ➢ **Full**: *The Prelude or, Growth of a Poet's Mind; An Autobiographical Poem.*
- ➢ **The Prelude** is an **autobiographical poem in blank verse.**
- ➢ Intended as the **introduction** to **The Recluse**, an unfinished work.
- ➢ **Highly personal**, revealing many **details of Wordsworth's life.**
- ➢ Began in **1798**, Wordsworth was **28 years old.**
- ➢ Never gave it a title, called it **"Poem to Coleridge".**
- ➢ The poem remained **unknown** until published after his **death** in 1850.
- ➢ The title **"The Prelude"** was given by his **widow Mary.**
- ➢ **The Prelude** was meant as **prologue** to a **three-part epic.**
- ➢ **Wordsworth** only completed **The Prelude** and **The Excursion.**
- ➢ **Planned to surpass Milton's Paradise Lost**, but left it incomplete.
- ➢ **The Recluse** would have been **three times longer** than **Paradise Lost.**
- ➢ Wordsworth was **plagued with agony** for not finishing the work.
- ➢ Planned project inspired by **"dear friend"** Coleridge.
- ➢ **Philosophical poem** on **Man, Nature, and Society.**
- ➢ Meant to show a poet's **sensations and opinions** in **retirement.**
- ➢ **Wordsworth** went to his grave, leaving **The Recluse unfinished.**
- ➢ **Coleridge's inspiration and interest are evident in his letters.**
- ➢ For instance, in 1799, he wrote to Wordsworth: *"I am anxiously eager to have you steadily employed on 'The Recluse'... I wish you would write a poem, in blank verse, addressed to those who, in consequence of the complete failure of the French Revolution, have thrown up all hopes of amelioration of mankind, and are sinking into an almost Epicurean selfishness, disguising the same under the soft titles of domestic attachment and contempt for visionary philosophies. It would do great good, and might form a Part of 'The Recluse'."* (STC to WW, Sept. 1799).
- ➢ Wordsworth **pays tribute to Coleridge** in his introduction to the edition of 1850: *"work [is] addressed to a dear friend, most*

> *distinguished for his knowledge and genius, and to whom the author's intellect is deeply indebted."*

➢ According to Monique R. Morgan's **"Narrative Means to Lyric Ends in Wordsworth's Prelude,"** *"Much of the poem consists of Wordsworth's interactions with nature that 'assure[d] him of his poetic mission.'*

➢ The goal of the poem is to demonstrate his fitness to produce great poetry, and The Prelude itself becomes evidence of that fitness."

➢ It traces the growth of the poet's mind by stressing the mutual consciousness and spiritual communion between the world of nature and man.

➢ Books of the 14-book Prelude
  - *Introduction – Childhood and School-Time*
  - *School-Time (Continued)*
  - *Residence at Cambridge*
  - *Summer Vacation*
  - *Books*
  - *Cambridge and the Alps*
  - *Residence in London*
  - *Retrospect – Love of Nature Leading to Love of Man*
  - *Residence in France*
  - *Residence in France (Continued)*
  - *Residence in France (Concluded)*
  - *Imagination and Taste, How Impaired and Restored*
  - *Imagination and Taste, How Impaired and Restored (Concluded)*
  - *Conclusion*

Questions:

Question 63

Match List I and List II List I

List I Author	List II Work
A. John Keats	I. Alastor
B. Willam Wordsworth	II Songs of Experience
C. PB Shelley	III. Comic
D. William Blake	IV. The Excursion

Choose the correct answer from the options given below:

1. A – Ill, B – I, C – IV, D – II
2. A – III, B – IV, C – 1, D – II
3. A – I, B – IV, C – III, D – II
4. A – IV, B – II, C – I, D – Ill

Explanations:
Answer: 2. A – III, B – IV, C – 1, D – II

"Alastor" is a poem by Percy Bysshe Shelley, published in 1816. It is a Gothic poem about a young poet's search for the ideal woman.

"The Excursion" is a long poem by William Wordsworth, published in 1814. It is part of Wordsworth's larger work "The Prelude" and tells the story of a group of travelers who discuss nature, humanity, and the role of art in society.

"Songs of Experience" is a collection of poems by William Blake, published in 1794.

"Comic" is indeed a poem by John Keats, published in 1817..

Arrange the following critical works in their chronological order of publication:

A. "Preface to Lyrical Ballads"
B. "A Defence of Rhyme"
C. "Life of Cowley"
D. "The Frontiers of Criticism"

Choose the correct answer from the options given below:

1. A, C, B and D
2. B, A, C and D
3. B, C, A and D
4. C, A, D and B

Explanations:
Answer: 3. B, C, A and D

Samuel Daniel (1562–1619) published the essay on English poetry *A Defence of Rhyme (1603).*

"Life of Cowley": This is a biography of the English poet Abraham Cowley, written by Samuel Johnson and first published in 1779.

"Preface to Lyrical Ballads": This is a critical essay written by William Wordsworth and originally published in 1800.

"The Frontiers of Criticism": This is a collection of essays by T.S. Eliot, published in 1961.

Question 65

Arrange the following lines of poetry in their chronological sequence:
- A.   "An aged man is but a paltry thing."
- B.   "The world is too much with us."
- C.   "Daddy, I have had to kill you."
- D.   "After great pain, a formal feeling comes -"

Choose the correct answer from the options below
1.   B, D, A, C
2.   D, B, A, C
3.   D, B, C, A
4.   **B, D, C, A**

Correct Explanations:
"The World Is Too Much with Us" is a sonnet by the English Romantic poet William Wordsworth. Composed circa **1802**, the poem was first published in Poems, in Two Volumes.

The American poet Emily Dickinson wrote "After great pain, a formal feeling comes" around **1862**.

"Sailing to Byzantium" is a poem by William Butler Yeats, first published in the **1928** collection "The Tower. *An aged man is but a paltry thing,/A tattered coat upon a stick, unless*"

"Daddy" is a poem written by American Confessional poet Sylvia Plath. The poem was written on October 12, **1962**, four months before her death and one month after her separation from Ted Hughes. "Daddy, I have had to kill you. In the waters off beautiful Nauset. I used to pray to recover you."

Match List I with List II

List I (Author)	List II (Text)
A. Robert Browning	I. Queen Mary
B.S. T. Coleridge	II.The Second Mrs Tanqueray
C. A. W. Pinero	III. Remorse
D. Alfred Tennyson	IV. The Borderers
E. William Wordsworth	V. Strafford

Choose the correct answer from the options given below:
1. **A-V; B-III; C-II; D-I; E-IV**
2. A-II; B-IV; C-III; D-V; E-I
3. A-III; B-V; C-II; D-I; E-IV
4. A-IV; B-II; C-I; D-V; E-III

Correct Explanations:
➢ ***The Second Mrs. Tanqueray* (1892) is a problem play by Arthur Wing Pinero.** It adopts the "Woman with a past" plot, popular in nineteenth century melodrama.
➢ ***Strafford* is an 1837 tragedy by the British writer Robert Browning.** It portrays the downfall and execution of Lord Strafford, the advisor to Charles I shortly before the English Civil War.
➢ ***Osorio* is a tragedy in blank verse by Samuel Taylor Coleridge.** It was written in 1797 but was unperformed following its rejection by Drury Lane Theatre. Coleridge revised and recast the play sixteen years later, giving it the new title of *Remorse*.
➢ ***Queen Mary and Harold*, by Alfred Lord Tennyson.**
➢ ***The Borderers*, by William Wordsworth.**

Arrange chronologically the following texts in terms of their years of first publication:

A. Edmund Spenser's The Faerie Queene
B. Coleridge and Wordsworth's Lyrical Ballads

C. Pablo Neruda's Canto General

D. Charles Baudelaire's The Flowers of Evil

Choose the correct answer from the options given below

1. A, B, C, D
2. **A, B, D, C**
3. B, C, A, D
4. D, A, B, C

Correct Explanations:

"The Faerie Queene" is an English epic poem by Edmund Spenser. Books I–III were first published in **1590,** then republished in 1596 together with books IV–VI.

"Lyrical Ballads", with a Few Other Poems is a collection of poems by William Wordsworth and Samuel Taylor Coleridge, first published in **1798.**

"Les Fleurs du mal" is a volume of French poetry by Charles Baudelaire. Les Fleurs du mal includes nearly all of Baudelaire's poetry, written in **1840** and ending with his death in August 1867.

"Canto General" is Pablo Neruda's tenth book of poems. It was first published in Mexico in **1950.**

Question 68

Arrange the following groups of poets in their chronological sequence in relation to English literary history:

A. The Imagist poets
B. The Cavalier poets
C. The Movement poets
D. The Lake poets

Choose the correct answer from the options given below

1. B, D, C, A
2. D, A, B, C
3. D, B, A, C
4. **B, D, A, C**

Correct Explanations:
The cavalier poets was a school of English poets of the 17th century, that came from the classes that supported King Charles I during the English Civil War (1642–1651). The best-known cavalier poets are Robert Herrick, Richard Lovelace, Thomas Carew, and Sir John Suckling.

The Lake Poets were a group of English poets who all lived in the Lake District of England, United Kingdom, in the first half of the nineteenth century. As a group, they followed no single "school" of thought or literary practice then known. The three main figures of what has become known as the Lakes School were **William Wordsworth, Samuel Taylor Coleridge, and Robert Southey.** They were associated with several other poets and writers, including Dorothy Wordsworth, Charles Lamb, Mary Lamb, Charles Lloyd, Hartley Coleridge, John Wilson, and Thomas De Quincey.

Imagism was a movement in early-20th-century Anglo-American poetry that favored precision of imagery and clear, sharp language. It is considered to be the first organized modernist literary movement in the English language. Imagist publications appearing between 1914 and 1917 featured works by many of the most prominent modernist figures in poetry and other fields, **including Pound, H.D. (Hilda Doolittle), Amy Lowell, Ford Madox Ford, William Carlos Williams, F. S. Flint, and T. E. Hulme.**

The Movement was a term coined in 1954 by J. D. Scott, literary editor of The Spectator, to describe a group of writers, including **Philip Larkin, Kingsley Amis, Donald Davie, D. J. Enright, John Wain, Elizabeth Jennings, Thom Gunn, and Robert Conquest.**

Question 69

Which of the following is not true about "Lyrical Ballads"?
1. It turns English Poetry away from the social and intellectual sophistication of the seventeenth and the eighteenth- century poetry.
2. **It is very particular about the form and structure of a poem.**
3. It takes poetry out of the confines of reason and intellect to the unravished and unspoilt beauties of nature.
4. It is a manifesto of Romantic poetry.

Correct Explanations:

The Preface to Lyrical Ballads is an essay, composed by William Wordsworth, for the second edition published in 1800 of the poetry collection Lyrical Ballads, and then greatly expanded in the third edition of 1802. It has come to be seen as a de facto manifesto of the Romantic movement.

The four guidelines of the manifesto include:

1. Ordinary life is the best subject for poetry. (Wordsworth uses common man's language.)
2. **Everyday language is best suited for poetry**
3. Expression of feeling is more important than action or plot
4. "Poetry is the spontaneous overflow of powerful feelings" that "takes its origin from emotion, recollected in tranquillity." - William Wordsworth

Question 70

Who said that? "There is, there can be and there ought to be the difference between the language of prose and metrical composition"?

1. John Dryden
2. **William Wordsworth**
3. S.T. Coleridge
4. T.S. Eliot

Correct Explanations:

What does Wordsworth say about the language of poetry?

- "Preface to the Lyrical Ballads" by William Wordsworth is an epoch-making contribution to English literature.
- It is a landmark of literary criticism. Wordsworth has declared a break of the Neo- classical tradition in English poetry through this piece.
- He has discussed the characteristics of a poet, his functions and his dominions elaborately.
- During the Neo-classical Age, the language of poetry was decorated and figurative.
- It dealt with the aristocratic way of life. But Wordsworth revolts against it. He changes the classical theory of poetry.
- He declares that a poet is a man speaking to men.
- The language of poetry is the language of common people.
- **He boldly proclaims that there is no essential difference between the language of prose and that of metrical composition. In fact,**

with the publication of this " preface ", Wordsworth started the
Romantic Revival.

Inane gaudiness" is a phrase used in connection with Neo-classicism by

1. **William Wordsworth**
2. S.T. Coleridge
3. Matthew Arnold
4. T.S. Eliot

Correct Explanations:
**The term "inane gaudiness" is actually used by William Wordsworth in
his "Preface to Lyrical Ballads" to criticize the artificiality of Neoclassical
poetry, not to praise it.**

Given below are two statements:

> **Statement I:** Wordsworth's "Intimations of Immortality from
> Recollections of Early Childhood" was published in 1807.
> **Statement II:** In "Intimations of Immortality from Recollections of
> Early Childhood." Wordsworth sums up his philosophy of childhood.

**In light of the above statements, choose the correct answer from the
options given below:**

> 1. Both Statement I and Statement II are false.
> 2. Both Statement I and Statement II are true.
> 3. Statement I is true, but Statement II is false.
> 4. Statement I is false, but Statement I is true

Explanations
Answer: 2. Both Statement I and Statement II are true.

"Ode: Intimations of Immortality from Recollections of Early Childhood" (also
known as "Ode", "Immortality Ode" or "Great Ode") is a poem by William
Wordsworth, completed in 1804 and **published in Poems, in Two Volumes
(1807).**

Wordsworth's praise of the child as the "best philosopher" was criticised by Coleridge and became the source of later critical discussion.

In 1802, Wordsworth wrote many poems that dealt with his youth. These poems were partly inspired by his conversations with his sister, Dorothy, whom he was living with in the Lake District at the time. **The poems, beginning with "The Butterfly" and ending with "To the Cuckoo", were all based on Wordsworth's recalling both the sensory and emotional experience of his childhood.** From "To the Cuckoo", he moved on to "The Rainbow", both written on 26 March 1802, and then on to "Ode: Intimation of Immortality from Recollections of Early Childhood".

Question 73

Arrange the correct chronological sequence of the publication of the following texts:

> A. Essay of Dramatic Poesy
> B. A Room of One's Own
> C. Culture and Anarchy
> D. The Lives of the Poets
> E. "Preface to the Lyrical Ballads"

Choose the correct answer from the options given below:

> 1. A, D, E, C, B
> 2. D, A, E, B, C
> 3. A, C, D, E, B
> 4. E, D, C, A, B

Explanations
Answer: 1. A, D, E, C, B

A. John Dryden's ***Essay of Dramatick Poesy*** was likely written in **1666** during the Great Plague of London and published in **1668**.
D. ***Lives of the Most Eminent English Poets*** (1779–8).
E. ***The Preface to Lyrical Ballads*** is an essay by William Wordsworth, first published in the second edition of the poetry collection Lyrical Ballads in **1800**.

C. ***Culture and Anarchy: An Essay in Political and Social Criticism*** is a series of periodical essays by Matthew Arnold, first published in Cornhill Magazine from 1867 to 1868 and later collected as a book in 1869. The preface was added in **1869**.

B. ***A Room of One's Own*** is an essay by Virginia Woolf, published in 1929, based on two lectures she gave in **1928** at Newnham College and Girton College, the first two colleges for women at Cambridge.

Question 74

Which among the following poems has not been composed by P.B. Shelley?

1. To Wordsworth
2. Mutability
3. Hymn to Intellectual Beauty
4. When We Two Parted

Explanations:
Answer: 4. When We Two Parted

"When We Two Parted", a poem of Lord Byron

"Hymn to Intellectual Beauty" is a poem written by Percy Bysshe Shelley in 1816 and published in 1817.

"Mutability" is a poem by Percy Bysshe Shelley, featured in the 1816 collection titled Alastor, or The Spirit of Solitude: And Other Poems.

In **"To Wordsworth,"** Percy Bysshe Shelley pays homage to the elder Romantic poet William Wordsworth (1770-1850), reflecting on the latter's advancing age and legacy..

Question 75

Chronologically arrange the following works on literary criticism in order of their publication:

A. An Apologie for Poetrie
B. The Art of Rhetorique
C. Preface to Lyrical Ballads

    D. An Essays in Criticism
    E. The Metaphysical Poets

Choose the correct answer from the options given below:

1. E,A,B,C,D
2. B,A,C,D,E
3. C,D,B,A, E
4. ACE D.B

Explanations:
Answer: 2. B,A,C,D,E **Corrected (B,A,D,C,E)**

Thomas Wilson (1524–1581), an esteemed English diplomat and judge, notably served as a privy councillor and Secretary of State to Queen Elizabeth I from 1577 to 1581. Renowned for his contributions to **English literature, his works "The Art of Logique" (1551) and "The Arte of Rhetorique" (1553)** stand as pioneering comprehensive studies on logic and rhetoric in English. Additionally, Wilson authored "A Discourse upon Usury" (1572) and became the first to translate Demosthenes into English, marking significant literary achievements of his time.

Sir Philip Sidney began his journey as a poet in 1578, with a relatively brief but impactful literary career spanning 7 to 8 years. His seminal work, **"The Defence of Poesy," also known under the titles "The Defence of Poesie" and "An Apologie for Poetrie,"** stands as a powerful testament to the value of poetry, penned by someone deeply versed in both the practice and the classical understanding of the art.

An Essay on Criticism is one of the first major poems written by the English writer Alexander Pope (1688–1744), published in 1711. It is the source of the famous quotations "To err is human; to forgive, divine", "A little learning is a dang'rous thing" (frequently misquoted as "A little knowledge is a dang'rous thing"), and "Fools rush in where angels fear to tread".

The Preface to Lyrical Ballads is an essay, composed by William Wordsworth, for the second edition published in **1800** of the poetry collection Lyrical Ballads, and then greatly expanded in the third edition of 1802. It came to be seen as a de facto manifesto of the Romantic movement.

***The Metaphysical Poets* by T.S. Eliot First published in the Times Literary Supplement, 20 October 1921**. By collecting these poems from the work of a generation more often named than read, and more often read than profitably studied, Professor Grierson has rendered a service of some importance.

SAMUEL TAYLOR COLERIDGE (1772–1834)

Hist Life:

- **Coleridge** was born in **Devonshire**, youngest of **thirteen children**.
- As a child, he was **unusually precocious** and reflective.
- His father died when **Coleridge was nine years old**.
- At **ten**, he obtained a place at **Christ's Hospital**.
- **Charles Lamb** was one of his **schoolmates**.
- **Coleridge** went to **Cambridge** in **1791**, influenced by **revolutionary ideas**.
- He abandoned **university** and enlisted in the **Light Dragoons**.
- After a few months, his **military career** ended.
- In **1794**, he returned to **Cambridge** and met **Southey**.
- **Coleridge and Southey** planned an **ideal republic** in America.
- Coleridge married **Southey's wife's sister**.
- He lectured, wrote poetry, and started a newspaper, **The Watchman**.
- In **1797**, Coleridge met **Wordsworth** and planned **Lyrical Ballads**.
- He briefly became a **Unitarian minister**.
- He received a **small annuity** from two **rich friends**.
- Coleridge studied **German philosophy** on the **Continent**.
- He lived in the **Lake District** for a time.
- **Coleridge** pursued a **restless and unhappy existence**.
- He turned to **journalism** and **lecturing**, but began to decline.
- His decline was caused by **opium-taking**.
- He **parted from his wife and children**, leaving them behind.
- From **1816**, Coleridge drifted, revealing his genius **sporadically**.
- He moved to **Mr. Gillman's house** in **Highgate** in **1816**.
- The house was like a **sympathetic inebriates' home**.
- There, he gradually **shook off opium-taking**.
- Spent his later years in **subdued content**.
- Friends often visited him, enjoying his **wandering intelligence**.
- **Coleridge** conversed with **luminous intelligence** in his later years.

> ➤ From **Highgate**, he issued **a few significant books**.
> ➤ His later works, despite faults, are among the **best in class**.

His Poetry:

> ➤ **Coleridge's poetical genius** blossomed briefly but **richly**.
> ➤ His best poems were composed within **1797–98**.
> ➤ First book, **Poems on Various Subjects** (1797), had **moderate merit**.
> ➤ Collaborated with **Wordsworth** on **Lyrical Ballads**.
> ➤ **Lyrical Ballads** contains **four poems** by **Coleridge**.
> ➤ **The Rime of the Ancient Mariner** is the most **noteworthy**.
> ➤ The **poem's origin** was discussed on **Quantock Hills**.
> ➤ **Coleridge's imagination** was fired with the **Ancient Mariner** story.
> ➤ **Dissolving pictures**: voyage, **albatross**, calm, and **storm**.
> ➤ The **Ancient Mariner** is without a **parallel** in style and imagination.
> ➤ In **1797**, Coleridge also wrote **Christabel** and **Kubla Khan**.
> ➤ Both **Christabel** and **Kubla Khan** remained unfinished until **1816**.
> ➤ **Christabel** tells a **vampire tale** involving **Christabel**.
> ➤ **Christabel's** indecision showed **Coleridge's fatal hesitation**.
> ➤ The **Christabel meter** is a **melodious octosyllabic couplet**.
> ➤ **Kubla Khan** is an **echo of a dream**.
> ➤ **Coleridge** dreamt the lines but was **distracted** before finishing.
> ➤ **Kubla Khan** begins with a **pleasure-dome** in **Xanadu**.
> ➤ The poem becomes a **dreamlike series** of dissolving views.
> ➤ **Kubla Khan** collapses into a **wild dervish-dance** of imagination.
> ➤ In **1797**, Coleridge also composed **Frost at Midnight** and **Love**.
> ➤ He wrote the **Ode to France** in the same **year**.
> ➤ In **1802**, he wrote the great **ode Dejection**.
> ➤ **Dejection** laments the loss of his **shaping spirit of Imagination**.
> ➤ **The Knight's Tomb** is one of his **few notable fragments**.
> ➤ **The remainder of his poems** were of **poorer quality**.
> ➤ His play **Remorse** was accepted at **Drury Lane Theatre**.
> ➤ **Byron recommended** Coleridge's play **Remorse**.
> ➤ **Remorse** succeeded on stage but is **literarily insignificant**.
> ➤ **Coleridge's creativity** was marked by **unfinished projects**.
> ➤ **Kubla Khan's unfinished state** reflects **Coleridge's distractions**.
> ➤ **The Christabel meter** influenced **later poets**.
> ➤ **Coleridge's imagination** shone in **short, intense bursts**.
> ➤ **His opium addiction** plagued his **productivity** and **completion**.
> ➤ **Coleridge's work** has a sense of **unfulfilled potential**.

- ➢ **Remorse's success** didn't translate into **lasting literary impact**.
- ➢ **Coleridge's decline** began with his **creative indecision**.
- ➢ **Coleridge's genius** remains, though often **fragmented** and incomplete.

His Works:

- ➢ *Lectures 1795 on Politics and Religion (1971);*
- ➢ ***The Watchman (1970);***
- ➢ *Essays on his Times in the Morning Post and the Courier (1978) in 3 vols;*
- ➢ ***The Friend (1969) in 2 vols;***
- ➢ *Lectures, 1808–1819, on Literature (1987) in 2 vols;*
- ➢ *Lay Sermons (1972);*
- ➢ ***Osorio (1797) (Play)***
- ➢ ***Biographia Literaria (1983) in 2 vols;***
- ➢ *Lectures 1818–1819 on the History of Philosophy (2000) in 2 vols;*
- ➢ *Aids to Reflection (1993);*
- ➢ ***On the Constitution of the Church and State (1976);***
- ➢ *Shorter Works and Fragments (1995) in 2 vols;*
- ➢ *Marginalia (1980 and following) in 6 vols;*
- ➢ *Logic (1981);*
- ➢ ***Table Talk (1990) in 2 vols;***
- ➢ *Opus Maximum (2002);*
- ➢ *Poetical Works (2001) in 6 vols (part 1 – Reading Edition in 2 vols; part 2 – Variorum Text in 2 vols; part 3 – Plays in 2 vols).*

Notable Poems:

- ➢ "Christabel"
- ➢ "Dejection: An Ode"
- ➢ "Frost at Midnight"
- ➢ "Kubla Khan"
- ➢ "The Rime of the Ancient Mariner"

The Rime of the Ancient Mariner (1798)

- ➢ **The Rime of the Ancient Mariner** is Coleridge's **longest poem**.
- ➢ Written in **1797-98**, published in **Lyrical Ballads** (1798).
- ➢ Revised version published in **1817** with **a gloss**.
- ➢ Considered the start of **British Romantic literature**.

- The poem recounts a sailor's **long sea voyage**.
- The **Mariner** stops a **Wedding-Guest** to tell his story.
- **Wedding-Guest's reaction** shifts from **impatience** to **fascination**.
- **Coleridge uses personification** and **repetition** for mood.
- **Three men** walk to a wedding; one is detained.
- The **Wedding-Guest** is transfixed by the Mariner's **"glittering eye"**.
- The Mariner recalls sailing from his **native harbor**.
- The **Wedding-Guest imagines** music from the wedding.
- The Mariner's voyage encounters a **storm and icy waters**.
- They meet an **Albatross**, which brings **good luck**.
- The Mariner shoots the **Albatross** with a **crossbow**.
- At first, the sailors **curse the Mariner** for killing the bird.
- When the fog lifts, they **praise the Mariner**.
- The ship becomes **stranded** in a **silent sea**.
- The ship is like a **"painted ship on a painted ocean."**
- The sailors see **slimy creatures** and **death fire**.
- A spirit **follows the ship** from the land of **mist**.
- Sailors blame the Mariner, **hang the Albatross** around his neck.
- **Parched and desperate**, the sailors **cannot speak**.
- The Mariner sees a **ship** on the horizon.
- He bites his arm to **moisten his tongue** and shouts.
- The ship holds **Death** and **Nightmare Life-in-Death**.
- They **roll dice; Life-in-Death** wins.
- The sailors **drop dead** one by one.
- Each sailor **curses the Mariner** with his **eye**.
- The **Wedding-Guest fears** the Mariner.
- The Mariner reassures him, saying he is **alive**.
- The Mariner is **surrounded by corpses** and **slimy sea**.
- He tries to **pray** but is stopped by a **"wicked whisper"**.
- For **seven days**, he **endures** the sight of the dead.
- The Mariner sees **beautiful water snakes** at **moonrise**.
- He **blesses** the creatures and **prays**.
- The **Albatross** falls from his neck into the sea.
- The Mariner's **curse** begins to **lift**.
- **The ship** moves again, but the crew remains **dead**.
- **Spirits possess the crew**, making them work the ship.
- The **spirits guide** the ship home to **England**.
- The Mariner hears **two voices** discussing his fate.
- The Mariner wakes to find the ship near **land**.

- ➤ **A hermit**, pilot, and boy approach in a boat.
- ➤ The **ship sinks**, and the Mariner is rescued.
- ➤ The **Mariner confesses** his sins to the **hermit**.
- ➤ The Mariner is compelled to **tell his tale** to others.
- ➤ The **Wedding-Guest** becomes a **"sadder and wiser man"**.
- ➤ The poem uses themes of **sin, guilt, and redemption**.
- ➤ The **Albatross** symbolizes **nature** and its connection to **humanity**.
- ➤ The **Mariner's journey** reflects a spiritual **awakening**.
- ➤ **Coleridge blends** the **supernatural** with **moral lessons**.
- ➤ The poem's structure uses **repetition** for dramatic **effect**.
- ➤ The poem is written in **ballad form** with **simple language**.
- ➤ The **Mariner's curse** is relieved through **repentance**.
- ➤ **Nature's beauty** and the **sublime** play central roles.
- ➤ The Mariner's story is about **punishment** and **forgiveness**.
- ➤ **The gloss** in later versions adds **explanatory notes**.
- ➤ **Coleridge** uses vivid imagery to create a sense of **awe**.
- ➤ The poem leaves readers with a sense of **mystery** and **wonder**.

Here are some of the most important lines from **"The Rime of the Ancient Mariner"** by Samuel Taylor Coleridge:

- ➤ **"Water, water, every where, / Nor any drop to drink."**
  - ○ This line captures the irony of the sailors' situation, surrounded by water yet dying of thirst.
- ➤ **"He prayeth best, who loveth best / All things both great and small; / For the dear God who loveth us, / He made and loveth all."**
  - ○ This expresses the moral lesson of the poem: the importance of love and respect for all creatures, great and small.
- ➤ **"The Albatross about my neck was hung."**
  - ○ A significant metaphor for guilt and burden, representing the consequences of the Mariner's action in killing the Albatross.
- ➤ **"With my crossbow / I shot the Albatross."**
  - ○ The pivotal moment of the poem, where the Mariner's fateful action brings doom upon the ship and crew.
- ➤ **"And a thousand thousand slimy things / Lived on; and so did I."**
  - ○ Reflects the Mariner's torment and isolation as he continues to live while surrounded by death.
- ➤ **"Alone, alone, all, all alone, / Alone on a wide, wide sea!"**

- o Emphasizes the Mariner's despair and complete isolation after the death of the crew.
- ➢ **"The fair breeze blew, the white foam flew, / The furrow followed free; / We were the first that ever burst / Into that silent sea."**
  - o Describes the ship's initial progress, setting the stage for the disaster to follow.
- ➢ **"A sadder and a wiser man, / He rose the morrow morn."**
  - o Refers to the Wedding-Guest, who has been deeply affected by the Mariner's story.
- ➢ **"Day after day, day after day, / We stuck, nor breath nor motion; / As idle as a painted ship / Upon a painted ocean."**
  - o This line highlights the crew's suffering as they are stuck in a windless, unmoving sea.
- ➢ **"The self-same moment I could pray; / And from my neck so free / The Albatross fell off, and sank / Like lead into the sea."**
- ➢ Marks the moment when the Mariner is spiritually freed from his guilt after blessing the sea creatures.

These lines represent key moments of **the Mariner's journey, guilt, isolation**, and eventual redemption.

Kubla Khan ((1797)1816)

- ➢ **Kubla Khan** was composed under the influence of **laudanum**.
- ➢ Coleridge claimed the poem came from an **opium-induced dream**.
- ➢ Planned poem was **200–300 lines**, but he forgot the rest.
- ➢ Interrupted by **"a person from Porlock"**, preventing completion.
- ➢ **Kubla Khan** was kept private until **published in 1816**.
- ➢ **Lord Byron** encouraged Coleridge to publish the poem.
- ➢ Coleridge's contemporaries questioned the poem's **origin story**.
- ➢ Critics later admired **Kubla Khan** as a **great poem**.
- ➢ Now viewed alongside **The Rime of the Ancient Mariner**.
- ➢ One of the best examples of **Romanticism** in **English poetry**.
- ➢ The poem is frequently **anthologized** and studied.
- ➢ The manuscript is exhibited at the **British Library, London**.
- ➢ **Kubla Khan**'s first stanza describes a **pleasure dome**.
- ➢ The second stanza explores an **Abyssinian maid's song**.
- ➢ The poem contrasts **natural vs. artistic creative power**.

- ➤ The third stanza shifts to a **first-person speaker**.
- ➤ The speaker dreams of **reviving the maid's song**.
- ➤ He imagines filling the **pleasure dome with music**.
- ➤ The audience would experience **religious ecstasy**.
- ➤ **Three irregular stanzas** move between different times.
- ➤ The first stanza describes **Xanadu**'s origin and geography.
- ➤ It mentions the **river Alph**, flowing through caves.
- ➤ Ten miles of **fortified land** surrounds **gardens and forests**.
- ➤ The second stanza describes a **mysterious canyon**.
- ➤ A **geyser erupts** from the canyon, feeding the **sacred river**.
- ➤ The river flows to the **caves** and reaches the **dark sea**.
- ➤ **Kubla Khan** hears a **prophecy of war** during the eruption.
- ➤ The **pleasure dome** reflects in the water near the geyser.
- ➤ The final couplet again describes the **pleasure dome**.
- ➤ The third stanza shifts to the speaker's **vision** of a woman.
- ➤ The woman plays a **dulcimer** in the speaker's vision.
- ➤ Reviving her song would **revive the pleasure dome**.
- ➤ Those hearing the song would experience **warning and awe**.
- ➤ The audience envisions an **alarming male figure**.
- ➤ The stanza ends with a **warning** after consuming **Paradise's food**.

Here are some important lines from **"Kubla Khan"** by Samuel Taylor Coleridge:

- ➤ **"In Xanadu did Kubla Khan / A stately pleasure-dome decree"**
  - o This opening line introduces the mythical and grand setting of the poem.
- ➤ **"Where Alph, the sacred river, ran / Through caverns measureless to man / Down to a sunless sea."**
  - o These lines describe the mysterious, fantastical landscape, emphasizing the river Alph and its journey to a dark, unknown sea.
- ➤ **"So twice five miles of fertile ground / With walls and towers were girdled round."**
  - o This highlights the vastness of Kubla Khan's domain, enclosed by walls and towers.
- ➤ **"And there were gardens bright with sinuous rills, / Where blossomed many an incense-bearing tree;"**

- - These lines evoke the lush, exotic gardens within the pleasure dome.
- ➤ **"A savage place! as holy and enchanted / As e'er beneath a waning moon was haunted / By woman wailing for her demon-lover!"**
  - - This describes a wild, mysterious place filled with enchantment and danger.
- ➤ **"And from this chasm, with ceaseless turmoil seething, / As if this earth in fast thick pants were breathing,"**
  - - These lines depict the powerful, turbulent energy emerging from the earth, symbolizing creativity and chaos.
- ➤ **"It was a miracle of rare device, / A sunny pleasure-dome with caves of ice!"**
  - - A striking image of contrast between the pleasure-dome and icy caves, blending opposites in the poem's dreamlike vision.
- ➤ **"And all who heard should see them there, / And all should cry, Beware! Beware! / His flashing eyes, his floating hair!"**
  - - These lines describe the speaker's vision of others reacting in awe and fear to a powerful figure.
- ➤ **"For he on honey-dew hath fed, / And drunk the milk of Paradise."**
  - - The closing lines suggest the speaker's mystical experience, having consumed divine food, representing ultimate inspiration.

These lines reflect the poem's central themes of **fantasy, imagination**, and the **mysterious interplay of nature and creativity**.

Christabel:

- ➤ **Christabel** is a long narrative ballad by **Samuel Taylor Coleridge**.
- ➤ **Part one** was written in **1797**, and part two in **1800**.
- ➤ **Three additional parts** were planned but never **completed**.
- ➤ Coleridge left Christabel out of **Lyrical Ballads** on **Wordsworth's advice**.
- ➤ Exclusion and incompletion made Coleridge doubt his **poetic power**.
- ➤ **Christabel** was published in **1816** with **Kubla Khan** and **The Pains of Sleep**.

- The poem uses an **accentual metric system** with **four accents per line**.
- **Christabel** encounters a stranger, **Geraldine**, in the **woods**.
- **Geraldine** claims she was **abducted by rough men**.
- **Christabel** pities **Geraldine** and takes her **home**.
- **Supernatural signs** suggest **Geraldine** is not what she **seems**.
- They spend the **night together**, with **ominous revelations**.
- Geraldine reveals a **terrible mark**, but its nature is **undefined**.
- **Christabel's father, Sir Leoline**, becomes **enthralled with Geraldine**.
- He orders a **grand procession** to celebrate her **rescue**.
- **Christabel**, under **enchantment**, starts realizing Geraldine's **malign nature**.
- The **unfinished poem** ends as **Christabel's suspicions grow**.

Osorio (1797) or Remorse (Play)

- **Osorio** is a **tragedy in blank verse** by **Coleridge**.
- Written in **1797**, it was **unperformed** after rejection by **Drury Lane**.
- Coleridge revised it **16 years later**, renaming it **Remorse**.
- **Remorse** achieved **critical and commercial success** in 1813.
- It ran for **twenty nights** at **Drury Lane Theatre**.
- The play was issued in **print three times** within the year.
- **Remorse** was a successful **revision** of **Osorio**.

Biographia Literaria (1817):

- The **two-volume autobiography** was published in **1817** by Coleridge.
- Its working title was 'Autobiographia Literaria'.
- Its subtitle, *'Biographical Sketches of My Literary Life and Opinions', alludes to The Life and Opinions of Tristram Shandy, Gentleman by Laurence Sterne.*
- **Wordsworth's poetry theory** and **Kant's imagination** influenced Coleridge's work.
- **Coleridge** coined the term **"esemplastic"** from **post-Kantian writers**.
- Influences include **F.W.J. von Schelling, David Hartley**, and **Associationist psychology**.
- **Coleridge's critical work** is in **24 chapters of Biographia Literaria**.
- **Biographia Literaria** was written between **1815–17**.

- ➤ Coleridge examines **criticism practice** and its **theory** in the text.
- ➤ **First volume** emphasizes **Coleridge's philosophical development**.
- ➤ He believed in the **"self-sufficing power of absolute Genius."**
- ➤ He compared **talent** and **genius** to an **"egg and an egg-shell."**
- ➤ **Coleridge defined "willing suspension of disbelief" in 1817** in *Biographia Literaria*.
- ➤ It is also referred to as **poetic faith** by Coleridge.
- ➤ This concept allows **artists to create worlds** separate from reality.
- ➤ **Suspension of disbelief** lets audiences **enjoy art** without focusing on its unreality.
- ➤ The idea originated in **Greco-Roman theater**, where it enabled **catharsis**.
- ➤ **The concept of untranslatability:**
- ➤ *"The infallible test of a blameless style, its untranslatability into other words of the same language without damage to its meaning."*

Chapter XIV:

- ➤ This chapter begins with Coleridge's views on **two cardinal points of poetry**.
- ➤ The **cardinal points** of poetry are:
  - ○ Ability to **evoke sympathy in the reader** by faithfully adhering to nature's truths.
  - ○ Ability to **express novelty by modifying with imagination's colours**.
- ➤ Subjects for these poems were to come from **ordinary life**.
- ➤ The **second type of poetry** where the incidents and agents were **supernatural**.
- ➤ These two cardinal points are the subject of poems in **"The Lyrical Ballads."**
- ➤ **Coleridge defended Wordsworth's poetic creed** in **Biographia Literaria**.
- ➤ Coleridge disagreed with **Wordsworth's ideas** on **poetic diction**.
- ➤ Coleridge supported **Lyrical Ballads' "language of real life"**.

Fancy and Imagination:

- ➤ **Kant, Fichte, and Schelling** coined the definition of **imagination**.
- ➤ **Imagination and fancy** differ fundamentally in **kind**.
- ➤ There is **no creative power** in **fancy**.
- ➤ Fancy only **combines perceptions into beautiful shapes**.

- ➤ **Imagination does not** merely **fuse or unify** perceptions.
- ➤ **Mechanical mixtures** and **chemical compounds** differ similarly.
- ➤ **Coleridge's imagination** has **two forms**: Primary and **Secondary**.
- ➤ **Primary imagination** perceives the **external world** through **senses**.

Fancy:

- ➤ **Coleridge regards fancy** as inferior to **imagination**.
- ➤ **Fancy** is a **creative power**, but less than imagination.
- ➤ It **combines things** into different shapes, not **fusing** them.
- ➤ **Imagination** fuses different elements into a **unified whole**.
- ➤ Fancy **brings together dissimilar images** from different sources.

Primary Imagination:

- ➤ **Imagination** differs from **fancy** in nature and function.
- ➤ **Coleridge** defines two forms of imagination: **Primary** and **Secondary**.
- ➤ **Primary imagination** perceives the **external world** through **senses**.
- ➤ We use **primary imagination** to perceive things **daily**.
- ➤ It perceives objects in both their **parts and whole**.
- ➤ **Primary imagination** is an **involuntary act** of the mind.
- ➤ The **mind receives impressions** and sensations **unconsciously**.
- ➤ **Primary imagination** imposes order on **sensory impressions**.
- ➤ It **shapes and sizes** impressions for **clear perception**.
- ➤ **Clear, coherent perception** becomes possible through **primary imagination**.

Secondary Imagination:

- ➤ **Primary imagination** is **universal** and present in **everyone**.
- ➤ **Secondary imagination** is unique to **artists** and creators.
- ➤ **Secondary imagination** enables **artistic creation**.
- ➤ It is **more active** and requires **conscious effort**.
- ➤ **Primary imagination** works with what is **perceived**.
- ➤ Provides **raw material** as sensations and **impressions**.
- ➤ **Secondary imagination** selects, orders, and **reshapes raw material**.
- ➤ Uses **will and intellect** to create **beautiful objects**.
- ➤ **Esemplastic power** shapes and **modifies external objects**.
- ➤ It exerts **plastic stress**, immersing them in **dreams and glory**.
- ➤ It **"dissolves, diffuses, and dissipates in order to create."**
- ➤ All **poetic activity** is based on **secondary imagination**.
- ➤ It **harmonizes opposites**, a **"magical, synthetic power."**

- ➤ Imagination integrates **soul, perception, intellect**, and **will**.
- ➤ Fuses **internal with external**, subjective with **objective**.
- ➤ Connects the **human mind** with **external nature**.
- ➤ Reconciles the **spiritual** with the **physical and material**.
- ➤ Imagination blends **emotion, intellect, and perception** into creation.

Questions:

Question 76

Who among the following used 'untranslatableness' in his famous work?

1. William Wordsworth in the Preface to Lyrical Ballads
2. Philip Sidney in Defense of Poesie
3. S.T. Coleridge in Biographia Literaria
4. Matthew Arnold in The Study of Poetry

Explanations:
Answer: 3.S.T. Coleridge in Biographia Literaria

The concept of untranslatability has its classical phrasing in book twenty-two of Coleridge's Biographia Literaria : "The infallible test of a blameless style, its untranslatability into other words of the same language without damage to its meaning." The Collected Poems of Yvor Winters.

Question 77

As mentioned in -My First Acquaintance with Poets' which poet does William Hazlitt describe as the "only person I ever knew who answered the idea of a man of genius"?

1. Coleridge
2. Wordsworth
3. Byron
4. Shelley

Explanations:
Answer: 1. Coleridge

In his essay "My First Acquaintance with Poets," William Hazlitt describes Samuel Taylor Coleridge as the "only person I ever knew who

answered the idea of a man of genius." Hazlitt was a great admirer of Coleridge's work and intellect, and their friendship lasted for many years. In the essay, Hazlitt also discusses his other literary acquaintances, including William Wordsworth and Charles Lamb.

Match List I with List II

List I (Author)	List II (Text)
A. Robert Browning	I. Queen Mary
B.S. T. Coleridge	II.The Second Mrs Tanqueray
C. A. W. Pinero	III. Remorse
D. Alfred Tennyson	IV. The Borderers
E. William Wordsworth	V. Strafford

Choose the correct answer from the options given below:

1. **A-V; B-III; C-II; D-I; E-IV**
2. A-II; B-IV; C-III; D-V; E-I
3. A-III; B-V; C-II; D-I; E-IV
4. A-IV; B-II; C-I; D-V; E-III

Correct Explanations:
- ➤ *The Second Mrs. Tanqueray* **(1892) is a problem play by Arthur Wing Pinero.** It adopts the "Woman with a past" plot, popular in nineteenth century melodrama.
- ➤ *Strafford* **is an 1837 tragedy by the British writer Robert Browning.** It portrays the downfall and execution of Lord Strafford, the advisor to Charles I shortly before the English Civil War.
- ➤ *Osorio* **is a tragedy in blank verse by Samuel Taylor Coleridg**e. It was written in 1797 but was unperformed following its rejection by Drury Lane Theatre. Coleridge revised and recast the play sixteen years later, giving it the new title of *Remorse*.
- ➤ *Queen Mary and Harol***d, by Alfred Lord Tennyson**.
- ➤ *The Borderers***, by William Wordsworth**.

Match List I with List II

LIST I	LIST II
A. "Negative Capability"	I. Matthew Arnold
B. "Sweetness and light"	II. Samuel Taylor Coleridge
C. "Esemplastic"	III. T.S. Eliot
D. "Dissociation of Sensibility"	IV. John Keats

Choose the correct answer from the options given below:
1. A-II, B-IV, C-I, D-III
2. A-II, B-I, C-IV, D-III
3. A-IV, B-III, C-II, D-I
4. A-IV, B-I, C-II, D-III

Explanations:
Ans: A-IV, B-I, C-II, D-III

A. "Negative Capability" - John Keats: Negative Capability is a term coined by John Keats in a letter to his brothers in 1817, where he described it as the ability to tolerate uncertainty and the mysterious without resorting to oversimplification, explanation or absolute knowledge.

B. "Sweetness and light" - Matthew Arnold: "Sweetness and light" is a phrase used by Matthew Arnold to describe the goal of cultural criticism, which is to help people to see the world more clearly, to appreciate beauty, and to lead better lives.

C. "Esemplastic" - Samuel Taylor Coleridge: Esemplastic is a term coined by Samuel Taylor Coleridge to describe the power of imagination to unify or combine different elements into a single, integrated whole.

D. "Dissociation of Sensibility" - T.S. Eliot: "Dissociation of Sensibility" is a term coined by T.S. Eliot in his essay "The Metaphysical Poets" to describe a separation of thought and feeling in 17th century poetry. Eliot argues that the poetry of Donne and his contemporaries is marked by a dissociation of sensibility, which is the result of the fragmentation of experience caused by the rise of rationalism and the scientific method.

Question 80

Match List I with List II

List I	List II
A. Egotistical sublime	I. Matthew Arnold
B. Willing suspension of disbelief	II. Joseph Addison
C. Touchstone	III. John Keats
D. Pleasures of the Imagination	IV. Samuel Taylor Coleridge

Choose the correct answer from the options given below:

1. (A)-(III), (B)-(IV), (C)-(I), (D)-(II)
2. (A)-(III), (B)-(IV), (C)-(II), (D)-(I)
3. (A)-(II), (B)-(IV), (C)-(I), (D)-(III)
4. (A)-(II), (B)-(IV), (C)-(I), (D)-(II)

Explanations
Answer: 1. (A)-(III), (B)-(IV), (C)-(I), (D)-(II)

Joseph Addison's philosophical essay "Pleasures of the Imagination," published in The Spectator (1712), takes a wary approach to the imagination. According to Addison, if employed properly, the imagination can be a means for one to avoid falling into slothful or illicit ways.

Suspension of disbelief is the avoidance—often described as willing—of critical thinking and logic in understanding something that is unreal or impossible in reality, such as something in a work of speculative fiction, in order to believe it for the sake of enjoying its narrative. **The phrase first appeared in English poet and aesthetic philosopher Samuel Taylor Coleridge's Biographia Literaria (1817),** where he suggested that if an author could infuse a "human interest and a semblance of truth" into a story with implausible elements, the reader would willingly suspend judgement concerning the implausibility of the narrative.

The 'egotistical sublime' is a phrase coined by John Keats to describe the poetry of William Wordsworth in an 1818 letter to Richard Woodhouse. The phrase expresses the **underlying self-centred nature of Wordsworth's poetry,** particularly his use of the narrative voice to convey his own conception of a singular truth. The egotistical sublime contrasts with Keat's perception of 'negative capability', which he believed to be the ideal and exemplified by the sonnets of William Shakespeare.

As a metaphor, a touchstone refers to any physical or intellectual measure by which the validity or merit of a concept can be tested. It is similar in use to an acid test, a litmus test in politics, or, from a negative perspective, a shibboleth where some consider the criterion to be out-of-date. **The word was introduced into literary criticism by Matthew Arnold in "Preface to the volume of 1853 poems" (1853)** to denote short but distinctive passages selected from the writings of the greatest poets, which he used to determine the relative value of passages or poems which are compared to them.

Question 81

Who among the following acknowledged that poetry is formed from the same elements as prose; the difference lies in the different combination of these elements and the difference of purpose?

1. John Dryden
2. Samuel Taylor Coleridge
3. Alexander Pope
4. Philip Sydney

Explanations:
Answer: 2. Samuel Taylor Coleridge

"The office of philosophical disquisition consists in just distinction; while it is the privilege of the philosopher to preserve himself constantly aware, that distinction is not division. In order to obtain adequate notions of any truth, we must intellectually separate its distinguishable parts; and this is the technical process of philosophy. But having so done, we must then restore them in our conceptions to the unity, in which they actually co-exist; and this is the result of philosophy. **A poem contains the same elements as a prose composition; the difference therefore must consist in a different combination of them, in consequence of a different object proposed.** *According to the difference of the object will be the difference of the combination. It is possible, that the object may be merely to facilitate the recollection of any given facts or observations by artificial arrangement; and the composition will be a poem, merely because it is distinguished from prose by metre, or by rhyme, or by both conjointly. In this, the lowest sense, a man might attribute the name of a poem to the well known enumeration of the days in the several months;*

> *Thirty days hath September,*

April, June, and November, &c.
and others of the same class and purpose. And as a particular pleasure is found
in anticipating the recurrence of sounds and quantities, all compositions that
have this charm superadded, whatever be their contents, may be entitled
poems." **BIOGRAPHIA LITERARIA VOLUME 2 CHAPTER 14**

Question 82

Which among the following are the titles of the periodicals?

    A. Dickens' Household Words
    B. S.T. Coleridge' Friend
    C. Richard Steele's Guardian
    D. Franz Kafka's The Metamorphosis
    E. Leigh Hunt's Indicator

Choose the correct answer from the options given below:

    1. (A) and (B) Only
    2. (B) and (C) Only
    3. (A), (B), (C) and (E) Only
    4. (C), (D) and (E) Only

Explanations:
Answer: 3. (A), (B), (C) and (E) Only

Charles Dickens, in the 1850s, took on the role of editor for the English
weekly magazine _Household Words_, named after a phrase from
Shakespeare's Henry V. Throughout its conception, Dickens considered
various titles such as The Robin, The Household Voice, The Comrade, The
Lever, and The Highway of Life before settling on Household Words.

In 1809, Samuel Taylor Coleridge embarked on his second venture into
publishing with _The Friend_, a weekly journal showcasing his broad
spectrum of interests from law to literary criticism. Coleridge's
disorganization and poor business acumen led to financial difficulties,
necessitating loans from affluent friends to continue the publication. Despite
initial support, including subscriptions from members of Parliament, The
Friend faced an inevitable decline due to Coleridge's financial
mismanagement.

Sir Richard Steele, in collaboration with Joseph Addison, co-founded *The Spectator*, following their initial project, ***The Tatler***. Launched on 12 April 1709, The Tatler was published three times a week under the pseudonym Isaac Bickerstaff. Steele aimed to critique societal pretenses and advocate for simplicity in life through The Tatler, which predominantly featured his writings. The magazine was discontinued in 1711 to escape political backlash, leading Steele and Addison to start The Spectator and later ***The Guardian***.

Leigh Hunt, an influential English critic and poet, co-founded ***The Examiner,*** a radical journal, becoming a nexus for the "Hunt circle" which included notable figures like William Hazlitt and Charles Lamb. Hunt played a crucial role in introducing poets like John Keats and Percy Bysshe Shelley to the public. Aside from *The Examiner,* Hunt edited ***The Reflector,*** a quarterly magazine, and ***The Indicator,*** a weekly publication that he likely filled with his literary contributions. He also briefly managed ***The Companion***, a weekly that focused on literature and the arts.

The Metamorphosis, a profound allegorical narrative by the esteemed Austrian author Franz Kafka, was first made available to the public in the German language as Die Verwandlung in the year 1915.

Question 83

Who has defined a poet in the following words:

"The poet, described in ideal perfection, brings the whole soul of man into activity, with the subordination of it faculties to each other according to their relative worth and dignity."

1. William Wordsworth
2. John Keats
3. Samuel Taylor Coleridge
4. P.B. Shelley

Explanations:
Answer: **3.** Samuel Taylor Coleridge

"The poet, described in ideal perfection, brings the whole soul of man into activity, with the subordination of its faculties to each other according to

their relative worth and dignity. *He diffuses a tone and spirit of unity, that blends, and (as it were) fuses, each into each, by that synthetic and magical power, to which I would exclusively appropriate the name of Imagination. This power, first put in action by the will and understanding, and retained under their irremissive, though gentle and unnoticed, control, laxis effertur habenis, reveals "itself in the balance or reconcilement of opposite or discordant" qualities: of sameness, with difference; of the general with the concrete; the idea with the image; the individual with the representative; the sense of novelty and freshness with old and familiar objects; a more than usual state of emotion with more than usual order; judgment ever awake and steady self-possession with enthusiasm and feeling profound or vehement; and while it blends and harmonizes the natural and the artificial, still subordinates art to nature; the manner to the matter; and our admiration of the poet to our sympathy with the poetry."*

[from Biographia Literaria, Chapter 14, by Samuel Taylor Coleridge, 9th Century, English Romantic Poet and Critic]

Question 84

Which statements among the following are not relevant to Biographia Literaria?

A. The first volume of the text recounts the author's friendship with Robert Southey and William Blake
B. Another edition of the text was published later in 1847 with his daughter Sara's appended notes
C. It is a work by S. T. Coleridge in two volumes
D. In this work, Coleridge discusses the difference between fancy and imagination
E. In the first volume, Coleridge acknowledges his teachers and philosophers including Aristotle and Plato

Choose the correct answer from the options given below:

1. A and B only
2. B and C only
3. A and E only
4. D and E only

Explanations:
Answer: 3. A and E only

Biographia Literaria

- **<u>Biographia Literaria, work by Samuel Taylor Coleridge, published in two volumes in 1817.</u>**
- **<u>Another edition of the work, to which Coleridge's daughter Sara appended notes and supplementary biographical material, was published in 1847.</u>**
- Originally titled 'Autobiographia Literaria' during its development.
- **<u>Influenced by William Wordsworth's poetry theories.</u>**
- Incorporates Kant's view on imagination's transformative power.
- Coleridge introduced "esemplastic" to describe imagination's role.
- Draws from post-Kantian thinkers, including F. W. J. von Schelling.
- Also influenced by empiricist philosophy and psychology.
- David Hartley's work notably shaped Coleridge's ideas.
- Explores Associationist psychology within literary criticism.
- Combines Romantic and Enlightenment thought in analysis.
- **<u>The first volume of the book recounts the author's friendship with poets Robert Southey and William Wordsworth.</u>**
- **<u>Describe the influences on his philosophical development, from his early teachers to such philosophers as Immanuel Kant, Johann Fichte, and Friedrich von Schelling</u>.**
- **<u>This section includes his well-known discussion of the difference between fancy and imagination</u>.**
- In the second volume Coleridge concentrates on literary criticism and proposes theories about the creative process and the historical sources of the elements of poetry.
- Began as preface to Coleridge's poem collection.
- Evolved into a literary autobiography of Coleridge.
- Covers education, studies, early literary pursuits.
- Critiques Wordsworth's theory from Lyrical Ballads' Preface.
- States Coleridge's own philosophical and poetic views.
- **The first volume culminates in his gnomic definition of the imagination or "esemplastic power"**
- The later chapters of the book deal with the nature of poetry and with the question of poetic diction raised by Wordsworth.

- **The book contains Coleridge's celebrated and vexed distinction between "imagination" and "fancy".**
- **Chapter XIV is the origin of the famous critical concept of the "willing suspension of disbelief" when reading poetic works.**

"The IMAGINATION ... I consider either as primary, or secondary. The primary IMAGINATION I hold to be the living Power and prime Agent of all human Perception, and as a repetition in the finite mind of the eternal act of creation in the infinite I AM.

At Jesus College, Coleridge was introduced to political and theological ideas then considered radical, including those of the poet **Robert Southey with whom he collaborated on the play The Fall of Robespierre. Coleridge joined Southey in a plan, later abandoned,** to found a utopian commune-like society, called Pantisocracy, in the wilderness of Pennsylvania.

Robert Southey (1774-1843)

- **Born** in **Bristol**, educated at **Westminster School and Oxford**.
- He led a **laborious life as a man of letters**.
- **Southey produced** a great mass of work of **considerable merit**.
- He lived most of his life at **Greta Hall, Keswick**.
- **Southey was made Poet Laureate** in **1813**.
- His **reputation as a poet** has **not been maintained**.
- Southey was closely linked to major **English Romantic poets**.
- He was a **friend and neighbor** of **William Wordsworth**.
- **Southey attended college** with **Samuel Taylor Coleridge**.
- **Ironically**, Southey never achieved significant success **as a poet**.
- Despite his talent, **Southey's poetry lacked widespread success**.
- **Several of Southey's poems** are considered **critically successful**.
- His **poetry suffered** from excessive mythologizing and allusion.
- **Poetic clarity** in Southey's work was often **sacrificed**.
- Hazlitt talks about **his experiences meeting and interacting with famous poets of his time, including Coleridge, Wordsworth, and Southey.**
- **Major Works:**
    - *Fall of Robespierre (1794)*
    - ***Joan of Arc: An Epic Poem (1796)***
    - *Poems (1797–1799)*
    - *Letters from Spain (1797)*

- *Devil's Thoughts (1799)*
- ***Thalaba the Destroyer (1801)***
- *Amadis de Gaula (1803)*
- *Madoc (1805)*
- ***Letters from England (1807)***
- *Palmerin of England (1807; translation)*
- *The Cid (1808; translation)*
- *The Curse of Kehama (1810)*
- *The Life of Nelson (1813)*
- ***Roderick, the Last of the Goths (1814)***
- *Wat Tyler: A Dramatic Poem (1817)*
- *Journal of a Tour in Scotland in 1819 (1929, posthumous)*
- *The Life of Wesley and the rise and progress of Methodism (c. 1820)*
- ***A Vision of Judgment (1821)***
  - The **Satanic School** was a term coined by **Robert Southey.**
  - **"monstrous combinations of horrors and mockery, lewdness and impiety with which English poetry has ... been polluted"**
  - **Byron and Shelley's works** exhibited a "***Satanic spirit of pride and audacious impiety.***"
  - **The Vision of Judgment (1822)** is a satirical poem in ottava rima by **Lord Byron.**
- ***Life of Cromwell (1821)***
- *Thomas More (1829)*
- *The Pilgrim's Progress with a Life of John Bunyan (1830)*
- *Cowper (1833)*
- *The Doctors (1834) – Includes the first published version of the fairytale-like "Goldilocks and the Three Bears."*
- *Select Lives of Cromwell and Bunyan (1846)*
- *The Inchcape Rock*

Question 85

Who among the following refers to Byron's works as "monstrous combinations of horrors and mockery, lewdness and impiety" ?

(1) Charles Lamb
(2) Robert Southey

(3) Mary Shelley
(4) Leigh Hunt

Explanations:
Answer: (2) Robert Southey

The **Satanic School** was a term coined by **Robert Southey** to describe a group of writers led by **Byron** and **Shelley**, whose works he believed exhibited a "Satanic spirit of pride and audacious impiety."

Southey introduced the term in his poem **A Vision of Judgement** (1821) as a form of moral criticism. However, **Byron** was amused by Southey's description, calling him an author of **"monstrous combinations of horrors and mockery, lewdness and impiety."** In response, Byron wrote his own **Vision of Judgment**, where he portrayed Southey as a scribbler praising weak kings. Byron also embraced the idea of the "Satanic" school and developed the concept of the **Byronic hero**—a tragic figure, like **Satan in Paradise Lost**, who is admirable even when flawed.

The **Byronic hero** eventually influenced other literary figures, such as **Charles Baudelaire**, whose **poète maudit** evolved from this archetype.

Thomas Carlyle criticized the movement, accusing **Byron** and **Shelley** of engaging in a "wrangle with the devil" without having the courage to confront him directly. In the materials surrounding his play **Manfred**, **Byron** suggested that these characters, though not paragons of traditional virtues, were beings of fire and spirit.

In part III, Southey sets out to chastise readers, authors and critics alike for their perpetuation of the "**monstrous combinations of horrors and mockery, lewdness and impiety with which English poetry has ... been polluted**," "intended as furniture for the brothel" (Southey X: 203).

Question 86

Which of the following works is NOT written by P. B. Shelley?

1. *The Mask of Anarchy*
2. *Queen Mab: A Philosophical Poem*
3. ***The Vision of Judgement***

4. *The Revolt of Islam*

Explanations:

The Vision of Judgment (1822) is a satirical poem written by **Lord Byron** in **ottava rima**, depicting a humorous dispute in Heaven over the fate of **King George III's soul**. Byron wrote it as a direct response to **Robert Southey's** poem, **A Vision of Judgement** (1821), which had imagined George III's soul triumphantly entering Heaven. Byron was provoked by the **High Tory** perspective of Southey's work and particularly by the preface, in which Southey attacked those who supported a **"Satanic school"** of poetry, accusing them of promoting a **"Satanic spirit of pride and audacious impiety."**

Lord Byron (1788-1824)

- **Lord Byron** was proud of his **ancestry and poetry**.
- His ancestors traced back to the **Norman Conquest**.
- Byron's grandfather was a **notorious admiral**.
- His father was a **rake** who married **Miss Gordon**.
- Byron's father **squandered** his Scottish heiress's **money**.
- Byron spent his **early years** in **Aberdeen**.
- At ten, he inherited **Newstead Abbey** and his **title**.
- Byron was educated at **Harrow** and **Cambridge**.
- He had a **dark, passionate nature**, with humor and affection.
- His **"Byronic" temperament** was not entirely affected.
- His mother was **foolish**, warping his temper with **frustrations**.
- Byron endured **tortures** trying to correct his **foot malformation**.
- After university, he indulged in **dissipation at Newstead**.
- He gloried in his **dare-devil reputation**, but paid for it.
- Byron traveled the **Continent** after tiring of loose pleasures.
- He took his seat in the **House of Lords**, but made no impact.
- His poem on travels made him **famous overnight**.
- Byron became a **society darling** due to youth and wit.
- He married a **great heiress**, but she left him in a year.
- Dark **rumors** spread about Byron's **conduct**.
- Byron left **England** in 1816 due to a **storm of abuse**.
- He spent his last years **wandering the Continent**.
- Byron supported the **Greek independence movement**.

> He died of **fever** in **Missolonghi**, given a grand funeral.

His Poetry

> **Byron's first volume, Hours of Idleness** (1807), was a **juvenile effort.**
> It received harsh criticism from **The Edinburgh Review.**
> **Byron retaliated** with **English Bards and Scotch Reviewers** (1809).
> The poem was **immature**, but showed **Byronic force** in couplets.
> Byron traveled for two years, resulting in **Childe Harold's Pilgrimage.**
> **Childe Harold**'s hero is a **romantic youth**, reflecting **Byron himself.**
> The poem described **popular beauty-spots** in **Spenserian stanzas.**
> **Childe Harold** brought Byron **fame**, which he later squandered.
> In between social events, Byron wrote **poetic tales** prolifically.
> **The Giaour** and **The Bride of Abydos** were published in **1813.**
> **The Corsair** and **Lara** followed in **1814.**
> **The Siege of Corinth** and **Parisina** were published in **1815.**
> These tales featured the **Byronic hero** and **Eastern settings.**
> Written in couplets, they imitated **Scott's metrical tales.**
> **Byron** supplanted **Scott**, though lacking Scott's masculine fervor.
> His verses were often **sickly**, yet vehemence imitated **passion.**
> **Byron left England** in 1816, hounded by **scandal.**
> His wanderings were chronicled in **Childe Harold's** third and fourth cantos.
> These cantos showed **firmer descriptions** and **sincere tone.**
> **Bitter pessimism** was apparent in the new cantos.
> During this time, he wrote **The Prisoner of Chillon** (1816).
> **Mazeppa** (1819) was Byron's **last metrical tale.**
> He wrote many **mediocre lyrics** during his **wanderings.**
> Byron also composed several **great satirical poems.**
> The most notable satire was **Beppo** (1818).
> **The Vision of Judgment** (1822) was directed at **Southey.**
> Byron's longest satire, **Don Juan**, was published **1819–1824.**
> **Don Juan** ranks among the **greatest satirical poems.**
> It was issued in **portions**, just as **Byron composed it.**
> **Don Juan** is a **picaresque novel** in verse form.
> The hero undergoes **many wanderings and adventures.**
> The poem was denounced as **vile and immoral** upon publication.

- ➤ Byron expressed his **wrath against the human race** in **Don Juan**.
- ➤ The satire's **strength and flexibility** were beyond question.
- ➤ **Bitter mockery, caustic comment**, and **rage** filled the poem.
- ➤ The stanzas, written in **ottava rima**, were as sharp as steel.
- ➤ **The style** was half-colloquial, disdainful of **poetical trappings**.
- ➤ Despite this, some passages reached **rare tenderness**.
- ➤ **Don Juan** became Byron's **most effective satire**.
- ➤ Byron's work combined **vigor, range**, and **effectiveness**.

His Drama

- ➤ **Byron's dramas** are blank-verse tragedies from his **later career**.
- ➤ They were composed while **Byron was in Italy**.
- ➤ The chief dramas include **Manfred** (1817) and **Marino Faliero** (1820).
- ➤ **The Two Foscari** and **Cain** were written in **1821**.
- ➤ **The Deformed Transformed** was written in **1824**.
- ➤ The dramas often feature a **Byronic hero**.
- ➤ **Cain** portrays an outcast defying the **world's censure**.
- ➤ **The Deformed Transformed** references **Byron's own deformity**.
- ➤ Byron showed **limited dramatic skill** in these works.
- ➤ He could only portray characters that **resembled himself**.
- ➤ The **blank verse** has **power and dignity**.
- ➤ However, it **lacks higher poetic inspiration**.

Major Works by Lord Byron:

- ➤ *Hours of Idleness (1807)*
  - o **His first book of poetry**
- ➤ *Lachin y Gair (1807)*
- ➤ *English Bards and Scotch Reviewers (1809)*
  - o The opening **parodies the first satire of Juvenal.**
  - o Byron used heroic couplets in imitation of Alexander Pope's The Dunciad.
  - o Attacked Wordsworth and Samuel Taylor Coleridge, and Francis Jeffrey.
  - o He praised such Neoclassical poets instead of Pope and John Dryden.
- ➤ *Childe Harold's Pilgrimage, Cantos I & II (1812)*
  - o The **poem was published** between **1812 and 1818**.
  - o **"I awoke one morning and found myself famous"**, said Byron.

- o That morning was **3rd March 1812**.
- o **Cantos I and II of Childe Harold's Pilgrimage** were first published.
- o Dedicated to **"Ianthe,"** it describes a **world-weary young man**.
- o The protagonist is **disillusioned** with a life of **pleasure**.
- o He looks for **distraction** in **foreign lands**.
- o The poem reflects the **melancholy and disillusionment** of its generation.
- o The title comes from **childe**, a medieval term for **knighthood candidate**.
- o The poem contributed to the **Byronic hero** cult.
- o It influenced **literature, music, painting**, and **European Romanticism**.
- o **Harold** wanders Europe, expressing his **feelings and ideas**.
- o In **Canto I**, Harold recounts **French savagery** in **Spain and Portugal**.
- o In **Canto II**, he admires **Greece's past**, now enslaved by **Turks**.
- o In **Canto III**, Harold visits **Waterloo**, the **Rhine**, and **Switzerland**.
- o **Switzerland's scenery** and historic associations **enchant** Harold.
- o In **Canto IV**, he journeys through **Italy**, lamenting its **heroic past**.
- o He mourns Italy's **vanished artistic past** and **subject status**.

- ➢ *The Giaour (1813)*
- ➢ *The Bride of Abydos (1813)*
- ➢ *The Corsair (1814)*
- ➢ *Lara, A Tale (1814)*
- ➢ *Hebrew Melodies (1815)*
- ➢ *The Siege of Corinth (1816)*
- ➢ *Parisina (1816)*
- ➢ **The Prisoner of Chillon (1816)**
  - o It is a 392-line **narrative poem** by Lord Byron.
  - o Written in 1816
  - o It chronicles the imprisonment of a **Genevois monk, François Bonivard**, from 1532 to 1536.
  - o **On 22 June 1816**, Byron and **Shelley sailed** on Lake Geneva.
  - o They visited **Château de Chillon**, touring its **dungeon**.
  - o **Byron was inspired** by Bonivard's story and wrote **The Sonnet of Chillon**.

- o Due to **rainfall**, Byron rested in **Ouchy after the tour**.
- o Byron composed the extended fable in **late June or July**.
- o The poem was likely completed by **2 July 1816**.
- o **The Prisoner of Chillon** was published on **5 December 1816**.
- o The protagonist is an **isolated figure** enduring **great sufferings**.
- o He finds solace in **nature's beauty**, a theme in **Byron's work**.
- o The poem reflects Byron's **travels and experiences**.
- o **The Prisoner of Chillon** is a **romantic verse-tale**.
- o The plot describes a **lone survivor's trials**.
- o His father was **burnt at the stake**, his brothers died.
- o Two brothers **died on the battlefield**, another was **burnt**.
- o The narrator is the **sole survivor** of the **family tragedy**.

- ➤ *The Dream (1816)*
- ➤ *Prometheus (1816)*
- ➤ *Darkness (1816)*
- ➤ ***Manfred (1817)***
  - o **Manfred: A dramatic poem is a closet drama written in 1816–1817.**
  - o Includes **supernatural elements**, reflecting the **ghost story popularity**.
  - o It is a **typical example** of **Gothic fiction**.
  - o **Byron began Manfred** in **late 1816** after ghost-story sessions.
  - o **Supernatural references** are **clear throughout** the poem.
  - o **Robert Schumann** musically adapted **Manfred** in **1852**.
  - o **Tchaikovsky** composed the **Manfred Symphony** based on the poem.
  - o **Nietzsche** was inspired by **Manfred** to create **"Manfred Meditation"** in 1872.
- ➤ *The Lament of Tasso (1817)*
- ➤ ***Beppo (1818)***
  - o Beppo: A Venetian Story is a lengthy poem by Lord Byron,
  - o Written in Venice in 1817.
  - o **Beppo** is Byron's first use of **Italian ottava rima**.
  - o It is a **precursor** to Byron's famous work, **Don Juan**.
  - o The poem contains **760 verses in 95 stanzas**.
  - o It tells the story of **Laura**, whose husband **Beppo** was lost.
  - o Laura takes on a **Cavalier Servente** according to Venetian customs.
  - o At the **Venetian Carnival**, they are observed by a **Turk**.

- o The **Turk** turns out to be her **missing husband, Beppo**.
- o **Beppo explains** his time as a **slave and pirate**.
- o Laura rejoins **Beppo** and befriends the **Count**.
- ➢ *Childe Harold's Pilgrimage (1818)*
- ➢ *Don Juan (1819–1824)*
  - o **Don Juan** is a **satirical epic poem** by **Lord Byron**.
  - o It portrays **Don Juan** as easily **seduced by women**.
  - o The poem is written in **ottava rima** with **sixteen cantos**.
  - o **Byron derived Don Juan** from the **Spanish legend**.
  - o **Published in 1819**, cantos I and II were **criticized as immoral**.
  - o At Byron's death in **1824**, sixteen cantos were **completed**.
  - o The **narrative** spans **sixteen thousand lines in seventeen cantos**.
  - o **Ottava rima** uses a **couplet rhyme scheme** for humor.
  - o **Don Juan** grows up in **Spain** with quarreling **parents**.
  - o After his father's **death**, Don Juan inherits a **fortune**.
  - o His **mother** educates him and shields him from **worldly evils**.
  - o **Don Juan** has an affair with **Julia**, leading to **his exile**.
  - o He leaves **Spain** after **Julia's husband** tries to kill him.
  - o Don Juan's ship **wrecks** in the **Mediterranean Sea**.
  - o **Don Juan** is the only survivor of the **lifeboat incident**.
  - o **Haidée**, a beautiful woman, **rescues** and falls for **Don Juan**.
  - o Haidée's **pirate father** sells Don Juan into **slavery**.
  - o A **Turkish princess** buys him as a **sex slave**.
  - o **Don Juan** escapes when the **Russians attack the Turks**.
  - o He becomes a **Russian war hero** fighting the **Turks**.
  - o **Catherine the Great** falls in love with **Don Juan**.
  - o **Catherine** rewards him and sends him to **England** as ambassador.
  - o In **England**, Byron mocks the **English aristocracy**.
  - o The poem ends with **Don Juan** possibly seducing another **woman**.
  - o Byron died before completing the **poem**, which is over **5000 lines**.
  - o **Don Juan** was scornfully **dedicated to Robert Southey**, Byron's rival.
  - o **Southey** was the **Poet Laureate of Britain** at the time.
  - o In stanza III Byron said:
    - ▪ *"You, Bob! are rather insolent, you know,*

- ▪ *At being disappointed in your wish*
- ▪ *To supersede all warblers here below,*
- ▪ *And be the only Blackbird in the dish;*
- ▪ *And then you overstrain yourself, or so,*
- ▪ *And tumble downward like the flying fish*
- ▪ *Gasping on the deck, because you soar too high, Bob,*
- ▪ *And fall, for lack of moisture quite a-dry, Bob!"*

➢ *Mazeppa (1819)*
   o **A long narrative poem about a seventeenth-century military leader of Ukraine.**
➢ *The Prophecy of Dante (1819)*
➢ *Fragment of a Novel (1819)*
   o It is an **unfinished 1819 vampire horror story** written by Lord Byron.
   o The story, also known as **"A Fragment" and "The Burial: A Fragment",**
   o It was one of the **first in English to feature a vampire theme.**
   o The main character was **Augustus Darvell.**
   o John William Polidori based his novella The Vampyre (1819), originally attributed in print to Lord Byron, on the Byron fragment.
➢ *Marino Faliero (1820)*
➢ *Sardanapalus (1821)*
   o **It is a tragedy drama.**
➢ *The Two Foscari (1821)*
   o **An Historical Tragedy** is a play that tells the story of Francesco Foscari.
➢ *Cain (1821)*
   o Cain is a **dramatic poem that tells the story of the biblical figure Cain.**
   o Cain is portrayed as a rebellious and envious figure struggling against the unjust authority of God.
   o The poem also delves into the themes of morality and free will.
➢ *The Vision of Judgment (1821)*
➢ *Heaven and Earth (1821)*
➢ *Werner (1822)*
➢ *The Age of Bronze (1823)*
➢ *The Island (1823)*
➢ *The Deformed Transformed (1824)*

> *Letters and journals, vol. 1 (1830)*
> *Letters and journals, vol. 2 (1830)*

Code 1:

🎶 **Byron's Last Hours of Idleness** spent on 🎤 **Singing English Bards** 👑 **Childe Harolds** who was a ▯ **Prisoner of Chillon**

📚 **Hours of Idleness (1807)**
📖 **English Bards and Scotch Reviewers (1809)**
📕 **Childe Harold's Pilgrimage, Cantos I & II (1812)**
🏰 **The Prisoner of Chillon (1816)**

Code 2:

🗻 **Manfred** the 🏔 **Childe** known as 🕺 **Don Juan** 🐎 **Mazeppa** who had the ⭐ **Vision of Southey**

🧗 **Manfred (1817)**
⛺ **Childe Harold's Pilgrimage (1818)**
🕴 **Don Juan (1819–1824)**
🐎 **Mazeppa (1819)**
👁 **The Vision of Judgment (1821)**

She Walks in Beauty (1814)

> **"She Walks in Beauty"** is a short lyrical poem by **Byron**.
> Written in **1814**, it is one of Byron's **famous works**.
> The poem was inspired by a **real-life event**.
> Byron attended a **party in London** on **11 June 1814**.
> **Mrs. Anne Beatrix Wilmot's** beauty struck Byron at the event.
> The poem was written the **following day** after the party.
> She inspired Byron's **unfinished epic poem about Goethe**.
> **Goethe** was a personal **hero** of Byron's.
> Byron referred to this unpublished work as his **magnum opus**.
> He switched **Goethe's gender**, using his **cousin's description**.

She walks in beauty, like the night
Of cloudless climes and starry skies;
And all that's best of dark and bright
Meet in her aspect and her eyes
Thus mellow'd to that tender light
Which heaven to gaudy day denies.

One shade the more, one ray the less,
Had half impair'd the nameless grace
Which waves in every raven tress,
Or softly lightens o'er her face;
Where thoughts serenely sweet express
How pure, how dear their dwelling-place.

And on that cheek, and o'er that brow,
So soft, so calm, yet eloquent,
The smiles that win, the tints that glow,
But tell of days in goodness spent,
A mind at peace with all below,
A heart whose love is innocent!

When We Two Parted (1816)

- ➢ It was written in **1816** by the British Romantic poet Lord Byron.
- ➢ It describes the **pain and disillusionment.**
- ➢ It follows a break-up between the speaker and his lover.

When we two parted
In silence and tears,
Half broken-hearted
To sever for years,
Pale grew thy cheek and cold,
Colder thy kiss;
Truly that hour foretold
Sorrow to this.

The dew of the morning
Sunk chill on my brow—
It felt like the warning
Of what I feel now.
Thy vows are all broken,
And light is thy fame;
I hear thy name spoken,
And share in its shame.

They name thee before me,
A knell to mine ear;
A shudder comes o'er me—

Why wert thou so dear?
They know not I knew thee,
Who knew thee too well—
Long, long shall I rue thee,
Too deeply to tell.

In secret we met—
In silence I grieve,
That thy heart could forget,
Thy spirit deceive.
If I should meet thee
After long years,
How should I greet thee?—
With silence and tears.

Questions

Question 87

Which among the following writers once remarked that "I awoke one morning and found myself famous" ?

    (1) Charles Lamb
    (2) P.B. Shelley
    (3) Lord Byron
    (4) John Keats

Explanations:
Answer: (3) Lord Byron

"I awoke one morning and found myself famous" is a line from the epic poem Childe Harold's Pilgrimage by Lord Byron. The line refers to the publication of the poem's first two cantos on March 3, 1812. The poem was an immediate success with the public and critics.

Childe Harold's Pilgrimage is about the travels and reflections of a young man who is dissatisfied. The poem was written after **Byron's travels and experiences abroad.** Some believe that the poem is the most explicit portrayal of Byron's personality.

"I awoke one morning and found myself famous", said Byron. That morning was 3rd March 1812, **the morning that Cantos I and II of Childe Harold's Pilgrimage were first published**. "*There, for the present, the poem stops; its reception will determine whether the author may venture to conduct his readers to the capital of the East*", Byron, 'Preface to the First and Second Cantos'.

Question 88

Who among the following wrote Mazeppa, a long narrative poem about a seventeenth-century military leader of Ukraine?

1. William Cowper
2. Lord Byron
3. P.B. Shelley
4. S.T. Coleridge

Explanations:
Answer 2: Lord Byron

Mazeppa is a narrative poem written by the English Romantic poet Lord Byron in 1819. It is based on a popular legend about the early life of Ivan Mazepa (1639–1709), who later became Hetman (military leader) of Ukraine. Byron's poem was immediately translated into French, inspiring a series of works in various art forms. Mazeppa's cultural legacy was revitalised with Ukraine's independence in 1991.

Question 89

Who is the author of "A Fragment" (1819), one of the earliest vampire stories in English?

1. P.B. Shelley
2. Lord Byron
3. Bram Stoker
4. Mary Shelley

Explanations:
Answer: 2. Lord Byron

"Fragment of a Novel" is an unfinished 1819 vampire horror story written by Lord Byron. The story, also known as "A Fragment" and "The Burial: A Fragment", was one of the first in English to feature a vampire theme. The main character was Augustus Darvell. John William Polidori based his novella

The Vampyre (1819), originally attributed in print to Lord Byron, on the Byron fragment.

Extra Perk:

P.B. Shelley: While Shelley is best known for his Romantic poetry, he also wrote several works that could be classified as Gothic, including:

➢ **"Zastrozzi" (1810):** This novel is a dark tale of revenge, featuring a villainous protagonist who seeks to destroy his half-brother.
➢ **"St. Irvyne" (1811):** This novel tells the story of a man who discovers the secret of immortality but finds that eternal life comes at a terrible cost.

Lord Byron: Byron was a prominent figure in the Romantic movement and also wrote several works that could be classified as Gothic, including:

● **"The Giaour" (1813):** This poem tells the story of a man who is haunted by guilt and seeks redemption through a series of violent acts.
● **"Manfred" (1817):** This play tells the story of a man who has made a pact with the devil and is tormented by guilt and despair.
● **"The Vampyre" (1819):** This short story, attributed to Byron but actually written by his physician, John William Polidori, tells the story of a man who becomes enamored with a mysterious woman who turns out to be a vampire.

Bram Stoker: Stoker is best known for his novel "Dracula" (1897), which is widely regarded as one of the greatest works of Gothic fiction.

Mary Shelley: In addition to "Frankenstein," Shelley also wrote several other works that could be classified as Gothic, including:

➢ **"Mathilda" (1819):** This novel tells the story of a young woman.
➢ **"Frankenstein; or, The Modern Prometheus" (1818):** This is Shelley's most famous work and is widely regarded as a masterpiece of Gothic literature. The novel tells the story of a scientist who creates a living being from dead body parts, with disastrous consequences.

Question 90

Choose the plays written by Lord Byron

A. Sardanapalus
B. Hellas

C. Cain
D. The Two Foscari: An Historical Tragedy
E. The Cenci

Choose the correct answer from the options given below:

1. A, B and C
2. B, C and E
3. A, B and D
4. A, C and D

Explanations:
Ans: A, C and D

Sardanapalus, Cain, and The Two Foscari: An Historical Tragedy are all plays written by Lord Byron.

Sardanapalus is a tragedy in which the king of Assyria, Sardanapalus, chooses to die with his beloved concubine Myrrha rather than face defeat at the hands of his enemies. The play explores themes of love, loyalty, and sacrifice.

Cain is a dramatic poem that tells the story of the biblical figure Cain, who is portrayed as a rebellious and envious figure struggling against the unjust authority of God. The poem also delves into the themes of morality and free will.

The Two Foscari: An Historical Tragedy is a play that tells the story of Francesco Foscari, the Doge of Venice, and his son Jacopo, who is wrongly accused of treason and exiled. The play explores themes of power, justice, and familial loyalty.

Extra Perk:

Hellas and The Cenci are both dramatic works written by Percy Bysshe Shelley.

Hellas is a verse drama that was published in 1822. It is a play that deals with the struggle for Greek independence from the Ottoman Empire. The play is divided into three parts and features a chorus that sings throughout the play.

The Cenci is a tragedy that was published in 1819. It is based on the true story of the Cenci family, who were a noble family in Rome.

Arrange the correct chronological sequence of the publication of the following texts:

> A. *September 1, 1939*
> B. *The Collar*
> C. *Beppo*
> D. *Paradise Lost*
> E. *Seeing Things*

Choose the correct answer from the options given below:

> 1. B, D. C, A. E
> 2. B. A, E, C, D
> 3. A, E, B. C, D
> 4. C, B. A, D, E

Explanations
Answer: 1. B, D. C, A. E

"The Collar" is a poem written by the Welsh poet George Herbert and was published in 1633 as part of his collection of poems titled The Temple.

Paradise Lost is a renowned epic poem composed in blank verse by the English poet John Milton (1608–1674) during the 17th century. The initial version was **published in 1667.**

Beppo: A Venetian Story is an extensive poem written by Lord Byron in 1817 while he was in Venice.

"September 1, 1939" is a poem by W. H. Auden, composed shortly after the German invasion of Poland that marked the commencement of World War II. It was initially published in The New Republic on October

18, 1939, and later included in Auden's collection titled Another Time (1940).

Seeing Things is the eighth collection of poetry by Seamus Heaney, the recipient of the 1995 Nobel Prize in Literature. It was published in 1991 and draws inspiration from the visions of the afterlife depicted in the works of Virgil and Dante Alighieri.

Question 92

In which year "She Walks in Beauty", a poem by Lord Byron, was composed?

     1. 1788
     2. 1824
     3. 1815
     4. 1814

Explanations:
Answer: 4. 1814

<u>"She Walks in Beauty" is a renowned short lyrical poem penned by Lord Byron in 1814,</u> celebrated for its iambic tetrameter structure and standing as one of Byron's signature pieces. The poem's inspiration is traced back to a personal experience of Byron. On June 11, 1814, during a social gathering in London, Byron was captivated by the distinct **beauty of Mrs. Anne Beatrix Wilmot, the spouse of his first cousin, Sir Robert Wilmot.** Her striking appearance left such an impression on him that he composed the poem the following morning.

Question 93

Match List I with List II

List I (Author)	List II (Work)
A. Ann Radcliff	I. The Deserted Village
B. Oliver Goldsmith	II. The Romance of the Forest
C. Swinburne	III. The Vision of Judgement
D. Lord Byron	IV. The Sisters

Choose the correct answer from the options given below:

1. A - III, B - II, C - I, D - IV
2. A - III, B - IV, C - I, D - II
3. A - II, B - IV, C - III, D - I
4. A - II, B - I, C - IV, D - II

Explanations:
Answer: 4. A - II, B - I, C - IV, D - II

Ann Radcliffe's _The Romance of the Forest_, published in 1791

Oliver Goldsmith's "The Deserted Village," published in 1770, is a pastoral elegy that laments the loss of rural life due to agrarian displacement, landlord greed, and social changes.

Lord Byron's "The Vision of Judgment" (1822) satirizes the heavenly debate over George III's soul with sharp wit in ottava rima. Reacting to Robert Southey's laudatory "A Vision of Judgement".

Percy Bysshe Shelley (1792-1822)

- **Shelley was born** in Sussex, heir to a **baronetcy**.
- Educated at **Eton and Oxford**, Shelley showed **eccentricity** early on.
- He frequented **graveyards**, studied **alchemy**, and read **dark books**.
- His pamphlet, **The Necessity of Atheism**, got him expelled.
- Shelley developed extreme ideas on **religion, politics, morality**.
- Despite his ideas, he was **unselfish and amiable** by nature.
- His early **unhappy marriage** caused a family **quarrel**.
- His father, **Sir Timothy Shelley**, settled an **annuity** on him.
- **The Examiner**, founded by **Leigh and John Hunt**, published **literary contributions** of **Shelley, Keats, and Hazlitt.**
- Shelley devoted himself to **writing and wandering** freely.
- In **1816**, his first wife committed **suicide**.
- He remarried **William Godwin's daughter** and settled in **Italy**.
- Italy inspired Shelley's **genius and creativity** to flourish.
- Shelley drowned in a **sudden squall** at age **thirty**.
- His body was **burned on the beach** where it was found.
- **Shelley's ashes** were laid beside **Keats' in Rome**.
- His **early death** was a great loss to **literature**.

- His **crude opinions** were evolving, and his **vision** was clearer.
- Shelley's **poetic abilities** were maturing into **great beauty**.
- His potential was likened to **seraph's wings** in **development**.
- **The grave claimed** a great victory with Shelley's **untimely death**.

Poetry:

- *Original Poetry by Victor and Cazire (collaboration with Elizabeth Shelley) – 1810*
- *Posthumous Fragments of Margaret Nicholson (collaboration with Thomas Jefferson Hogg) – 1810*
- *The Devil's Walk – 1812*
- ***Queen Mab – 1813***
- ***Alastor, or The Spirit of Solitude – 1815 (published 1816)***
- ***Mont Blanc – 1816 (published 1817)***
- ***Mutability – 1816***
- ***Hymn to Intellectual Beauty – 1817***
- ***The Revolt of Islam – 1817 (published 1818)***
- ***Ozymandias – 1818***
- *Rosalind and Helen – 1818 (published 1819)*
- *Lines Written Among the Euganean Hills – 1818 (published 1819)*
- *England in 1819 – 1819 (published 1839)*
- *Love's Philosophy – 1819*
- ***Ode to the West Wind – 1819 (published 1820)***
- ***The Mask of Anarchy – 1819 (published 1832)***
- *Julian and Maddalo – 1819 (published 1824)*
- *Peter Bell the Third – 1820 (published 1839)*
- *Letter to Maria Gisborne – 1820 (published 1824)*
- ***To a Skylark – 1820***
- *The Cloud – 1820*
- *The Sensitive Plant – 1820*
- ***The Witch of Atlas – 1820 (published 1824)***
- ***Adonais – 1821***
- *Epipsychidion – 1821*
- *Music, When Soft Voices Die – 1821 (published 1824)*
- *One Word is Too Often Profaned – 1822 (published 1824)*
- *A Dirge – 1822 (published 1824)*
- ***The Triumph of Life (unfinished) – 1822 (published 1824)***
- *Posthumous Poems – 1824*

Drama:
- ***The Cenci – 1819***
- ***Prometheus Unbound – 1820***
- *Oedipus Tyrannus; Or, Swellfoot The Tyrant – 1820*
- *Charles the First (unfinished) – 1822*
- **Hellas – 1822**

Fiction:
- ***Zastrozzi – 1810***
- *St. Irvyne; or, The Rosicrucian – 1810 (published 1811)*
- *Short Prose Works:*
- *The Assassins, A Fragment of a Romance – 1814*
- *The Coliseum, A Fragment – 1817*
- *The Elysian Fields: A Lucianic Fragment – 1818*
- *Una Favola (A Fable) – 1819 (originally in Italian)*

Essays:
- ***The Necessity of Atheism (with T. J. Hogg) – 1811***
- *Poetical Essay on the Existing State of Things – 1811*
- *An Address, to the Irish People – 1812*
- *Declaration of Rights – 1812*
- *A Letter to Lord Ellenborough – 1812*
- *A Vindication of Natural Diet – 1813*
- *A Refutation of Deism – 1814*
- *Speculations on Metaphysics – 1814*
- ***On the Vegetable System of Diet – 1814–1815 (published 1929)***
- *On a Future State – 1815*
- *On The Punishment of Death – 1815*
- *Speculations on Morals – 1817*
- *On Christianity (incomplete) – 1817 (published 1859)*
- *On Love – 1818*
- *On the Literature, the Arts and the Manners of the Athenians – 1818*
- *On The Symposium, or Preface to The Banquet Of Plato – 1818*
- *On Frankenstein – 1818 (published 1832)*
- *On Life – 1819*
- *A Philosophical View of Reform – 1819–20 (first published 1920)*
- ***A Defence of Poetry – 1821 (published 1840)***

Chapbooks:
- *Wolfstein; or, The Mysterious Bandit – 1822*
- *Wolfstein, The Murderer; or, The Secrets of a Robber's Cave – 1830*

Translations:

> *The Banquet (or The Symposium) of Plato – 1818 (first published unbowdlerised 1931)*
> *Ion of Plato – 1821*
> *Collaborations with Mary Shelley:*
> *History of a Six Weeks' Tour – 1817*
> *Proserpine – 1820*
> *Midas – 1820*

Code 1: 🌳 **Zassi Nessy** grows 🥕 **vegetables** in **Mabalastor** 🌿
Zastrozzi – *1810*
The Necessity of Atheism (with T. J. Hogg) – *1811*
On the Vegetable System of Diet – *1814–1815* (published *1929*)
Alastor, or The Spirit of Solitude – *1815* (published *1816*)

Code 2: 🐱 **Beautiful Mumtaj** in **Islamabad** and 🏺 **Ozymandiaz Cenci** in the **West Wind**
Queen Mab – *1813*
Ozymandias – *1818*
The Cenci – *1819*
Ode to the West Wind – *1819* (published *1820*)

Code 3: 🐦 **Skylark Mask** in the play 🎭 **Prometheus** 🔥
To a Skylark – *1820*
The Mask of Anarchy – *1819* (published *1832*)
Prometheus Unbound – *1820*

Code 4: 🧙 **The Witch** and 🌐 **Atlas** defend and **triumph Poetry** ✒️
against 🗡 **Hellas**
The Witch of Atlas – *1820* (published *1824*)
Adonais – *1821*
A Defence of Poetry – *1821* (published *1840*)
Hellas – *1822*
The Triumph of Life (unfinished) – *1822* (published *1824*)

> *Zastrozzi – 1810*
>   o **Zastrozzi: A Romance** is a **Gothic novel.**
> *The Necessity of Atheism (with T. J. Hogg) – 1811*
> *Queen Mab – 1813*
>   o Nine cantos with seventeen notes.
>   o It is the first large poetic work written by Shelley
> *On the Vegetable System of Diet – 1814–1815 (published 1929)*

- ***Alastor, or The Spirit of Solitude – 1815 (published 1816)***
  - The poem had **no title** when Shelley passed it to **Peacock**.
  - The poem is **720 lines long** and is considered **a major work**.
  - It is one of **Shelley's first major poems**.
  - **Peacock suggested** the name **Alastor**, from **Roman mythology**.
  - **Peacock defined Alastor** as "evil genius".
  - The poem was titled **Alastor** based on **Peacock's suggestion**.
- ***Mont Blanc – 1816 (published 1817)***
- ***Mutability – 1816***
  - Appeared in **1816 collection** *Alastor, or The Spirit of Solitude*.
  - Half of the poem is **quoted in Mary Shelley's** *Frankenstein* (1818).
  - **Shelley's authorship** is not **acknowledged** in the **novel**.
  - **Leigh Hunt's poem** in the novel is **acknowledged by name**.
  - Eight lines from **"Mutability"** are quoted in **Chapter 10** of *Frankenstein*.
  - Quoted when **Victor Frankenstein climbs Glacier Montanvert** in **Swiss Alps**.
    - *"We rest. – A dream has power to poison sleep;*
    - *We rise. – One wandering thought pollutes the day;*
- ***Hymn to Intellectual Beauty – 1817***
  - **Written during summer 1816** while Percy and **Mary Shelley** stayed with **Byron**.
  - The location was **near Lake Geneva, Switzerland**.
- ***The Revolt of Islam – 1817 (published 1818)***
- ***Ozymandias – 1818***
  - It is a sonnet.
  - It was first published in The Examiner of London's 11 January 1818 issue.
- ***The Cenci – 1819***
  - It is a verse drama in five acts.
  - The story centers on **Count Francesco Cenci**, known for **depravity**.
  - He throws a **party** and announces the **deaths of two sons**.
  - His daughter **Beatrice** is another victim of his **cruelty**.
  - **Beatrice** seeks help from **Orsino**, a priest she once loved.

- o **Orsino** and the **Cenci family** plot to **murder the count**.
- o The conspirators are **discovered**, and **Orsino evades capture**.
- o The rest of the **conspirators are tried** and **executed**.
- o **Beatrice enlists** Orsino to **murder her father**.
- o The story highlights **family tragedy and betrayal**.
- ➤ *Ode to the West Wind – 1819 (published 1820)*
  - o The speaker invokes the **"wild West Wind"** to hear him.
  - o The wind is called the **"destroyer and preserver"** of life.
  - o It stirs violent storms and the **"dying year"** dirge.
  - o The wind moves the **Mediterranean** and **cleaves the Atlantic** ocean.
  - o The speaker wishes to be carried like a **leaf or cloud**.
  - o He pleads to be lifted like a **wave, leaf, or cloud**.
  - o The speaker asks the wind to **"make me thy lyre"**.
  - o He asks the wind to **scatter his words** across mankind.
  - o The speaker concludes, **"If winter comes, can spring be far behind?"**
- ➤ *The Mask of Anarchy – 1819 (published 1832)*
  - o It is a British political poem.
  - o Following the Peterloo Massacre of that year.
- ➤ *To a Skylark – 1820*
  - o It was published **alongside** his lyrical drama **Prometheus Unbound**.
  - o The poem is inspired by **Shelley and Mary's walk** near **Livorno**.
  - o It describes the **skylark's appearance** and **song**.
  - o **Mary Shelley** recalled the event that inspired **Shelley's poem**.
  - o They spent **springtime** near **Leghorn (Livorno)**, Italy.
  - o They heard the **skylark caroling** on a **beautiful summer evening**.
    - ▪ *Hail to thee, blithe Spirit!*
    - ▪ *Bird thou never wert,*
    - ▪ *That from Heaven, or near it,*
    - ▪ *Pourest thy full heart*
    - ▪ *In profuse strains of unpremeditated art.*

> *Do you know who wrote "The Skylark"?*
> *John Clare – "The Skylark"*
> *Matthew Arnold – "The Scholar-Gipsy"*
> *Percy Bysshe Shelley – "To a Skylark"*
> *Christina Rossetti – "The Skylark"*

- ➤ **Prometheus Unbound – 1820**
  - o A **four-act** lyrical drama.
  - o Shelley's play is a closet drama.
  - o **Prometheus**, who defies the gods and **gives fire to humanity**.
  - o He is subjected to **eternal punishment** and suffering **at the hands of Zeus**.
  - o **Demogorgon is depicted as a mysterious and powerful being who represents the forces of fate and destiny.**
- ➤ **The Witch of Atlas – 1820 (published 1824)**
- ➤ **Adonais – 1821**
  - o **Full**: *Adonais: An Elegy on the Death of John Keats, Author of Endymion, Hyperion.*
  - o **A pastoral elegy.**
  - o The poem, which is in 495 lines in 55 Spenserian stanzas.
  - o It is a pastoral elegy in the English tradition of John Milton's Lycidas.
  - o The **speaker weeps** for **Adonais**, god of beauty and desire.
  - o **Adonais** has died due to **another god's jealousy**.
  - o The speaker calls **Urania**, Adonais' **mother**, to his deathbed.
  - o The speaker admonishes **Urania** for not **saving his life**.
  - o He summons **nature, Greek gods, and Romantic poets** to mourn.
  - o The speaker asks **everyone to mourn** the **beautiful youth**.
  - o After long mourning, the speaker says **weeping is over**.
  - o The youth has **gone to a better place**, joining **eternity**.
  - o The afterlife means the **youth isn't truly dead**.
  - o The speaker reasons, there's **no reason to cry**.
  - o The youth's **work lives on**, comforting the **speaker**.
  - o Famous **dead poets** arrive to **mourn Adonais**.
  - o **Adonais** will become **King** in the **afterlife**.
  - o The speaker instructs mourners to **visit Rome** where he's buried.
  - o They see **Rome's ruins** and the field **where Adonais rests**.
  - o The beauty of the **field comforts** the mourners.

- o The speaker remains **unconsoled**, wishing to join **Adonais**.
- o The poem ends with the speaker's **soul seeing Adonais' spirit**.
- ➢ *A Defence of Poetry – 1821 (published 1840)*
  - o The essay was written in **1821**.
  - o It was published posthumously in 1840 in *Essays, Letters from Abroad, Translations and Fragments* by Edward Moxon in London.
  - o It contains Shelley's famous assertion that "*poets are the unacknowledged legislators of the world*".
  - o This essay was written in **response** to the article written by his friend, **Thomas Love Peacock**, entitled *"The Four Ages of Poetry"*, published in 1820.
  - o Shelley's argument for poetry is written within the context of Romanticism.
  - o Shelley states that *"ethical science arranges the elements which poetry has created,"*.
  - o It leads to a moral, civil life, and poetry acts in a way that *"awakens and enlarges the mind itself by rendering it the receptacle of a thousand unapprehended combinations of thought"*.
  - o **Shelley says** language reflects the human impulse for **order**.
  - o **Language reproduces** the **rhythmic** and **orderly** in human expression.
  - o **Harmony and unity** are instinctively embraced in **creativity**.
  - o *"Every man in the infancy of art, observes an order which approximates more or less closely to that from which highest delight results..."*
  - o This "faculty of approximation" allows the observer to experience the beautiful by establishing a *"relation between the highest pleasure and its causes"*.
  - o Those who possess this skill *"in excess are poets"* responsible for conveying to the public the *"pleasure"* of their experiences.
  - o **Language** follows poetic precepts of **order, harmony, unity**.
  - o **Admiration of beauty** has an important **social aspect**.
  - o **The mind in creation is as a fading coal which some invisible influence, like an inconstant wind, awakens to transitory brightness."**
  - o **Communication** extends beyond **self-awareness to self-evaluation**.
  - o Poetry and arts are involved in **social activities**.

- o **Shelley praised Plato and Jesus** for imaginative **use of language**.
- o They imagined the **inconceivable** through their **linguistic abilities**.
- o **Language** expresses a desire for **beauty and delight**.
- o Shelley believed that:
    - Poets are the authors of language, music, dance, architecture, statuary, and painting.
    - Poets are the **institutors of laws** and the founders of civil society.
- o **Social and linguistic** order is not the **sole product of the rational faculty**.
- o Language is **"arbitrarily produced by the imagination"**.
- o It reveals *"the before unapprehended relations of things and perpetuates their apprehension"* of higher beauty and truth.
- o Shelley's states that *"poets are the unacknowledged legislators of the world"*.
- o It suggests his awareness of *"the profound ambiguity inherent in linguistic means, which he considers at once as an instrument of intellectual freedom and a vehicle for political and social subjugation."*

➢ *Hellas – 1822*
- o Hellas is a **verse drama**.
- o Shelley wrote it while living in Pisa, with a view to raising money for the **Greek War of Independence**.

➢ *The Triumph of Life (unfinished) – 1822 (published 1824)*
- o **The last major work**.
- o Shelley wrote the poem at Casa Magni in Lerici, Italy.
- o The poem was first published in the collection **Posthumous Poems (1824)**
- o **The Triumph of Life consists of 548 lines in terza rima.**
- o **J. Hillis Miller**, a leading deconstructionist, analyzes **Shelley's "The Triumph of Life"**.
- o He provides a **deconstructionist reading** of the **poem's themes and structure**.

Questions:

Question 94

P.B. Shelley's Adonais laments the death of :

(1) John Keats
(2) Mary Shelley
(3) Robert Byron
(4) Leigh Hunt

Explanations:
Answer: (1) John Keats

Adonais: An Elegy on the Death of John Keats, Author of Endymion,
Hyperion, etc. is a pastoral elegy composed by Percy Bysshe Shelley in 1821
to honor **John Keats**, and it is widely recognized as one of Shelley's finest and
most celebrated works.

Question 95

**Who among the following was not associated with Cockney School of
Poetry?**

1. John Keats
2. P.B. Shelley
3. Leigh Hunt
4. William Blake

Explanations:
Answer: 4. William Blake

The **"Cockney School"** refers to a group of poets and essayists active in
England during the early 19th century. The term originated from **hostile
reviews** in **Blackwood's Magazine** in 1817, with **Leigh Hunt** as the main
target, though **John Keats** and **William Hazlitt** were also included. Of the
group, only **Keats** could be considered a true "cockney," while **Hazlitt** wasn't
even born in **London**. The controversy eventually led to the death of **John
Scott** in a duel.

William Blake was not included in the Cockeney School of Poetry.

Match List I and List II List I

List I Author	List II Work
A. John Keats	I. Alastor
B. Willam Wordsworth	II Songs of Experience
C. PB Shelley	III. Comic
D. William Blake	IV. The Excursion

Choose the correct answer from the options given below:

1. A – III, B – I, C – IV, D – II
2. A – III, B – IV, C – 1, D – II
3. A – I, B – IV, C – III, D – II
4. A – IV, B – II, C – I, D – III

Explanations:
Answer: 2. A – III, B – IV, C – 1, D – II

"Alastor" is a poem by Percy Bysshe Shelley, published in 1816. It is a Gothic poem about a young poet's search for the ideal woman.

"The Excursion" is a long poem by William Wordsworth, published in 1814. It is part of Wordsworth's larger work "The Prelude" and tells the story of a group of travelers who discuss nature, humanity, and the role of art in society.

"Songs of Experience" is a collection of poems by William Blake, published in 1794. It is a companion volume to "Songs of Innocence" and explores the darker side of human experience, including themes of oppression, corruption, and mortality.

"Comic" is indeed a poem by John Keats, published in 1817. It is a satirical poem that mocks the futility of human ambition and the transience of earthly pleasures.

Which two of the following poets defended poetry against Plato's denigration of Poetry?

A. John Dryden

B. P.B. Shelley
C. T.S. Eliot
D. Philip Sidney

Choose the most appropriate answer from the options given below

1. (B) and (D) Only
2. (B) and (C) Only
3. (A) and (B) Only
4. (C) and (A) Only

Explanations:
Answer: 1. (B) and (D) Only

The poets who defended poetry against Plato's denigration of poetry are P.B. Shelley and Philip Sidney. Both Shelley and Sidney wrote influential works that argued for the value and significance of poetry. Shelley, in his essay "A Defence of Poetry," emphasized the role of poetry in inspiring moral and social progress. Sidney, in his work "The Apology for Poetry," defended poetry as a powerful form of art that has the ability to teach, delight, and elevate the soul. They countered Plato's criticism and championed the importance of poetry in human culture and society.

Question 98

Who among the following compared 'the mind in creation' to 'a fading coal'?

1. Wordsworth
2. Coleridge
3. **Shelley**
4. Keats

Correct Explanations:
This statement is not entirely accurate. The correct quote from Shelley's "A Defence of Poetry" is: "A man, to be greatly good, must imagine intensely and comprehensively; he must put himself in the place of another and of many others; the pains and pleasures of his species must become his own. The great instrument of moral good is the imagination; and poetry administers to the effect by acting upon the cause. Poetry enlarges the circumference of the imagination by replenishing it with thoughts of ever new delight, which have the power of attracting and assimilating to their own nature all other thoughts, and which form new intervals and interstices whose void forever

craves fresh food. Poetry strengthens the faculty which is the organ of the moral nature of man, in the same manner as exercise strengthens a limb. **A poet, to be great, must be capable of mingling in the affections of his characters; he must be capable of being in them and in himself; he must be capable of "suffering" as well as of "doing." The mind in creation is as a fading coal which some invisible influence, like an inconstant wind, awakens to transitory brightness."**

Question 99

Which among the following is an incomplete poem by P.B. Shelley?

1. **"The Triumph of Life"**
2. "Ode to the West-wind"
3. "Queen Mab"
4. "The Daemon of the World"

Correct Explanations:
The Triumph of Life was the last major work by Percy Bysshe Shelley before his death in 1822. **The work was left unfinished.** Shelley wrote the poem at Casa Magni in Lerici, Italy in the early summer of 1822. He modelled the poem, written in terza rima, on Petrarch's Trionfi and Dante's Divine Comedy.

Question 100

Identify the poems termed as "pastoral elegies" :

A. Lycidas
B. In Memory of W.B. Yeats
C. Adonais
D. Thyrsis
E. In Memoriam

Choose the most appropriate answer from the options given below :
1. C, D and E only
2. **A, C and D only**
3. B, C and E only
4. A, B and C only

Correct Explanations:

Lycidas, a poem by John Milton, written in 1637 for inclusion in a volume of elegies published in 1638 to commemorate the death of Edward King, Milton's contemporary at the University of Cambridge, who had drowned in a shipwreck in August 1637. The poem mourns the loss of a virtuous and promising young man about to embark upon a career as a clergyman. Milton muses on fame, the meaning of existence, and heavenly judgment, adopting **the conventions of the classical pastoral elegy** (Lycidas was a shepherd in Virgil's Eclogues).

Adonais, a pastoral elegy by Percy Bysshe Shelley, was written and published in 1821 to commemorate the death of his friend and fellow poet John Keats earlier that year..

Thyrsis, an elegiac poem by Matthew Arnold, was first published in Macmillan's Magazine in 1866.

Question 101

J Hillis Miller. one of the leading exponents of deconstruction, does a deconstructionist reading of which of the following poems of P. B. Shelley?

1. **"The Triumph of Life"**
2. "Ode to the West Wind"
3. "Revolt of Islam"
4. "The Witch of Atlas"

Correct Explanations:

➢ The Triumph of Life was the last major work by Percy Bysshe Shelley before his death in 1822.
➢ The work was left unfinished. Shelley wrote the poem at Casa Magni in Lerici, Italy in the early summer of 1822.
➢ He modelled the poem, written in terza rima, on Petrarch's Trionfi and Dante's Divine Comedy.
➢ Shelley was working on the poem when he accidentally drowned on 8 July 1822 during a storm on a voyage from Leghorn.
➢ The poem was first published in the collection Posthumous Poems (1824) published in London by John and Henry L. Hunt which was edited by his wife Mary Shelley, who emphasised the importance of the work.

- ➢ **J. Hillis Miller touches on The Triumph of Life in his essay "The Critic as Host",** where he argues that the poem 'contains within itself, jostling irreconcilably with one another, both logocentric metaphysics and nihilism'.
- ➢ Shelley's poem presents the mirror image or, perhaps it would be better to say, something like photographic negative, of the Platonic system of light and dark.

Question 102

Who among the following characters personifies necessity in P. B. Shelley's Prometheus Unbound?

1. Prometheus
2. Demogorgon
3. Jove
4. Jeus

Explanations:
Ans: Demogorgon

In P. B. Shelley's Prometheus Unbound, the character who personifies necessity is Demogorgon. **Demogorgon is depicted as a mysterious and powerful being who represents the forces of fate and destiny.** In the play, Prometheus seeks the help of Demogorgon to overthrow Jove, the tyrannical ruler of the gods, and to bring about a new era of freedom and enlightenment. Demogorgon's appearance in the play is brief but significant, as he symbolizes the inexorable power of fate that ultimately leads to the downfall of oppressive regimes and the triumph of the human spirit.

Question 103

Match List I with List II

LIST I	LIST II
A. Plato	I. Rhetoric
B. Aristotle	II. Symposium
C. P. B. Shelley	III. Apology of Poetry
D. Philip Sydney	IV. Defence of Poetry

Choose the correct answer from the options given below:

1.   A-I, B-II, C-III, DIV
2.   A-III, B-II, C-IV, D-I
3.   A-IV, B-III, C-II, D - I
4.   A-II, B-I, C-IV, D-III

Explanations:
Ans: A-II, B-I, C-IV, D-III

Plato's "Symposium" is a philosophical text that explores the nature of love and desire through a series of speeches delivered by guests at a symposium, or drinking party.

Aristotle's "Rhetoric" is a treatise on the art of persuasion.

P.B. Shelley's "Defence of Poetry" is a critical essay in which he argues that poetry is a powerful force for social and political change.

Philip Sidney's "Apology for Poetry" is a work of literary criticism in which he defends poetry against its critics.

Question 104

Arrange the works in chronological sequence:

A.   Matthew Arnold's Culture and Anarchy
B.   Thomas Browne's The Anatomy of Melancholy
C.   Thomas Hobbes' Leviathan
D.   Walter Pater's Studies in the History of the Renaissance
E.   PB Shelley's Defense of Poesie

Choose the correct answer from the options given below:

1.   B, C, E, A, D
2.   A, B, C, D, E
3.   C, D, E, A, B
4.   D, C, B, A, E

Explanations:
Ans: B, C, E, A, D

> *Thomas Browne's The Anatomy of Melancholy (1621).*
> *Thomas Hobbes' Leviathan (1651).*
> *Matthew Arnold's Culture and Anarchy (1869).*
> *Walter Pater's Studies in the History of the Renaissance (1873).*
> *PB Shelley's Defense of Poesie (written in 1821, published in 1840).*

Question 105

Which of the following works is NOT written by P. B. Shelley?

1. *The Mask of Anarchy*
2. *Queen Mab: A Philosophical Poem*
3. ***The Vision of Judgement***
4. *The Revolt of Islam*

Explanations:
"The Vision of Judgement" is a poem by the English poet Lord Byron.
"A Vision of Judgement" is a poem by the English poet Robert Southey..
Other Explanations:

"The Mask of Anarchy" is a political poem written by Shelley in 1819 in response to the Peterloo Massacre, and it calls for non-violent resistance against oppression.

"Queen Mab: A Philosophical Poem" was written by Shelley in 1813, and it is a utopian poem that advocates for radical political and social reform.

"The Revolt of Islam" is an epic poem written by Shelley in 1817, and it tells the story of a young woman named Laon who leads a revolution against an oppressive government. The poem is considered one of Shelley's most significant works, reflecting his radical political and social views.

Question 106

Who among the following has composed the lyrical drama Hellas?

1. Lord Byron
2. **P. B. Shelley**
3. William Wordsworth
4. John Keats

Explanations:

"Hellas" is a lyrical drama written by the English poet Percy Bysshe Shelley. It was first published in 1822 and was Shelley's vision of a world revolution that would lead to a utopian society..

Which among the following poems has not been composed by P.B. Shelley?

1. To Wordsworth
2. Mutability
3. Hymn to Intellectual Beauty
4. When We Two Parted

Explanations:
Answer: 4. When We Two Parted

"When We Two Parted", a poem of Lord Byron

"Hymn to Intellectual Beauty" is a poem written by Percy Bysshe Shelley in 1816 and published in 1817.

"Mutability" is a poem by Percy Bysshe Shelley, featured in the 1816 collection titled Alastor, or The Spirit of Solitude: And Other Poems..

In **"To Wordsworth,"** Percy Bysshe Shelley pays homage to the elder Romantic poet William Wordsworth (1770-1850), reflecting on the latter's advancing age and legacy.

John Keats (1795-1821)

His Life and Career:

- ➤ **Keats was born in London**, son of a livery stable keeper.
- ➤ He attended **private school in Enfield**, apprenticed to a surgeon.
- ➤ In **1814**, he moved to **London for medical studies**.
- ➤ His **poetical talent emerged**, overshadowing his interest in surgery.

- He met **Leigh Hunt**, radical journalist, in **1815**.
- **Hunt introduced him to Shelley** and other poets.
- His **first poetry volume** in **1817** gained **little notice**.
- **Keats' health began failing** due to **family tendency to consumption.**
- He met **Fanny Brawne** and was **briefly engaged.**
- **His illness worsened**, leading to mental and physical distress.
- His **letters to Fanny** were **published posthumously in 1879.**
- His **second volume (1818)** was harshly **criticized by Tory journals.**
- **Keats seemed unaffected**, though it probably **impacted his health.**
- In **1820**, he **left England for warmer climates**, died in **Rome (1821).**
- **At 17**, Keats discovered **Spenser**, influencing his poetic journey.
- His first attempt at poetry was **Imitation of Spenser (1813).**
- His first book, **Poems (1817)**, showed **little merit.**
- The **poems followed** Shenstone, Gray, and **Byron's style.**
- **Endymion (1818)** is an **early, flawed work** of 4000 lines.
- Despite its flaws, **Endymion shows Keats' budding style.**
- Hostile reviews **targeted the weaknesses** in **Endymion.**
- **Keats' health** was already declining during these **attacks.**
- His **third and final volume** contained many first-rate poems.
- **Isabella, or The Pot of Basil (1818)** was an **advance in style.**
- The poem had **fewer stylistic lapses**, with **sentimental pathos.**
- **The Eve of St. Agnes (1818) is adorned with poetic imagination.**
- It's often considered **Keats' masterpiece**, rich in **fancy and imagery.**
- **Hyperion (1818)** tells of **primordial battles** between gods.
- **Hyperion** remains unfinished, reflecting **Keats' failing strength.**
- The poem's **style is sublime** but showed **his grip loosening.**
- **The Eve of St. Mark (1819)** remains **unfinished.**
- It contains **brilliant descriptive passages** and **improvement in style**.
- **Lamia (1819)** is based on **Burton's Anatomy of Melancholy.**
- **Lamia** is his **weakest longer poem**, showing **stylistic lapses.**
- Keats' phrases **"plead yourself"** and **"labyrinth you"** exceed poetic limits.
- His best work includes **many shorter poems** of supreme beauty.
- His **great odes: To a Nightingale, On a Grecian Urn**, and **To Autumn.**
- **La Belle Dame sans Merci** is a **lyrical ballad**, a **masterpiece.**

- ➤ In **1819**, Keats collaborated on a drama, **Otho the Great.**
- ➤ He started, but **did not finish, King Stephen.**
- ➤ **The Cap and Bells**, an **unfinished fairy-tale**, is **below his standard.**
- ➤ **Keats' failing health** didn't stop his **creative output.**
- ➤ He **struggled emotionally**, reflected in his **letters to Fanny.**
- ➤ **Leigh Hunt's support** couldn't save **Keats from harsh criticism.**
- ➤ **Quarterly Review** attacked Keats **for radical affiliations.**
- ➤ Keats sought **refuge in writing**, ignoring **negative reviews.**
- ➤ His **final days** were spent **in despair** over his illness.
- ➤ **Endymion's complexity** showed **Keats' ambition** despite **criticism.**
- ➤ **Keats' love of Spenser** fueled **his early poetic ventures.**
- ➤ **Hyperion's grand scale** challenged Keats' **strength** and resolve.
- ➤ **The Eve of St. Mark** hints at **Keats' evolving descriptive power.**
- ➤ **The great odes** reveal **Keats' poetic peak**, especially in **1819.**
- ➤ His short works show **Keats' mastery of lyrical ballads.**
- ➤ **Endymion's flaws** reflected **Keats' poetic immaturity.**
- ➤ **Keats found solace** in writing **despite personal despair.**
- ➤ **His letters** provide insight into **his emotional struggles.**
- ➤ **Fanny Brawne's engagement** brought **both joy and pain.**
- ➤ **Rome's beauty** inspired Keats' **final moments.**
- ➤ **Keats' legacy** endures despite **his short life and illness.**
- ➤ His **poetic contributions** rank him among **the greatest poets.**
- ➤ Anthony Burges's novel **"Abba Abba" is a fictionalized account of the final days of Keats's life.**

Poetry:
- ➤ ***Sleep and Poetry (1816)***
- ➤ ***Endymion (1817)***
  - ○ **Dedicated** this poem to the late poet **Thomas Chatterton.**
  - ○ The poem begins with, "***A thing of beauty is a joy for ever.***"
  - ○ Endymion is written in **rhyming couplets in iambic pentameter.**
  - ○ It is also known as **heroic couplets.**
  - ○ **Endymion, the shepherd** beloved of the moon goddess **Selene.**
  - ○ Elaborates on the original story and renames Selene "Cynthia" (an alternative name for Artemis).
  - ○ Divided into **four books**, each approximately **1,000 lines** long.
  - ○ The scene depicts **trees, rivers, shepherds, and sheep.**
  - ○ The shepherds **pray to Pan**, the **god of shepherds.**
  - ○ The youths **sing and dance**, while elders **discuss Elysium.**

- o **Endymion**, a **"brain-sick shepherd-prince"**, is in a trance.
- o His sister **Peona takes him away** to rest.
- o Endymion **sleeps at Peona's resting place**.
- o Upon waking, **Endymion tells Peona** about **Cynthia**.
- o He expresses **his deep love** for **Cynthia**.

➢ *Isabella or The Pot of Basil (1818)*
- o **Isabella or the Pot of Basil** (1818) is by **John Keats**.
- o It is **adapted from Boccaccio's Decameron** (IV, 5).
- o **Isabella** is forced to marry a **nobleman** but loves **Lorenzo**.
- o Her **brothers murder Lorenzo** and **bury his body**.
- o **Lorenzo's ghost** reveals his **death in Isabella's dream**.
- o **Isabella exhumes the body** and buries his head in **basil pot**.
- o She tends the **basil obsessively** while **pining for Lorenzo**.
- o The poem **preceded The Eve of Saint Agnes** by Keats.
- o Both poems are **medieval romances** with **dangerous love**.
- o It was **published in 1820**, with other **works by Keats**.
- o The poem **inspired Pre-Raphaelite artists**, including **Hunt and Millais**.

➢ *Hyperion (1818, unfinished)*
- o *Hyperion, a Fragment* is an **abandoned/unfinished** epic poem.
- o Published in **Lamia, Isabella, The Eve of St. Agnes (1820)**.
- o Based on **Titanomachia**, showing the **Titans' despair** after defeat.
- o **Keats wrote it** from late **1818 to spring 1819**.
- o He abandoned it for **"too many Miltonic inversions"**.
- o Keats was **nursing his brother**, who died of tuberculosis.
- o **Tom Keats died on 1 December 1818** from tuberculosis.
- o **The Fall of Hyperion** continued the ideas, published posthumously.

➢ *The Eve of St. Agnes (1819)*
- o **42 Spenserian stanzas** set in the **Middle Ages**.
- o It was written by John Keats in 1819 and published in 1820.
- o **St. Agnes** is the **patron saint of virgins** and **died a martyr**.
- o **St. Agnes' Eve** is **January 20th**, with her feast day **January 21st**.
- o The **poem references divinations** mentioned by **John Aubrey's Miscellanies (1696)**.
- o On a **chilly night**, an **elderly beadsman prays** in a chapel.
- o **Madeline longs for Porphyro**, her **family's sworn enemy**.
- o She hopes for **sweet dreams of her lover** on **St. Agnes' Eve**.

- o **Porphyro sneaks into the castle**, seeking **Angela's help.**
- o **Angela reluctantly helps** him and **gathers food** for them.
- o **Porphyro hides** in Madeline's room and **watches her sleep.**
- o **He prepares a feast** while Madeline **dreams of him.**
- o Madeline wakes, thinking **Porphyro is part of her dream.**
- o Upon realizing, she says **she cannot hate his deception.**
- o Madeline feels abandoned if **Porphyro leaves her behind.**
- o **Porphyro promises his love** and to **take her home.**
- o They **flee the castle**, passing by **drunken revelers.**
- o **Angela's death** is revealed in the **poem's final stanza.**
- o The **beadsman dies**, sleeping among **his ashes cold.**
- o The poem ends with their **escape into the night** together.

- ➢ *Lamia (1819)*
- ➢ *The Cap and Bells (1819, unfinished)*
- ➢ *The Fall of Hyperion: A Dream (1819, unfinished)*
  - o **The Fall of Hyperion** is an epic poem by **Keats.**
  - o **Keats reworked and expanded lines** from **Hyperion.**
  - o The poem was **abandoned before Keats's death.**
  - o It begins with a **lyrical argument**, introducing a **dream or vision.**
  - o The poem is divided into **three scenes** before its **fragmentation.**
  - o The first scene shows the narrator at a **post-Edenic feast.**
  - o It recalls **"sensory delight"** from **Sleep and Poetry** and **Ode on a Grecian Urn.**
  - o The narrator drinks **"transparent juice"** and falls into a **deep sleep.**
  - o He awakens before a **temple**, with gates to the **East.**
  - o A mysterious figure, **Moneta**, challenges him to **climb stairs.**
  - o The poet experiences **painful death**, similar to **Apollo's pain.**
  - o The poet must **overcome suffering** to avoid **false poets' mistakes.**
  - o After reaching the top, **Moneta questions him** on poetry and visions.
  - o This scene reflects **Sleep and Poetry**, condemning **false poets.**
  - o After passing the test, **Moneta shows a vision** of **Titans and Hyperion.**
  - o The scene ends with **Hyperion rising**, leading to the **previous fragment.**
  - o **Hyperion's rise** concludes the **poet narrator's vision.**

Odes:

- _Ode to Apollo (1815)_
- **_"Comic"_ is indeed a poem by John Keats, published in 1817.**
- _Robin Hood (To a Friend) (1818)_
- _Lines on the Mermaid Tavern (1818)_
- _Ode to Maia (1818)_
- _Bards of Passion and of Mirth (1818)_
- _Ode to Fanny (1819)_
- **_Ode on a Grecian Urn_**
  - **Keats composed "Ode on a Grecian Urn" in May 1819.**
  - It was **first published anonymously** in **Annals of the Fine Arts**.
  - Keats' collection represents **a new development of the ode**.
  - The poem was **inspired by Benjamin Haydon's articles**.
  - **Keats' understanding of Greek virtues** influenced his writing.
  - He **describes a Greek urn** in **five ten-line stanzas**.
  - **Two scenes** are described: a lover's pursuit and a sacrifice.
  - The urn proclaims, **"'Beauty is Truth, Truth Beauty.'"**
  - Critics debate whether these lines **adequately end the poem**.
  - Discussions include the **speaker's role and material objects' inspiration**.
  - The poem explores the **relationship between reality and idealism**.
  - Contemporary critics **did not well receive** the ode.
  - The poem **was praised only from mid-19th century** onwards.
  - Now, it's **considered one of the best English odes**.
  - **20th-century critics** were divided over the **final proclamation**.
  - However, they **agreed on the poem's beauty**.
  - Some critics perceive **specific inadequacies** in the poem.

> _Thou still unravish'd bride of quietness,_
>   _Thou foster-child of silence and slow time,_
> _Sylvan historian, who canst thus express_
>   _A flowery tale more sweetly than our rhyme:_
> _What leaf-fring'd legend haunts about thy shape_
>   _Of deities or mortals, or of both,_
>   _In Tempe or the dales of Arcady?_
>   _What men or gods are these? What maidens loth?_
> _What mad pursuit? What struggle to escape?_
>   _What pipes and timbrels? What wild ecstasy?_

Heard melodies are sweet, but those unheard
*   Are sweeter; therefore, ye soft pipes, play on;*
Not to the sensual ear, but, more endear'd,
*   Pipe to the spirit ditties of no tone:*
Fair youth, beneath the trees, thou canst not leave
*   Thy song, nor ever can those trees be bare;*
*   Bold Lover, never, never canst thou kiss,*
Though winning near the goal yet, do not grieve;
*   She cannot fade, though thou hast not thy bliss,*
*   For ever wilt thou love, and she be fair!*

Ah, happy, happy boughs! that cannot shed
*   Your leaves, nor ever bid the Spring adieu;*
And, happy melodist, unwearied,
*   For ever piping songs for ever new;*
More happy love! more happy, happy love!
*   For ever warm and still to be enjoy'd,*
*   For ever panting, and for ever young;*
All breathing human passion far above,
*   That leaves a heart high-sorrowful and cloy'd,*
*   A burning forehead, and a parching tongue.*

Who are these coming to the sacrifice?
*   To what green altar, O mysterious priest,*
Lead'st thou that heifer lowing at the skies,
*   And all her silken flanks with garlands drest?*
What little town by river or sea shore,
*   Or mountain-built with peaceful citadel,*
*   Is emptied of this folk, this pious morn?*
And, little town, thy streets for evermore
*   Will silent be; and not a soul to tell*
*   Why thou art desolate, can e'er return.*

O Attic shape! Fair attitude! with brede
*   Of marble men and maidens overwrought,*
With forest branches and the trodden weed;
*   Thou, silent form, dost tease us out of thought*
As doth eternity: Cold Pastoral!

> *When old age shall this generation waste,*
> *Thou shalt remain, in midst of other woe*
> *Than ours, a friend to man, to whom thou say'st,*
> ***"Beauty is truth, truth beauty,—that is all***
> ***Ye know on earth, and all ye need to know."***

- ➢ ***Ode on Indolence***
    - ○ The poem **describes indolence,** synonymous with **"avoidance" or "laziness."**
    - ○ Written when **Keats was focused on material prospects.**
    - ○ Keats said **its composition brought him great pleasure.**
    - ○ **Ode on Indolence** was not **published until 1848.**
    - ○ The poem uses **ten-line stanzas with a unique rhyme scheme.**
    - ○ The rhyme scheme starts with **Shakespearian quatrain** (ABAB).
    - ○ The poem **ends with a Miltonic sestet** (CDECDE), like other odes.
- ➢ ***Ode on Melancholy***
    - ○ The poem describes the poet's perception of **melancholy.**
    - ○ It consists of **three stanzas,** each with **ten lines.**
    - ○ **"Ode on Melancholy"** addresses how to cope with **sadness.**
    - ○ The **first stanza** advises against trying to **forget sadness.**
    - ○ **Lethe,** river of forgetfulness, represents **forgetting sorrow.**
    - ○ Avoid **suicide** or fascination with **death symbols.**
    - ○ Doing so makes the **soul drowsy** instead of **alert** to suffering.
    - ○ The second stanza instructs to **find beauty** during **melancholy fits.**
    - ○ **Natural beauty,** like roses and rainbows, **overwhelms sorrow.**
    - ○ Look into the **eyes of a beloved** to find comfort.
    - ○ **Third stanza** connects **pleasure and pain** as inseparable.
    - ○ **Beauty dies,** joy is fleeting, **pleasure turns to poison.**
    - ○ The shrine of melancholy is inside **the temple of Delight.**
    - ○ Only when overwhelmed by **joy,** sadness **reveals itself.**
    - ○ **Sadness emerges** by "burst[ing] Joy's grape" in **delight.**
    - ○ **He who tastes sadness** will know melancholy's full might.
    - ○ Melancholy is only accessible through **delight's inner sadness.**
    - ○ Those who embrace it will **"taste the sadness"** of melancholy.
    - ○ The speaker describes **melancholy's power** through **cloudy trophies.**

- o True understanding of **melancholy comes** from overwhelming joy.
- ➢ *Ode to a Nightingale*
    - o **Keats' poem** was published in **Lamia, Isabella, and Other Poems** (1820).
    - o It's a **meditation on art and life**, inspired by a **nightingale's song**.
    - o The **bird's song brings visionary happiness** to the **poet**.
    - o **Human grief, sickness**, and the **transience of youth** are contrasted.
    - o The **nightingale's song symbolizes art** that **outlasts mortal life**.
    - o The **bird nests in the poet's garden**, inspiring his **reflection**.
    - o **Human suffering** contrasts the poet's **joy in communing** with the bird.
    - o The nightingale's **song symbolizes the eternal nature of art.**
- ➢ *Ode to Psyche*
    - o The poem marks a departure from **Keats's early work.**
    - o **A mortal woman is a Psyche** in John Keats' "Ode to Psyche"
    - o **Early poems** often depict **escapes into pleasant imagination.**
    - o Keats uses imagination to **revive Psyche** and become **Eros (love)**.
    - o He seeks to **resurrect Psyche** through his creative **dedication.**
    - o Keats dedicates an **"untrodden region" of his mind** to Psyche.
    - o The poem reflects **Keats's desire to worship** the neglected goddess.
- ➢ *To Autumn*
    - o **"To Autumn"** was composed by **John Keats** in **1819.**
    - o It was published in **1820**, alongside **Lamia** and **The Eve of St. Agnes.**
    - o **"To Autumn"** is the last of Keats's **"1819 odes".**
    - o Keats wrote it after a **walk near Winchester** in autumn.
    - o The poem marked the **end of his poetic career.**
    - o Keats died in **Rome**, a year after the poem's publication.
    - o The speaker addresses **Autumn's abundance and intimacy with the sun.**
    - o **Autumn is personified** as a **goddess** sitting on the granary floor.
    - o She is often seen **sleeping in fields** or watching a **cider press.**

- o The speaker tells Autumn to **listen to her own music**, not spring's.
- o Twilight brings sounds of **gnats, lambs, crickets, and robins**.
- o Swallows **gather for migration**, singing from the skies.

Sonnets:

- ➤ *To Byron (1814)*
- ➤ *To Chatterton (1815)*
- ➤ ***On First Looking into Chapman's Homer (1815)***
  - o It is a sonnet.
  - o It tells of the author's astonishment while reading the works of the ancient Greek poet Home
- ➤ *On Sitting Down to Read King Lear Once Again (1818)*
- ➤ *When I Have Fears (1818)*

Songs:

- ➤ *Hymn to Apollo (1816)*
- ➤ *You Say You Love (1817)*
- ➤ ***La Belle Dame sans Merci (1819)***
  - o **"La Belle Dame sans Merci"** is a ballad from **1819**.
  - o *"The Beautiful Lady Without Mercy"*
  - o The title comes from **Alain Chartier's** 15th-century **La Belle Dame sans Mercy**.
  - o The poem is a **classic example** of **Keats' focus on love and death**.
  - o It tells of a **fairy who seduces** and condemns a **knight**.
  - o The fairy inspired **femme fatale imagery** in 19th-century **art**.
- ➤ *The Eve of St. Mark (1819)*

Keats's Letters:

- ➤ Keats wrote letters to **Bailey, George & Thomas Keats, Tyler, Woodhouse**.
- ➤ **Keats wrote 252 letters** in total during his lifetime.
- ➤ **"Egotistical sublime"** describes **Wordsworth's self-centered poetry**.
- ➤ **Keats** used the phrase in **1818** in a letter to **Woodhouse**.
- ➤ It refers to **Wordsworth's narrative voice** conveying **his singular truth**.
- ➤ **Keats** contrasted this with **"negative capability"** as the ideal.
- ➤ **Shakespeare's sonnets** exemplified **"negative capability"**, according to Keats.
- ➤ **Keats** believed in **less self-centered** and more **imaginative poetry**.

Negative Capability

- ➢ The term **Negative Capability** was used briefly in a letter.
- ➢ The phrase became public after **Keats' letters were collected**.
- ➢ Keats wrote this **letter to his brothers** on **22 December 1817**.
- ➢ In **1817**, Keats introduced **Negative Capability** in a letter.
- ➢ He was influenced by **Shakespeare's work** and described it.
- ➢ Keats describes **Negative Capability** as "being in uncertainties, mysteries, doubts."
- ➢ **"Negative"** is not pejorative but relates to **artistic potential**.
- ➢ **Negative Capability** explains why great writers accept **uncertainty**.
- ➢ It describes the **pursuit of artistic beauty over philosophical certainty**.
- ➢ **Philosophers and poets** use the term to explain truths **beyond reason**.
- ➢ Keats used **"negative"** to express **potential in absence** of possession.
- ➢ **Passivity** and accepting doubt are key to **literary achievement**.
- ➢ **Beauty trumps reason**, according to **Keats' view of poetic greatness**.

Questions:

Question 108

Which work of John Keats is dedicated to Thomas Chatterton ?

1. Lamia
2. Endymion
3. Hyperion
4. Ode on a Grecian Urn

Explanations:
Answer: 2. Endymion

Endymion (1817)
- ➢ **Dedicated** this poem to the late poet **Thomas Chatterton**.
- ➢ The poem begins with, "***A thing of beauty is a joy for ever.***"
- ➢ Endymion is written in **rhyming couplets in iambic pentameter**.
- ➢ It is also known as **heroic couplets**.
- ➢ **Endymion, the shepherd** beloved of the moon goddess **Selene**.

The lives of which of the following writers have been the subject matter of novels by Anthony Burgess?

- A. Milton
- B. Marlowe
- C. Shelley
- D. Keats

Choose the correct answer from the options given below:

1. A and B only
2. A and D only
3. B and C only
4. B and D only

Explanations:
Answer: 4. B and D only

Anthony Burgess, in addition to being a novelist and critic, was also a scholar of English literature. He was particularly interested in the lives and works of Romantic poets, **including Christopher Marlowe, Percy Bysshe Shelley, and John Keats**. Burgess wrote several novels that revolve around these poets, often exploring their lives, works, and the historical contexts in which they lived.

For example, his novel **"A Dead Man in Deptford" explores the life and death of Marlowe,** while "Byrne" is a fictionalized account of Shelley's life. Burgess's novel **"Nothing Like the Sun" is a fictionalized biography of William Shakespeare** that also features Marlowe as a character. Finally, **his novel "Abba Abba" is a fictionalized account of the final days of Keats's life.** In each of these novels, Burgess uses his extensive knowledge of literature and history to create rich and complex portraits of these writers and the worlds in which they lived.

Question 110

Arrange the following terms in their chronological sequence of appearance:

- A. dissociation of sensibility
- B. unreliable narrator
- C. theatre of cruelty
- D. egotistical sublime

Choose the correct answer from the options given below:

1. D, A, B, C
2. D, A, C, B
3. D, B, A, C
4. B, D, A, C

Correct Explanations:

D. According to the Romantic English poet John Keats (1795-1821), artists of fixed opinions suffered from "egotistical sublime," obsessing over singular truths to the point that they were unable to produce characters and storylines that convincingly diverged from their personal world views.

A. Dissociation of sensibility is a literary term first used by T. S. Eliot in his essay "The Metaphysical Poets" (1921).

C. The Theatre of Cruelty (1931-1936) is a form of theatre generally associated with Antonin Artaud. Artaud, who was briefly a member of the surrealist movement, outlined his theories in The Theatre and Its Double.

B. An unreliable narrator is a narrator whose credibility is compromised. They can be found in fiction and film and range from children to mature characters. The term was coined in 1961 by Wayne C. Booth in The Rhetoric of Fiction.

Question 111

Given below are two statements;

Statement I: The term "Negative Capability" was coined by John Keats,
Statement II: While analysing the term "Dissociation of sensibility", T. S. Eliot proclaims that Hamlet is an artistic failure.

In light of the above statements, choose the correct answer from the options given below:

1. Both Statement II and I are true
2. Both Statements I and Statement II are false
3. **Statement I is true, but Statement II is false**

4. Statement I is false, but Statement II is true

Correct Explanations:

Statement I: Negative capability is a phrase first used by Romantic poet John Keats in 1817 to explain the capacity of the greatest writers to pursue a vision of artistic beauty even when it leads them into intellectual confusion and uncertainty, as opposed to a preference for philosophical certainty over artistic beauty.

Statement II: Dissociation of sensibility is a literary term first used by T. S. Eliot in his essay "The Metaphysical Poets". It refers to the way in which intellectual thought was separated from the experience of feeling in seventeenth century poetry.

Statement III: Hamlet and His Problems is an essay written by T.S. Eliot in 1919 that offers a critical reading of Hamlet. The essay first appeared in Eliot's The Sacred Wood: Essays on Poetry and Criticism in 1920. T.S. Eliot has called it as an artistic failure because of the fact that there is delay on the part of Hamlet in executing the revenge. There are many critics who interpret Hamlet in terms of revenge motif where the prince makes an unnecessary delay. **Eliot's critique gained attention partly due to his claim that Hamlet is "most certainly an artistic failure." Eliot also popularised the concept of the objective correlative—a mechanism used to evoke emotion in an audience—in the essay.**

Question 112

Match List I with List II

LIST I	LIST II
A. "Negative Capability"	I. Matthew Arnold
B. "Sweetness and light"	II. Samuel Taylor Coleridge
C. "Esemplastic"	III. T.S. Eliot
D. "Dissociation of Sensibility"	IV. John Keats

Choose the correct answer from the options given below:

1. A-II, B-IV, C-I, D-III
2. A-II, B-I, C-IV, D-III

3. A-IV, B-III, C-II, D-I
4. A-IV, B-I, C-II, D-III

Explanations:
Ans: A-IV, B-I, C-II, D-III

A. "Negative Capability" - John Keats.
B. "Sweetness and light" - Matthew Arnold.
C. "Esemplastic" - Samuel Taylor Coleridge.
D. "Dissociation of Sensibility" - T.S. Eliot.

Question 113

Match List I with List II

List I	List II
A. Egotistical sublime	I. Matthew Arnold
B. Willing suspension of disbelief	II. Joseph Addison
C. Touchstone	III. John Keats
D. Pleasures of the Imagination	IV. Samuel Taylor Coleridge

Choose the correct answer from the options given below:

1. (A)-(III), (B)-(IV), (C)-(I), (D)-(II)
2. (A)-(III), (B)-(IV), (C)-(II), (D)-(I)
3. (A)-(II), (B)-(IV), (C)-(I), (D)-(III)
4. (A)-(II), (B)-(IV), (C)-(I), (D)-(II)

Explanations
Answer: 1. (A)-(III), (B)-(IV), (C)-(I), (D)-(II)

Joseph Addison's philosophical essay "Pleasures of the Imagination," published in The Spectator (1712.

Suspension of disbelief is the avoidance—often described as willing—of critical thinking and logic in understanding something that is unreal or impossible in reality, such as something in a work of speculative fiction, in order to believe it for the sake of enjoying its narrative. **The phrase first appeared in English poet and aesthetic philosopher Samuel Taylor Coleridge's Biographia Literaria (1817).**

The 'egotistical sublime' is a phrase coined by John Keats to describe the poetry of William Wordsworth in an 1818 letter to Richard Woodhouse.

As a metaphor, a touchstone refers to any physical or intellectual measure by which the validity or merit of a concept can be tested. The word was introduced into literary criticism by Matthew Arnold in "Preface to the volume of 1853 poems" (1853) to denote short but distinctive passages selected from the writings of the greatest poets, which he used to determine the relative value of passages or poems which are compared to them.

Question 114

According to Greek Mythology, who is a Psyche in John Keats' "Ode to Psyche"?

1. A mortal woman
2. Cupid
3. An immortal woman
4. Venus

Explanations:
Answer: 1. A mortal woman

"Ode to Psyche" stands out as one of John Keats's early masterpieces, forming part of his 1820 anthology, Lamia, Isabella, The Eve of St. Agnes, and Other Poems. Drawing inspiration from the **ancient myth of Psyche, a mortal beloved by the god Cupid**, Keats crafts a four-stanza ode that delves deep into themes of love and self-reflection.

Leigh Hunt (1784-1859) & His Examiner (1808)

> **Leigh Hunt** was an **English essayist, critic, and poet**.
> He was **editor of influential journals** during the periodical's peak.
> Hunt was a **friend and supporter of Shelley and Keats**.
> His best-known poems include **"Abou Ben Adhem" and "Jenny Kissed Me"**.
> Hunt's poems reflect his **knowledge of French and Italian verse**.
> His defense of Keats in **The Examiner** anticipated **Aesthetic movement views**.

- ➢ **Notable Work:**
    - o *Autobiography (1850;* in part a rewriting of Lord Byron and Some of His Contemporaries, 1828).
    - o *Juvenilia (1801).*
    - o *The Story of Rimini (1816).*
    - o *Foliage (1818) and Hero and Leander, and Bacchus and Ariadne (1819).*
- ➢ **Examiner (1808)**: Launched by **Leigh Hunt and his brother** advocating **abolition and reform**.
- ➢ Hunt was **imprisoned in 1813** for attacking the **prince regent**.
- ➢ In prison, **Hunt wrote for liberty**, viewed as a **martyr**.
- ➢ Released in **1815**, Hunt moved to **Hampstead**, meeting **Keats and Shelley**.
- ➢ The **Examiner defended Romantic poets** against **Blackwood's Magazine**.
- ➢ The Examiner supported the new Romantic poets against attacks by **Blackwood's Magazine on "the Cockney school of poetry,"** supposedly led by Hunt.
- ➢ **Reflector (1810–11)** combined **political writing with art and theatre criticism**.
- ➢ **Imagination and Fancy (1844)** compares **painting and poetry**, Hunt's **critical work**.
- ➢ **Indicator (1819–21)** published **Hunt's best essays** on various topics.
- ➢ **The Companion (1828)** continued Hunt's **weekly periodical writings**.
- ➢ Hunt **wrote for periodicals** until his **death**, leaving a lasting impact.

Question 115

Which among the following are the titles of the periodicals?

A. Dickens' Household Words
B. S.T. Coleridge' Friend
C. Richard Steele's Guardian
D. Franz Kafka's The Metamorphosis
E. Leigh Hunt's Indicator

Choose the correct answer from the options given below:

1. (A) and (B) Only
2. (B) and (C) Only

3. (A), (B), (C) and (E) Only
4. (C), (D) and (E) Only

Explanations:
Answer: 3. (A), (B), (C) and (E) Only

Charles Dickens, in the 1850s, took on the role of editor for the English weekly magazine _Household Words_, named after a phrase from Shakespeare's Henry V. Throughout its conception, Dickens considered various titles such as The Robin, The Household Voice, The Comrade, The Lever, and The Highway of Life before settling on Household Words.

In 1809, Samuel Taylor Coleridge embarked on his second venture into publishing with _The Friend_, a weekly journal showcasing his broad spectrum of interests from law to literary criticism..

Sir Richard Steele, in collaboration with Joseph Addison, co-founded _The Spectator_, following their initial project, **_The Tatler_**. Launched on 12 April 1709. The magazine was discontinued in 1711 to escape political backlash, leading Steele and Addison to start The Spectator and later **_The Guardian_**.

Leigh Hunt, an influential English critic and poet, co-founded **_The Examiner_,** a radical journal, becoming a nexus for the "Hunt circle" which included notable figures like William Hazlitt and Charles Lamb. Hunt played a crucial role in introducing poets like John Keats and Percy Bysshe Shelley to the public. Aside from _The Examiner_, Hunt edited **_The Reflector_,** a quarterly magazine, and **_The Indicator_,** a weekly publication that he likely filled with his literary contributions. He also briefly managed **_The Companion_**, a weekly that focused on literature and the arts.

The Metamorphosis, a profound allegorical narrative by the esteemed Austrian author Franz Kafka, was first made available to the public in the German language as Die Verwandlung in the year 1915.

John Clare (1793-1864)

> ➢ **John Clare (1793-1864)** was an **English poet.**
> ➢ **Son of a farm laborer**, he celebrated the **English countryside**.
> ➢ His poetry reflects **sorrow at the countryside's disruption**.

- ➤ Clare's work was **re-evaluated in the late 20th century**.
- ➤ He's now recognized as a **significant 19th-century poet**.
- ➤ **Jonathan Bate called Clare** "the greatest laboring-class poet."
- ➤ Poems Descriptive of Rural Life and Scenery – 1820
- ➤ The Village Minstrel – 1821
- ➤ The Shepherd's Calendar; with Village Stories, and Other Poems – 1827
- ➤ The Rural Muse – 1835

John Clare's notable poems and prose pieces include:

- ➤ Poems Descriptive of Rural Life and Scenery (1820)
- ➤ The Village Minstrel, and Other Poems (1821)
- ➤ The Shepherd's Calendar (1827)
- ➤ The Rural Muse (1835)
- ➤ "Don Juan" (Asylum period work)
- ➤ "Child Harold" (Asylum period work)
- ➤ "A Favourite Place" (Later work)

List of Poems by John Clare:

- ➤ **First Love**
- ➤ Winter Walk
- ➤ **Badger**
- ➤ I am
- ➤ Autumn
- ➤ John Clare
- ➤ An Invite to Eternity
- ➤ **The Skylark**
- ➤ Nightwind
- ➤ Adieu
- ➤ All nature has a feeling
- ➤ Spring
- ➤ Sheep in winter
- ➤ **The Gipsy Camp**
- ➤ Death
- ➤ Poems Descriptive of Rural Life and Scenery
- ➤ Sonnet
- ➤ Summer
- ➤ The Secret
- ➤ Winter

Question 116

Identify the poet of the following poems :

(a) The Skylark (b) The Badger (c) The Gypsy Camp (d) First Love

    1. P.B. Shelley
    2. John Clare
    3. Lord Byron
    4. Robert Burns

Explanations:
Answer: 2. John Clare

Charles Lamb (1775-1834)

- ➢ **Lamb was born in London**, his father worked in Middle Temple.
- ➢ **Lamb was timid** and educated at Christ's Hospital.
- ➢ **He was a fellow-pupil** of Coleridge, a lifelong friend.
- ➢ **Speech impediment** prevented him from entering the Church.
- ➢ **Worked at the South Sea House**, then East India House (1792).
- ➢ **Mental illness ran in his family**, and affected Lamb briefly.
- ➢ **Sister Mary Lamb murdered their mother in 1796.**
- ➢ **Lamb devoted his life** to caring for his sister.
- ➢ **He retired in 1825**, after thirty years of service.
- ➢ **Known for humor, pathos, and goodwill** in literature.
- ➢ **Lamb started as a poet**, writing moderate pieces like *The Old Familiar Faces*.
- ➢ **His tragedy, John Woodvil (1801)**, was unsuccessful on stage.
- ➢ **Collaborated with his sister** on *Tales from Shakespeare* (1807).
- ➢ **Lamb's critical work** had insight and literary taste.
- ➢ **First essay published in London Magazine (1820)**, signed "Elia."
- ➢ **Essays of Elia (1823)** and *Last Essays of Elia (1833)* followed.
- ➢ **Essays are unequaled**, ranging from chimneysweeps to old china.
- ➢ **Lamb's essays are egotistical** yet artless and artful.
- ➢ **Personal recollections** are woven into his subjects.
- ➢ **His style is old-fashioned**, echoing older writers like Browne.
- ➢ **Uses long, curious words** with frequent exclamations and parentheses.
- ➢ **His humor is airy and precise**, elfish in tone.

- ➢ **Lamb's pathos is delicate**, sometimes deepening into sorrow.
- ➢ **His essay, Dream-Children**, expresses deep regret and emotion.
- ➢ **No essayist is as personal**, yet universally appealing.
- ➢ **His writing blends humor and pathos** seamlessly.
- ➢ **The joy comes from Lamb's voice**, not the subject matter.
- ➢ **Lamb's egotism is unique**, but never alienates the reader.
- ➢ **His essays show great humanity**, along with literary skill.
- ➢ **Lamb's style combines old-fashioned prose** with a modern touch.

Selected Works:

- ➢ *Blank Verse, poems, 1798*
- ➢ *A Tale of Rosamund Gray and Old Blind Margaret, 1798*
- ➢ *John Woodvil, verse drama, 1802*
- ➢ ***Tales from Shakespeare, 1807***
  - o **Tales from Shakespeare written by Charles and Mary Lamb** in 1807.
  - o **The book was intended for young persons** while retaining Shakespeare's language.
  - o **Mary retold the comedies, Charles the tragedies**.
  - o **Omitted the complex historical tales** including all Roman plays.
  - o **Modified for children without censoring**, but subplots removed.
  - o **Sexual references were removed** for young audience sensitivity.
  - o **They wrote the preface together**, ensuring consistency in tone.
  - o **Mary didn't receive credit till 1838**, after the seventh edition.
  - o **Marina Warner mentions this in the 2007 edition introduction.**
  - o **The book may be challenging for early 21st-century children.**
  - o **Still faithful to the original**, useful when learning Shakespeare.
  - o **Alternatives exist, but Lamb's retelling remains uniquely faithful.**
- ➢ *The Adventures of Ulysses, 1808*
- ➢ ***Specimens of English Dramatic Poets who Lived About the Time of Shakespeare, 1808***
- ➢ ***On the Tragedies of Shakespeare, 1811***
- ➢ ***Witches and Other Night Fears, 1821***
- ➢ *The Pawnbroker's Daughter, 1825*
- ➢ *Eliana, 1867*

- ➢ *Essays of Elia, 1823*
  - o **Essays of Elia** first published in book form in 1823.
  - o **Last Essays of Elia (1833)** issued by publisher Edward Moxon.
  - o **Essays first appeared in The London Magazine (1820-1825)**.
  - o **Lamb's essays were very popular** throughout the nineteenth century.
  - o **Essays have a personal and conversational tone**, charming readers.
  - o **Essays "established Lamb as the most delightful essayist."**
  - o **Lamb is "Elia"** and his sister Mary is "Cousin Bridget."
  - o **Lamb used "Elia" for an essay on the South Sea House.**
  - o **Elia was the last name of an Italian man.**
  - o **American editions were published in Philadelphia in 1828.**
  - o **American publishers reprinted English works without copyright restrictions.**
  - o **The American collection preceded the British counterpart by five years.**
  - o **Lamb's style influenced by Sir Thomas Browne and Robert Burton.**
  - o **Later pieces collected under a body called "Eliana."**
  - o List of Essays:
    - ▪ *"The South-Sea House"*
    - ▪ *"Oxford In The Vacation"*
    - ▪ *"Christ's Hospital Five-And-Thirty Years Ago"*
    - ▪ *"The Two Races Of Men"*
    - ▪ *"New Year's Eve"*
    - ▪ *"My Relations"*
    - ▪ *"Mackery End, In Hertfordshire"*
    - ▪ *"Modern Gallantry"*
    - ▪ *"The Old Benchers Of The Inner Temple"*
    - ▪ *"Grace Before Meat"*
    - ▪ *"On The Artificial Comedy Of The Last Century"*
    - ▪ *"On The Acting Of Munden"*.
- ➢ *The Last Essays of Elia, 1833*

Questions:

Match List I and List II List I

List I Essayist	List II Essay
A. George Orwell	I. "On the Artificial Comedy of the Last Century"
B. Michel de Montaigne	II. 'Why I Write"
C. Charles Lamb	III. "A Modest Proposal"
E. Jonathan Swift	IV. "On the Cannibals"

Choose the correct answer from the options given below:

1. A – Ill, B – IV, C – III, D – I
2. A – II, B – IV, C – I, D – Ill
3. A – IV, B – III, C – II, D – I
4. A – II, B – III, C I, D – IV

Explanations:
Answer: 2. A–II, B – IV, C – I, D – Ill

The correct sequence of the publication dates for these essays is:

1. **Michel de Montaigne - "On the Cannibals" (1580)**
2. **Charles Lamb - "On the Artificial Comedy of the Last Century" (1822)**
3. **Jonathan Swift - "A Modest Proposal" (1729)**
4. **George Orwell - 'Why I Write" (1946)**

Charles Lamb used the pseudonym Elia for writing in which of the following periodicals?

1. **London Magazine**
2. The Edinburg Review
3. The Quarterly Review
4. Athenaeum

Correct Explanations:

Charles Lamb (1775-1834) was an English essayist and writer who used the pseudonym "Elia" for his work in the London Magazine periodicals. Lamb began using the name "Elia" in 1820 when he wrote a series of essays for the magazine titled "Essays of Elia." These essays, which were published over the course of two years, covered a variety of topics, including literature, poetry, and social commentary.

Question 119

Find the chronological order of the writers in terms of the period they belonged to:

- A. Richard Steele
- B. Charles Lamb
- C. John Dryden
- D. Francis Bacon
- E. Matthew Arnold

Choose the correct answer from the options given below:

1. ABCDE
2. BDECA
3. CBDAE
4. **DCABE**

Explanations:
1. Francis Bacon (1561-1626)
2. John Dryden (1631-1700)
3. Richard Steele (1672-1729)
4. Charles Lamb (1775-1834)
5. Matthew Arnold (1822-1888)

Question 120

What is the correct chronological sequence of the following English non-fictional prose writers according to their years of birth?

A. Joseph Addison
B. Francis Bacon
C. Charles Lamb

D. Virginia Woolf

E. Matthew Amold

Choose the correct answer from the options given below:

1. A. D. C. B. E
2. B. A. C. E. D
3. C. A. D. E. B
4. D. C. B, A, E

Explanations

Answer: 2. B. A. C. E. D

- ➤ **Sir Francis Bacon (1561-1626).**
- ➤ **Joseph Addison (1672-1719).**
- ➤ **Charles Lamb (1775-1834).**
- ➤ **Matthew Arnold (1822-1888).**
- ➤ **Virginia Woolf (1882-1941).**

Question 121

What is the correct chronological sequence of the following texts?

A. "The Advancement of Learning"

B. "An Apology for Poetry"

C. "The Uses of the Spectator"

D. "My Relations"

E. "How it Strikes a Contemporary**

Choose the correct answer from the options given below:

1. A, B, C, D, E
2. B, A, C, D, E
3. C, A, D, E, B
4. D, C, B, A, E

Explanations

Answer: 2. B, A, C, D, E

The Defence of Poesie, literary criticism by Sir Philip Sidney, written about 1582 and published posthumously in 1595..

The Advancement of Learning (full title: Of the Proficience and Advancement of Learning, Divine and Human) is a 1605 book by Francis Bacon.

The Spectator was a daily publication founded by Joseph Addison and Richard Steele in England, lasting from 1711 to 1712.

Essays of Elia is a collection of essays written by Charles Lamb; it was first published in book form in 1823, with a second volume, Last Essays of Elia, issued in 1833 by the publisher Edward Moxon. **My Relations** is an essay part of this collection.

Men and Women is a collection of fifty-one poems in two volumes by Robert Browning, first published in 1855.

Question 122

Match List I with List II

List I	List II
A. Charles Lamb	I. Imaginary Conversations
B. William Hazlitt	II. Specimens of the English Dramatic Poets who Lived about the Time of Shakespeare
C. Walter Savage Landor	III. Characters of Shakespeare's Plays
D. Thomas Love Peacock	IV. Gryll Grange

Choose the correct answer from the options given below:

 1. A-III. B-I, C-IV. D-II
 2. A-I, B-II. C-III. D-IV
 3. A-II, B-III, C-I. D-IV
 4. A-IV, B-I. C-II. D-III

Explanations:
Answer: 3. A-II, B-III, C-I. D-IV

I. "Imaginary Conversations" is a collection of dialogues written by Walter Savage Landor, first published in 1824..

II. "Specimens of the English Dramatic Poets who Lived about the Time of Shakespeare" is a work by Charles Lamb, published in 1808..

III. "Characters of Shakespeare's Plays" is a book written by William Hazlitt, published in 1817.

IV. "Gryll Grange" is a novel by Thomas Love Peacock, first published in 1861.

Question 123

Which of the following were written by Thomas Love Peacock?

A. Headlong Hall
B. Nightmare Abbey
C. Imaginary Conversations
D. The Spirit of the Age
E. Specimens of the English Dramatic Poets who Lived about the Time of Shakespeare

Choose the Correct answer from the options given below

1. A and B
2. B and D
3. C and D
4. D and E

Explanations:
Answer: 1. A and B

Headlong Hall is a novella written by Thomas Love Peacock in 1815 and published in 1816.

Nightmare Abbey, published in 1818, is a satirical novella by Thomas Love Peacock that playfully mocks contemporary literary trends.

Imaginary Conversations, written by Walter Savage Landor.

The Spirit of the Age, published in 1825, is a collection of character sketches by William Hazlitt.

In addition to co-authoring Tales From Shakespeare with his sister, Charles Lamb contributed to the rediscovery of Shakespeare's contemporaries.

William Hazlitt (1778-1830)

- Hazlitt **was born in Shropshire**, son of a Unitarian minister.
- He initially **intended to be a painter** but shifted to writing.
- **Friend of Coleridge**, sharing revolutionary ideals.
- His **outspoken nature** led to many quarrels and controversies.
- **Produced a large body of political and literary works**.
- Key works include **The Characters of Shakespeare's Plays (1817)**.
- Also, **Lectures on the English Poets (1818)** and **The Spirit of the Age (1825)**.
- **Life of Napoleon (1828)**, though long, holds little value.
- **Literary criticism shows great ability and insight**.
- His criticism is **more balanced than Coleridge's**, broader than Lamb's.
- **More reasoned and scientific** than De Quincey's.
- **Political views sometimes clouded** his judgment in criticism.
- Despite this, **Hazlitt's criticism can often be trusted**.
- His **writing style is clear, readable**, and suited to his purpose.
- His style can express **passion for literature** when necessary.
- **Hazlitt felt a keen zest** for the good in English literature.

Notable Works:
- *A View of the English Stage (1818):*
    - His collected dramatic criticism appeared in 1818.
- *The Round Table, 2 vol. (1817):*
    - He also contributed to several journals, including Leigh Hunt's Examiner;
    - This association led to the publication of The Round Table, 2 vol. (1817),
    - 52 essays, of which 40 were by Hazlitt.
- *Characters of Shakespeare's Plays:*
    - In 1817, Hazlitt published his Characters of Shakespeare's Plays,
    - Met with immediate approval in most quarters.

- o However, he became involved in several quarrels, often with his friends,
- o Resulting from the forcible expression of his views in the journals.
- ➤ ***On the English Poets (1818) and On the English Comic Writers (1819)***
  - o **Made new friends**, including Shelley and Keats.
  - o **Consolidated his reputation as a lecturer** during this time.
  - o Delivered **courses On the English Poets (1818)** and **English Comic Writers (1819)**.
  - o Published a **collection of political essays**.
  - o **Said this about Coleridge "only person I ever knew who answered the idea of a man of genius"**
- ➤ ***Lectures on the Dramatic Literature of the Age of Elizabeth:***
  - o It was prepared in 1819.
  - o He devoted himself to essays for various journals, notably **John Scott's London Magazine**.
- ➤ ***Liber Amoris, or, The New Pygmalion (1823):***
  - o Hazlitt lived apart from his wife after the end of 1819,
  - o They were divorced in 1822.
  - o He fell in love with the daughter of his London landlord,
  - o Hazlitt described his suffering in the strange Liber Amoris
- ➤ ***Table Talk (1821) and The Plain Speaker (1826):***
  - o Many of his best essays were written during this difficult period.
  - o **"On the Pleasure of Painting."**
  - o The use of the pronoun "I" here, along with the personal subject matter, indicates Hazlitt's mastery of the familiar essay.
- ➤ ***Others were afterward edited by his son, William, as Sketches and Essays (1829)***
- ➤ ***An Essay on the Principles of Human Action***
- ➤ ***Literary Remains (1836)***
- ➤ ***Winterslow (1850) and by his biographer, P.P. Howe, as New Writings (1925–27).***
- ➤ ***Sketches of the Principal Picture Galleries in England (1824).***

Major Publications of William Hazlitt

- ➤ *An Essay on the Principles of Human Action (1805)*
- ➤ *Free Thoughts on Public Affairs (1806)*
- ➤ *A Reply to the Essay on Population, by the Rev. T. R. Malthus (1807)*

> ➤ ***The Round Table: A Collection of Essays on Literature, Men, and Manners (with Leigh Hunt; 1817)***
> ➤ ***Characters of Shakespeare's Plays (1817)***
> ➤ *Lectures on the English Poets (1818)*
> ➤ ***A View of the English Stage (1818)***
> ➤ *Lectures on the English Comic Writers (1819)*
> ➤ *Political Essays, with Sketches of Public Characters (1819)*
> ➤ *Lectures Chiefly on the Dramatic Literature of the Age of Elizabeth (1820)*
> ➤ ***Table-Talk (1821–22; "Paris" edition, with somewhat different contents, 1825).***
> ➤ *Characteristics: In the Manner of Rochefoucault's Maxims (1822)*
> ➤ *Liber Amoris: or, The New Pygmalion (1823)*
> ➤ ***The Spirit of the Age (1825)***
> ➤ *The Plain Speaker: Opinions on Books, Men, and Things (1826)*
> ➤ *Notes of a Journey Through France and Italy (1826)*
> ➤ *The Life of Napoleon Buonaparte (four volumes; 1828–1830)*

Questions:

Question 124

As mentioned in -My First Acquaintance with Poets' which poet does William Hazlitt describe as the "only person I ever knew who answered the idea of a man of genius"?

1. Coleridge
2. Wordsworth
3. Byron
4. Shelley

Explanations:
Answer: 1. Coleridge

In his essay "My First Acquaintance with Poets," William Hazlitt describes Samuel Taylor Coleridge as the "only person I ever knew who answered the idea of a man of genius."

Question 125

Who wrote the essay "My First Acquaintance with Poets"?

1. Charles Lamb
2. **William Hazlitt**
3. Thomas De Quincey
4. John Ruskin

Correct Explanations:
William Hazlitt, a British essayist, wrote the essay "My First Acquaintance with Poets" in 1823. The essay recounts Hazlitt's early encounters with poets and his appreciation for their work.

Question 126

An Essay on the Principles of Human Action was written by

1. Charles Lamb
2. Jean Jacques Rousseau
3. William Godwin
4. **William Hazlitt**

Explanations:

An Essay on the Principles of Human Action is a book by William Hazlitt.

Question 127

Match List I with List II

List I (Work)	List II (Author)
A. The English Comic Writers	I. David Hume
B. Essays Moral and Political	II. William Hazlitt
C. The Second Sex	III. Robert Wilson Lynd
D. The Pleasures of Ignorance	IV. Simone de Beauvoir

Choose the correct answer from the options given below:

1. A - II, B - I, C - IV, D - II
2. A - I, B - III, C - II, D - IV
3. A - IV, B - II, C - I, D - III •
4. A - III, B - I, C - II, D - IV

Explanations:

Answer: 1. A - II, B - I, C - IV, D - II

- **William Hazlitt wrote <u>Lectures on "the English Comic Writers</u>.**
- **David Hume's _Essays, Moral, Political, and Literary (1758)_.**
- **_The Second Sex_, penned by French existentialist philosopher Simone de Beauvoir** in 1949.
- **Robert Wilson Lynd's List of Works**
  - _The Mantle Of The Emperor (1906) with Ladbroke Black_
  - _On Not Being A Philosopher_
  - _Irish and English (1908)_
  - _Home Life in Ireland (1909)_
  - _Rambles in Ireland (1912)_
  - _The Book of This and That (1915)_
  - _If the Germans Conquered England (1917)_
  - _Old and New Masters (1919)_
  - _Ireland a Nation (1919)_
  - _The Art of Letters (1920)_
  - _The Passion of Labour (1920) New Statesman articles_
  - **_The Pleasures of Ignorance (1921)_**

Thomas De Quincey (1785-1859)

- **De Quincey was born in Manchester**, son of a wealthy merchant.
- He inherited wealth, but was **improvident and unreliable financially**.
- **Educated at Manchester Grammar School** and later **Oxford**.
- At Oxford, he excelled in **Greek** and began using **opium** in 1804.
- Used **opium to alleviate neuralgia pain**, leading to dependency.
- **Struggled financially** and earned a precarious living from journalism.
- Lived in the **Lake District (1809–30)** and became close with literary figures.
- His **opium use was excessive**, but he produced much work.
- Later moved to **Edinburgh** and became loosely associated with **Blackwood's Magazine**.
- **Buried in Edinburgh**, where he spent his final years.
- His work must be **"rigorously sifted"**; much is hack-work, some excellent.
- He wrote **no lengthy book**, similar to fellow opium-eater Coleridge.

- His fame rests on **Confessions of an English Opium-Eater (1821)**.
- **Confessions** is chaotic, a series of visions, part real, part dreamlike.
- The book has **passages of great power and beauty**.
- Other notable works: **The English Mail-coach, Suspiria de Profundis**, and **Murder considered as One of the Fine Arts**.
- Much of his work is **dreary and diffuse** with flat humor.
- **Wide knowledge**, though sometimes flawed by inaccuracy.
- His style can be **vulgar and tawdry**, but occasionally brilliant.
- When inspired, his **English has strength and sweetness**.
- At his best, he uses **elaborate style and imagery** without losing control.
- His **rhythm and melody** are often supreme in literature.
- He could **"blow through bronze"** and **"breathe through silver"**.
- His style is both **impressive and profound** at its height.
- The **passages we admire** have unity and lyric-like passion.
- He achieves **thrilling and profound effects** through rhythm and beauty.
- His best work features **studied rhythm and solemn beauty**.
- His diction is often **simple**, yet profoundly moving.
- De Quincey's writing can achieve **melody and deep emotion**.
- His work is a **mix of mediocrity and greatness**, requiring careful reading.

Major publications of Thomas De Quincey

- ***Confessions of an English Opium-Eater (1821)***
- ***On the Knocking at the Gate in Macbeth (1823)***
- *Walladmor (1825)*
- *On Murder Considered as one of the Fine Arts (1827)*
- *Klosterheim, or the Masque (1832)*
- *Lake Reminiscences (1834–40)*
- ***Revolt of the Tartars (1837)***
- *The Logic of Political Economy (1844)*
- *Suspiria de Profundis (1845)*
- ***The English Mail-Coach (1849)***
- *Autobiographic Sketches (1853)*
- ***Essays on the Poets, and Other English Writers (1853)***

> *"There is, first, the literature of knowledge; and, secondly, the literature of power. The function the first is - to teach; the function of*

the second is — to move : the first is a rudder, the second an oar or a sail."

Confessions of an English Opium-Eater (1821)

- ➤ **Confessions of an English Opium-Eater** is by **Thomas De Quincey**.
- ➤ It's **an autobiographical account** of his laudanum addiction.
- ➤ **De Quincey's first major work**, gaining overnight fame.
- ➤ First **published anonymously in 1821** in the London Magazine.
- ➤ Released as a **book in 1822 and revised in 1856**.
- ➤ **Part I** begins with a notice **"To the Reader."**
- ➤ The narrative presents **"a remarkable period in my life."**
- ➤ **Preliminary Confessions** focus on **childhood and youth experiences**.
- ➤ Emotional and psychological factors **precede opium addiction**.
- ➤ Describes time as a **homeless runaway in Oxford Street**.
- ➤ **Part II** starts with a **brief introduction and connecting passage**.
- ➤ **The Pleasures of Opium** describes his **positive drug experiences**.
- ➤ Covers the years **from 1804 until 1812**.
- ➤ **Introduction to the Pains of Opium** brings more autobiography.
- ➤ Takes De Quincey **from youth to maturity**.
- ➤ **The Pains of Opium** reveals his **nightmares and suffering**.
- ➤ A final **Notice to the Reader** clarifies the book's **chronology**.

On the Knocking at the Gate in Macbeth (1823)

- ➤ "On the Knocking at the Gate in Macbeth" is an essay by **Thomas De Quincey**.
- ➤ First published in the **October 1823 edition** of The London Magazine.
- ➤ The essay is less than **2,000 words long** but impactful.
- ➤ Called **"De Quincey's finest single critical piece"**.
- ➤ Also considered **"one of the most penetrating critical footnotes"**.
- ➤ Critics dismissing De Quincey's work often **praise this essay**.
- ➤ Concerns **Act II, Scene 3** in Shakespeare's *Macbeth*.
- ➤ The **murder of King Duncan** precedes Macduff and Lennox's arrival.
- ➤ De Quincey describes the **knocking at the gate** as impactful.
- ➤ The knocking creates **"awfulness and solemnity"** for the murderer.
- ➤ De Quincey attempts a **psychological interpretation** of this effect.
- ➤ **Foreshadows later psychological criticism** of Shakespeare.

- ➤ Horace Ainsworth Eaton called the essay **"penetrating and philosophic"**.
- ➤ De Quincey's conclusions are **as significant as Coleridge's or Hazlitt's**.
- ➤ He also examines his **response to the play's impact**.
- ➤ This essay parallels De Quincey's **"On Murder Considered as one of the Fine Arts"**.
- ➤ De Quincey's psychological insight **revolutionized Shakespearean criticism**.

Questions:

Question 128

Identify the author who stated the following lines -

"There is, first, the literature of knowledge; and, secondly, the literature of power. The function the first is - to teach; the function of the second is — to move : the first is a rudder, the second an oar or a sail."

1. Alexander Pope
2. Samuel Johnson
3. Thomas de Quincey
4. Philip Sidney

Explanations:
Answer: 3. Thomas de Quincey

This was said in his work *Essays on the Poets, and Other English Writers* (1953)

Question 129

Which two of the following are the titles of the sections in Thomas De Quincey's 'The English Mail – Coach'?

A. The Glory of Mobility
B. The Vision of Sudden Death
C. The Glory of Motion
D. The Vision of Unexpected Truth

Choose the correct answer from the options given below:

1. A and B only
2. A and D only
3. B and C only
4. B and D only

Explanations:

Answer: 3. B and C only

The English Mail-Coach is an essay by the English author Thomas De Quincey. A "three-part masterpiece" and "one of his most magnificent works," it first appeared in 1849 in Blackwood's Edinburgh Magazine, in the October (Part I) and December (Parts II and III) issues.

The essay is divided into three sections:

Part I, "The Glory of Motion
Part II, "The Vision of Sudden Death.
Part III, "Dream Fugue.

Question 130

Which of the following works have been authored by Thomas De Quincey?

A. Confessions of An English Opium Eater
B. The French Revolution
C. Hudibras
D. Autobiography
E. Suspiria De Profoundis

Choose the correct answer from the options given below:

1. A, B and C
2. A, C and D
3. A, D and E
4. A, B and D

Explanations:

Ans: A, D and E

- ***Confessions of An English Opium Eater*** - a memoir in which De Quincey.
- ***Suspiria De Profundis*** - a collection of essays by De.
- ***Autobiographic Sketches,*** sometimes referred to as the Autobiography of Thomas De Quincey, is a work first published in 1853.

Extra Perk:

- ***The French Revolution*** is a historical work authored by Thomas Carlyle.
- ***Hudibras* is a satirical poem written by Samuel Butler.**
- ***Thoughts on Education* is a treatise on education written by John Locke.**

Jane Austen (1775-1817)

- **Jane Austen was the daughter** of a Hampshire clergyman.
- She **was educated at home** with careful reading material.
- Her **life was unexciting**, involving pilgrimages to different residences.
- Jane lived near **Southampton where most novels** were written.
- Her first published works were issued anonymously.
- She died before **gaining adequate recognition** for her work.
- The **chronology of her novels** is difficult to trace.
- **Northanger Abbey** was her first novel, finished in 1798.
- It was published **after her death in 1818**.
- **Northanger Abbey** begins as a burlesque of terror novels.
- The incidents in the novel are **commonplace, but masterfully satiric**.
- **Pride and Prejudice** (1797) shares similar methods to Northanger Abbey.
- The heroine has **no extraordinary qualities**, yet is charming.
- **Pride and Prejudice** gently critiques **rank and wealth**.
- **Sense and Sensibility** (1798) follows the same general methods.
- A long pause followed, **as no publisher would issue** her work.
- **Sense and Sensibility** finally appeared in **1811**.
- **Mansfield Park, Emma**, and **Persuasion** were written after.
- If there's development, it's in avoiding **anything unusual**.
- **Plots are severely unromantic**, capturing everyday life.
- Her first novel began as a **burlesque but became serious**.
- Later novels, like **Emma**, focus on **ordinary existence**.

- ➤ **Only the highest art** could make such plots attractive.
- ➤ Her characters are developed with **minuteness and accuracy**.
- ➤ She often introduces **convincing clergymen** characters.
- ➤ Characters like **Mr. Collins** and **Miss Bates** are memorable.
- ➤ Her characters are **not types but individuals**.
- ➤ Her portrayal relies on **acute observation and quiet irony**.
- ➤ **Male characters** are softer, while females are **excellently portrayed**.
- ➤ **Jane Austen's place** in fiction is **remarkable and enduring**.
- ➤ Her **qualities are slow to be recognized** but grow on readers.
- ➤ She avoids **loud or garish** elements in her fiction.
- ➤ **The taste for her fiction** grows strong after appreciation.
- ➤ **Jane Austen earned a foremost place** in literature.
- ➤ **Northanger Abbey** humorously critiques **romantic imagination**.
- ➤ **Pride and Prejudice** examines **social class and personal growth**.
- ➤ **Sense and Sensibility** deals with **romantic ideals and reality**.
- ➤ **Mansfield Park** focuses on **morality and personal integrity**.
- ➤ **Emma** showcases a heroine's **self-awareness and social meddling**.
- ➤ **Persuasion** reflects **maturity, regret, and second chances**.
- ➤ Austen's style is **smooth, unobtrusive**, and delicately satirical.
- ➤ Her novels feature **ordinary middle-class** people and situations.
- ➤ Her later works refine **everyday life with subtle art**.
- ➤ **Northanger Abbey** parodies the gothic **novel of terror**.
- ➤ **Pride and Prejudice** displays **sharp wit** and social observations.
- ➤ Austen's humor lies in **her characters' subtle flaws**.
- ➤ **Emma's** irony and humor stem from **social misunderstandings**.
- ➤ **Mansfield Park** explores **the balance between duty and desire**.
- ➤ **Her characters are consistently alive** and richly developed.
- ➤ **Austen's reputation grew steadily** after her works were revisited.
- ➤ **F. R. Leavis wrote, "The Great Tradition" (1948),** where he names **Jane Austen, George Eliot, Henry James, and Joseph Conrad** as the great English novelists, alongside Charles Dickens, Nathaniel Hawthorne, Herman Melville, and Edgar Allan Poe.

Novels

- ➤ *Sense and Sensibility (1811)*
- ➤ *Pride and Prejudice (1813)*
- ➤ *Mansfield Park (1814)*
- ➤ *Emma (1815)*

> ➢ *Northanger Abbey (1818, posthumous)*
> ➢ *Persuasion (1818, posthumous)*
> ➢ *Lady Susan (1871, posthumous)*

Unfinished fiction
- *The Watsons (1804)*
- *Sanditon (1817)*

Code:

🧳 **Austen Watsons** have 😟 **Sense** and 🍦 **Pride** for 🧳 **Walking** in the 🌳 **Park** with 👧 **Emma** who lives in 🏰 **Northanger Abbey** and they both ✉️ **Persuaded** 👩 **Lady Susan** to join with them.

First Work: 📘 **Sense and Sensibility**
Second Work: 📖 **Pride and Prejudice**
Middle Works: 🌳 **Mansfield Park** 👧 **Emma** 🏰 **Northanger Abbey**
Second Last Work: ✉️ **Persuasion**
Last Work: 👩 **Lady Susan**

Or

SS-PP-Man Em-Nora-PerSusan-WatSan

Posthumous Works: 🏰 **Northanger Abbey**, ✉️ **Persuasion**, 👩 **Lady Susan**
Code: Abbey Persuade Lady Susan.

Unfinished Works: 🏖️ **White Sand**
Code: White Sand.

Sense and Sensibility (1811)

- ➢ Published in **1811**.
- ➢ It was published **anonymously**;
- ➢ **By A Lady** appears on the title page where the author's name might have been.

- **Dashwood sisters, Elinor (age 19) and Marianne (age 16½)**, as they come of age.
- They have an older half-brother, **John,** and a younger sister, **Margaret (age 13).**
- **The novel is set in South West England, London, and Sussex, probably between 1792 and 1797.**
- **Sense and Sensibility** focuses on the Dashwood family.
- Elinor represents **good sense**, Marianne represents **sensibility**.
- The Dashwoods become **destitute** after their father's death.
- John Dashwood, their half-brother, inherits **Norland Park**.
- John's **greedy wife Fanny** dissuades him from helping his sisters.
- The family moves to **Barton Cottage** in Devonshire.
- Marianne meets **Colonel Brandon**, 20 years her senior.
- She discourages Brandon's attention, preferring **John Willoughby**.
- **Willoughby** deserts her for an heiress, breaking her heart.
- Marianne eventually marries the sensible **Colonel Brandon**.
- Elinor forms an attachment with **Edward Ferrars**.
- Edward is secretly engaged to **Lucy Steele** for years.
- Edward is disowned but offered a **clergyman position** by Brandon.
- Elinor believes **Edward** has married someone else.
- **Lucy** marries Edward's brother, **Robert**, instead.
- **Edward** proposes to Elinor, and she accepts.
- Both sisters marry wisely and find happiness in the end.

Pride and Prejudice (1813)

- **Elizabeth Bennet** learns the consequences of **hasty judgments**.
- **Mr. Bennet's estate** is **entailed**, passing only to **male heirs**.
- The **Bennet family** risks **poverty** without an advantageous **marriage**.
- Famous opening line: "**It is a truth universally acknowledged...**"
- **Mrs. Bennet** aims to marry one daughter to **Mr. Bingley**.
- **Bingley** is charmed by **Jane**, but **Darcy** is aloof to **Elizabeth**.
- **Darcy's pride** and **Elizabeth's prejudice** keep them apart.
- **Mr. Collins** proposes to **Elizabeth**, who **refuses** him.
- **Collins** marries **Elizabeth's friend Charlotte** instead.
- **Elizabeth** meets **Wickham**, who shares **false stories** about **Darcy**.
- **Bingley** suddenly leaves, causing **Elizabeth** to **resent Darcy** more.
- **Darcy** grows fond of **Elizabeth** and **proposes**, but is **rejected**.
- **Elizabeth accuses Darcy** of ruining **Bingley** and **Jane's relationship**.
- **Darcy** reveals **Wickham's attempt** to elope with his **sister**.

- ➢ **Elizabeth** starts to see **Darcy** in a **different light**.
- ➢ **Lydia Bennet** elopes with **Wickham**, causing a family scandal.
- ➢ **Elizabeth** fears **Lydia's elopement** will ruin her family's reputation.
- ➢ **Darcy** helps persuade **Wickham** to **marry Lydia**.
- ➢ **Darcy's involvement** is kept secret, but **Elizabeth** finds out.
- ➢ **Bingley returns** and gets engaged to **Jane**, with **Darcy's encouragement**.
- ➢ **Darcy proposes again**, and **Elizabeth accepts** this time.
- ➢ **Marriage** provides financial security and resolves **Bennet family concerns**.
- ➢ **Darcy's love** for **Elizabeth** overcomes **social class differences**.
- ➢ **Elizabeth's initial prejudice** against **Darcy** is proven wrong.
- ➢ **Wickham** is revealed as **untrustworthy** and manipulative.
- ➢ **Darcy redeems himself** by helping **Lydia** and **Wickham**.
- ➢ The novel contrasts **superficial** and **genuine character traits**.
- ➢ **Elizabeth's character growth** involves reevaluating **first impressions**.
- ➢ The marriage of **Jane** and **Bingley** represents **romantic fulfillment**.
- ➢ **Darcy and Elizabeth's marriage** completes the novel's **moral resolution**.

Mansfield Park (1814)

- ➢ **Mansfield Park** was published in **three volumes** in **1814**.
- ➢ It's the **most serious** of **Austen's novels** with **religious themes**.
- ➢ **Fanny Price** is a **self-effacing cousin** living with the **Bertram family**.
- ➢ **Fanny's moral strength** earns her **acceptance** and **marriage** to **Edmund Bertram**.
- ➢ The novel explores **religion**, **duty**, and **moral strength**.
- ➢ **Mansfield Park** centers around **Fanny Price**, a poor, timid girl.
- ➢ Fanny is raised by her wealthy **Bertram relatives** at **Mansfield Park**.
- ➢ **Sir Thomas Bertram**, head of the family, oversees Fanny's upbringing.
- ➢ **Edmund Bertram**, the younger son, becomes Fanny's moral guide and friend.
- ➢ **Maria and Julia Bertram**, Fanny's cousins, are selfish and vain.
- ➢ **Henry and Mary Crawford** arrive, causing romantic complications at Mansfield.
- ➢ **Henry** flirts with **Maria**, even though she's engaged to **Mr. Rushworth**.
- ➢ **Edmund** falls for **Mary Crawford**, despite her lack of true morals.
- ➢ **Fanny** disapproves of **Henry's flirtations** and **Edmund's infatuation**.
- ➢ **Henry Crawford** proposes to **Fanny**, but she refuses his offer.

- ➤ **Maria** elopes with **Henry**, bringing scandal to the Bertram family.
- ➤ **Sir Thomas Bertram** realizes **Fanny's true worth** and moral character.
- ➤ **Edmund** sees **Mary's moral flaws** and ends their relationship.
- ➤ **Fanny marries Edmund**, receiving love and respect from the Bertrams.

Emma (1815)

- ➤ **Emma** is about **youthful hubris** and **romantic misunderstandings**.
- ➤ Set in the **fictional village of Highbury** and nearby estates.
- ➤ Published in **December 1815**, with the date listed as **1816**.
- ➤ **Austen explores** genteel women's lives in **Georgian–Regency England**.
- ➤ **Emma** is a **comedy of manners**, depicting social **and marital issues**.
- ➤ **Austen aimed** to create a heroine *"I am going to take a heroine whom no one but myself will much like.."*
- ➤ **Emma Woodhouse**, *"handsome, clever, and rich, with a comfortable home and a happy disposition... had lived nearly twenty-one years in the world with very little to distress or vex her.,"* opens the novel.
- ➤ **Emma is spoiled**, overestimates her matchmaking **abilities**.
- ➤ Her character is **headstrong, self-satisfied**, and meddlesome.
- ➤ Emma is **blind to dangers** of interfering in others' lives.
- ➤ Her **imagination and perceptions** frequently lead her astray.
- ➤ The novel **depicts issues** of **marriage, sex, age, and status**.
- ➤ **Summary:**
  - o **Emma Woodhouse**, a wealthy, clever, and **self-assured young woman**.
  - o She enjoys **matchmaking** despite her **lack of romantic experience**.
  - o **Mr. Knightley**, Emma's wise and sensible **family friend**.
  - o Emma **befriends Harriet Smith**, a naïve girl of **unknown parentage**.
  - o She discourages Harriet's interest in **farmer Robert Martin**.
  - o Emma encourages Harriet's **infatuation with Mr. Elton**, the vicar.
  - o **Mr. Elton proposes to Emma**, revealing his **true intentions**.
  - o **Frank Churchill**, a charming and **mysterious young man**, visits Highbury.
  - o Emma begins to **fancy herself in love** with Frank.
  - o Frank is secretly engaged to **Jane Fairfax**, another key character.
  - o Harriet develops **feelings for Mr. Knightley**, further complicating matters.

- o **Emma realizes her love** for **Mr. Knightley** too late.
- o **Mr. Knightley** proposes to Emma, **declaring his love**.
- o Harriet reunites with **Robert Martin**, her **true match**.
- o **Emma marries Mr. Knightley**, learning humility and **true love**.

Northanger Abbey (1818, posthumous)

- ➤ **Northanger Abbey** was published posthumously in **1817**.
- ➤ It was written around **1798–1799**, possibly titled **Susan**.
- ➤ The manuscript was sold to publisher **Richard Crosby** in 1803.
- ➤ The novel satirizes **polite society** and **Gothic tales of terror**.
- ➤ **Catherine Morland**, a country parson's daughter, gains **worldly wisdom**.
- ➤ She first experiences **fashionable society** in **Bath**.
- ➤ At **Northanger Abbey**, she learns not to trust **Gothic thrillers**.
- ➤ **Catherine's character growth** reflects her journey to **maturity**.
- ➤ Summary:
    - o **Catherine Morland**, the naive heroine, loves **Gothic novels**.
    - o Catherine visits **Bath** with wealthy neighbors, the **Allens**.
    - o She befriends **Isabella Thorpe**, who pursues Catherine's brother **James**.
    - o **John Thorpe**, Isabella's brother, shows romantic interest in **Catherine**.
    - o Catherine meets **Henry Tilney**, a charming clergyman, and his sister **Eleanor**.
    - o **General Tilney** invites Catherine to visit **Northanger Abbey**, their home.
    - o Catherine's imagination runs wild with **Gothic-inspired suspicions**.
    - o She believes **General Tilney** murdered his wife in the abbey.
    - o **Henry Tilney** confronts Catherine about her **wild accusations**.
    - o **General Tilney** discovers Catherine's modest status and sends her away.
    - o **Henry** defies his father's disapproval and proposes to **Catherine**.
    - o **Catherine** realizes the dangers of confusing **fiction** with **reality**.
    - o The novel satirizes **Gothic fiction** and **romantic exaggerations**.
    - o **Northanger Abbey** explores themes of **innocence**, **imagination**, and **social expectations**.

Persuasion (1818, posthumous)

- ➤ **Persuasion** was published posthumously in **1818** by **Austen**

- It was written between **1815–16**, alongside **Northanger Abbey**.
- **Persuasion** contains **subdued satire** and **comedy of character**.
- The novel tells the story of **second chances** in love.
- **Anne Elliot** and **Captain Wentworth** rekindle their love after **eight years**.
- **Anne** was previously **persuaded** to reject **Wentworth's proposal**.
- **Wentworth** returns from the **Napoleonic Wars**, now socially acceptable.
- He is now an **eligible suitor**, acceptable to **Anne's snobbish family**.
- **Anne** realizes her love for **Wentworth** remains **strong**.
- The novel explores **class**, **rank**, and **reawakened love** in society.
- **Summary:**
  - **Anne Elliot**, the heroine, is **intelligent**, **sensible**, and **reserved**.
  - **Anne** was persuaded to reject **Frederick Wentworth's** earlier proposal.
  - **Anne's family** faces financial troubles due to **Sir Walter's extravagance**.
  - They rent out their estate, **Kellynch Hall**, to **Admiral Croft**.
  - **Captain Wentworth**, now successful, returns as **Admiral Croft's brother-in-law**.
  - **Anne** still loves **Wentworth**, but he seems interested in others.
  - **Louisa Musgrove**, a young lively girl, captures **Wentworth's attention**.
  - **Louisa** suffers a serious fall, bringing **Anne** and **Wentworth** closer.
  - **Anne** remains calm and capable, impressing **Wentworth** with her strength.
  - **Anne's cousin**, **William Elliot**, reappears, showing romantic interest in her.
  - **Anne** learns that **William Elliot** has selfish motives, deceiving her.
  - **Captain Wentworth** writes **Anne** a heartfelt letter, declaring his love.
  - **Anne and Wentworth** finally reunite, rekindling their past love.
  - The novel ends with **Anne** and **Wentworth's happy marriage**.

Lady Susan (1871)

- Lady Susan is a short epistolary novel.
- Possibly written in 1794 but not published until 1871.
- Describes the schemes of the title character.

- ➢ **Lady Susan Vernon** is a charming, manipulative, and widowed woman.
- ➢ She visits her brother-in-law, **Charles Vernon**, at **Churchill** estate.
- ➢ **Lady Susan** tries to manipulate **Reginald De Courcy** into marrying her.
- ➢ She schemes to marry her daughter, **Frederica**, to **Sir James Martin**.
- ➢ **Frederica** resists, seeking refuge at the **Vernon household**.
- ➢ **Lady Susan** manipulates men, using charm for selfish gains.
- ➢ **Reginald De Courcy** falls for **Lady Susan**, despite his family's warnings.
- ➢ **Lady Susan's plans unravel** when **Frederica's feelings** become clear.
- ➢ **Lady Susan** eventually marries **Sir James**, abandoning **Reginald**.

Questions:

Question 131

Arrange the following women novelists in chronological order (by date of birth):

- A. Anne Bronte
- B. Jane Austen
- C. Ann Radcliffe
- D. Fanny Burney
- E. Maria Edgeworth

Choose the correct answer from the options given below:

1. B, A, D, C, E
2. C, D, B, E, A
3. D, C, E, B, A
4. A, B, C, E, D

Explanations:
Answer: 3. D, C, E, B, A

Fanny Burney (1752-1840): Major works: "Evelina" (1778), "Cecilia" (1782), "Camilla" (1796), "The Wanderer" (1814)

Maria Edgeworth (1768-1849): Major works: "Castle Rackrent" (1800), "Belinda" (1801), "The Absentee" (1812)

Ann Radcliffe (1764-1823): Major works: "The Castles of Athlin and Dunbayne" (1789), "The Mysteries of Udolpho" (1794), "The Italian" (1797)

Jane Austen (1775-1817): Major works: "Sense and Sensibility" (1811), "Pride and Prejudice" (1813), "Mansfield Park" (1814), "Emma" (1815), "Persuasion" (1818), "Northanger Abbey" (1818)

Anne Bronte (1820-1849): "Agnes Grey" (1847), "The Tenant of Wildfell Hall" (1848).

Question 132

Match List I with List II:

List I	List II
(A) "Willing to wound. and yet afraid to strike."	(I) Irony
(B) It is a truth universally acknowledged that a single man in possession of a good fortune must be in want of a wife."	(II) Simile
(C) "Thou still unravished bride of quietness./Thou foster child of silence and slow time."	(III) Antithesis
(D) "And ice. mast-high. come floating by. as green as emerald."	(IV) Assonance

Choose the correct answer from the options given below:
1. **(A)-(III), (B)-(I), (C)-(IV), (D)-(II)**
2. (A)-(II), (B)-(III), (C)-(I), (D)-(IV)
3. (A)-(I), (B)-(IV). (C)-(II), (D)-(III)
4. (A)-(III), (B)-(II). (C)-(IV). (D)-(I)

Correct Answer Explanation:
Antithesis: It is used in writing or speech either as a proposition that contrasts with or reverses some previously mentioned proposition or when two opposites are introduced together for a contrasting effect. This is based on the logical phrase or term.
Example: A contrast is sharply made. *Willing to wound and yet afraid to strike.*

Irony: It is the juxtaposition of what on the surface appears to be the case and what is the case or to be expected; it is an important rhetorical device and literary technique.

Example: Jane Austen's Pride and Prejudice begins with the proposition, "*It is a truth universally acknowledged, that a single man in possession of a good fortune, must be in want of a wife*"

Assonance: In prosody, repetition of stressed vowel sounds within words with different end consonants, as in the phrase "quite like." It is unlike rhyme, in which initial consonants differ, but both vowel and end-consonant sounds are identical, as in the phrase "quite right." Many common phrases, such as "mad as a hatter," "free as a breeze," or "high as a kite," owe their appeal to assonance. As a poetic device, internal assonance is usually combined with alliteration (repetition of initial consonant sounds) and consonance (repetition of end or medial consonant sounds) to enrich the texture of the poetic line.
Example: In the first stanza, the speaker stands before an ancient Grecian urn and addresses and uses assonance. He is preoccupied with its depiction of pictures frozen in time. It is the "still unravish'd bride of quietness," the "foster-child of silence and slow time." He also describes the urn as a "historian" that can tell a story.

Simile: It is a figure of speech comparing two, unlike entities. In the simile, unlike the metaphor, the resemblance is explicitly indicated by the words "like" or "as." The common heritage of similes in everyday speech usually reflects simple comparisons based on the natural world or familiar domestic objects, as in "He eats like a bird," "He is as smart as a whip," or "He is as slow as molasses." In some cases, the original aptness of the comparison is lost, as in the expression "dead as a doornail."
Example: "And ice. mast-high. come floating by. as green as emerald."

Question 133

"I recognise that its heroine is a little prig and its hero a pompous ass, but I do not care."

About which novel by Jane Austen does Somerset Maugham make this statement

1. Pride and Prejudice
2. Northanger Abbey
3. Sense and Sensibility
4. **Mansfield Park**

Explanations:

The novel by Jane Austen about which Somerset Maugham makes this statement is "Mansfield Park".

In his statement, Somerset Maugham is expressing his fondness for "Mansfield Park", despite his recognition that its heroine is a little prig (a person who is self-righteous and moralistic) and its hero a pompous ass (a person who is arrogant and conceited).

Find the chronological order of the writers in terms of their years of birth:

- A. Jane Austen
- B. Henry Fielding
- C. James M. Barrie
- D. Richard Doddridge Blackmore
- E. William Makepeace Thackeray

Choose the correct answer from the options given below:

1. ABCDE
2. **BAEDC**
3. CDABE
4. DBAEC

Explanations:
1. Henry Fielding (1707)
2. Jane Austen (1775)
3. William Makepeace Thackeray (1811)
4. Richard Doddridge Blackmore (1825)
5. James M. Barrie (1860)

In which novel of Jane Austen is Captain Frederick Wentworth a character?

    1. Emma
    2. Northanger Abbey
    3. Mansfield Park
    4. Persuasion

Explanations
Answer: 4. Persuasion

Persuasion is Jane Austen's final completed novel, published on December 20, 1817, alongside Northanger Abbey, six months after her death, though the title page bears the date 1818. The story revolves around **Anne Elliot**, a 27-year-old Englishwoman whose family decides to rent their home to an admiral and his wife to reduce their expenses and debt. **Captain Frederick Wentworth,** the wife's brother, was engaged to Anne in 1806, but the engagement was broken at the persuasion of her friends and family. Almost eight years later, Anne and Captain Wentworth, both single and unattached, reunite, leading to humorous encounters and a second chance at love and marriage for Anne.

> **Northanger Abbey- Catherine Morland**.
> **Mansfield Park- Fanny Price**.
> **"Emma- Emma Woodhouse, Miss Taylor, Mr Weston, Harriet Smith,** Robert Martin.

Question 136

Which among the following is not a character from Jane Austen's novel Persuasion?

    1. Sir Walter Elliot
    2. Lady Russell
    3. Miss Crawford
    4. Frederick Wentworth

Explanations:
Answer: 3. Miss Crawford

> Sir Walter Elliot, from *Persuasion*
> Captain Frederick - *Persuasion*.
> Lady Russell from *Persuasion*.

➤ Mary Crawford in "Mansfield Park".

➤ Mrs. Norris, the formidable antagonist in *Mansfield Park*.

➤ George Knightley in *Emma*.

➤ Elizabeth Bennet, the cherished protagonist of *Pride and Prejudice*,

➤ Fitzwilliam Darcy, from *Pride and Prejudice*.

➤ In *Sense and Sensibility*, Elinor Dashwood.

➤ Diana Parker from Austen's unfinished work *Sanditon*.

➤ Isabella Thorpe in *Northanger Abbey*.

➤ Lady Susan Vernon in Austen's novella *Lady Susan*.

Maria Edgeworth (1768-1849)

➤ **Maria Edgeworth** was an **Anglo-Irish writer** of **adults' and children's literature.**

➤ She was one of the first **realist writers** in **children's literature.**

➤ Edgeworth was significant in **the evolution of the novel** in **Europe.**

➤ She held views on **estate management, politics, and education.**

➤ She corresponded with **Sir Walter Scott** and **David Ricardo.**

➤ Lived in **England** until 1782, then moved to **Edgeworthstown, Ireland.**

➤ At 15, she assisted her father in **managing his estate.**

➤ She gained knowledge of **rural economy** and the **Irish peasantry.**

➤ This knowledge was the **backbone of her novels.**

➤ **Domestic life** at Edgeworthstown was **busy and happy.**

➤ Encouraged by her father, **Maria began writing.**

➤ She wrote in the **common sitting room.**

➤ Her 21 siblings provided **material and an audience** for her stories.

Notable Works:

➤ *Letters for Literary Ladies – 1795*

➤ *The Parent's Assistant – 1796*

➤ *Practical Education – 1798*

➤ ***Castle Rackrent – 1800 (novel)***

➤ ***Belinda – 1801 (novel)***

➤ ***Leonora – 1806***

➤ ***Tales of Fashionable Life – 1809 and 1812***

➤ *Ennui – 1809 (novel)*

➤ *The Absentee – 1812 (novel)*

➤ *Patronage – 1814 (novel)*

➤ *Harrington – 1817 (novel)*

> ➢ *Ormond – 1817 (novel)*
> ➢ *Helen – 1834 (novel)*

Usage Policy for NerdSchool Notes

Created by: Instructors from NerdSchool
Owned by: NERDSTABLE PVT LTD

The following notes are the intellectual property of **NERDSTABLE PVT LTD** and are made available exclusively to students who have paid for access. By using these notes, you agree to the terms and conditions outlined below:

Policy of Usage:

Personal Use Only: These notes are intended for your **personal study and exam preparation**. You are permitted to **read** and **print** them for your own reference.

No Unauthorized Distribution or Sale: You **may not sell**, **distribute**, or **replicate** these notes in any form, whether digitally or physically. This includes sharing copies with others, regardless of the medium (online platforms, printed materials, etc.).

No Plagiarism: You **may not claim** the contents of these notes as your own. Any form of direct publication or submission under your name, without proper citation, is strictly prohibited.

Non-Transferable Access: Access to these notes is restricted to the individual purchaser. **Sharing your login credentials** or any other means of access to these materials with others is a violation of this policy.

Additional Guidelines:

For Educational Use Only: These notes are designed to help students succeed in their academic exams and should be used responsibly. They are meant to supplement your learning, not to replace the guidance of instructors or textbooks.

No Commercial Use: The content in these notes cannot be used for **commercial purposes**. This includes using the material in any form of paid tutoring or educational courses that you offer without the explicit permission of NERDSTABLE PVT LTD.

Proper Attribution: If you wish to reference any part of these notes in your own academic work, proper **citation** must be made to **NerdSchool and NERDSTABLE PVT LTD**.

Legal Action: Any violation of these terms, including unauthorized distribution or commercial use, may result in **legal action**.